COMMENTARIES ON LIVING
Third Series

Commentaries on Living

Third Series

From the Notebooks of
J. Krishnamurti

Edited by
D. RAJAGOPAL

A publication supported by
THE KERN FOUNDATION

Quest Books
Theosophical Publishing House

Wheaton, Illinois ♦ Madras, India

CONTENTS

Commentaries on Living

Third Series

Does Thinking Begin with Conclusions?

THE HILLS across the lake were very beautiful, and beyond them rose the snow-covered mountains. It had been raining all day; but now, like an unexpected miracle, the skies had suddenly cleared, and everything became alive, joyous and serene. The flowers were intense in their yellow, red and deep purple, and the raindrops on them were like precious jewels. It was a most lovely evening, full of light and splendour. The people came out into the streets, and along the lake, children were shouting with laughter. Through all this movement and bustle there was enchanting beauty, and a strange, all-pervading peace.

There were several of us on the long bench facing the lake. A man was talking in rather a high voice, and it was impossible not to overhear what he was saying to his neighbour. "On an evening like this I wish I were far away from this noise and confusion, but my job keeps me here, and I loathe it." People were feeding the swans, the ducks and a few stray sea-gulls. The swans were pure white and very graceful. There wasn't a ripple on the water now, and the hills across the lake were almost black; but the mountains beyond the hills were aglow with the setting sun, and the vivid clouds behind them seemed passionately alive.

"I am not sure I understand you," my visitor began, "when you say that knowledge must be set aside to understand truth." He was an elderly man, much travelled and well-read. He had spent a year or so in a monastery, he explained, and had wandered all over the world, from port to port, working on ships, saving money and gathering knowledge. "I don't mean mere book knowledge," he went on; "I mean the knowledge that men have gathered but have not put down on paper, the mysterious tradition that's beyond scrolls and sacred books. I have dabbled in occultism, but that has always seemed to me rather stupid and superficial. A good microscope is vastly more beneficial than the clairvoyance of a man who sees superphysical things. I have read some of the great historians, with their theories and their visions, but . . . Given a first-rate mind and the capacity to accumulate knowledge, a man should be able to do immense good. I know it isn't the fashion, but I have a sneaking compulsion to reform the world, and knowledge is my passion. I have always been a passionate person in many ways, and now I am consumed with this urge to know. The other day I read something of yours which intrigued me, and when you said that there must be freedom from knowledge, I decided to come and see you—not as a follower, but as an inquirer."

To follow another, however learned or noble, is to block all understanding, isn't it?

"Then we can talk freely and with mutual respect."

If I may ask, what do you mean by knowledge?

"Yes, that's a good question to begin with. Knowledge is everything that man has learnt through experience; it is what he has gathered by study, through centuries of struggle and pain, in the many fields of endeavour, both scientific and psychological. As even the greatest historian interprets history according to his learning and mood, so an ordinary scholar like me may translate knowledge into action, either 'good' or 'bad'. Though we are not concerned with action at the moment, it is inevitably related to knowledge, which is what man has experienced or learnt through thought, through meditation, through sorrow. Knowledge is vast; it is not only written down in books, but it exists in the individual as well as in the collective or racial consciousness of man. Scientific and medical information, the technical 'knowhow' of the material world, is rooted principally in the consciousness of western man, just as in the consciousness of eastern man there is the greater sensitivity of unworldliness. All this is knowledge, embracing not only what is already known, but what is being discovered from day to day. Knowledge is an additive, deathless process, there is no end to it, and it may therefore be the immortal that man is after. So I can't understand why you say that all knowledge must be set aside if there is to be the understanding of truth."

The division between knowledge and understanding is artificial, it really doesn't exist; but to be free of this division, which is to perceive the difference between them, we must find out what is the highest form of thinking, otherwise there will be confusion.

Does thinking begin with a conclusion? Is thinking a movement from one conclusion to another? Can there be thinking, if thinking is positive? Is not the highest form of thinking negative? Is not all knowledge an accumulation of definitions, conclusions and positive assertions? Positive thought, which is based on experience, is always the outcome of the past, and such thought can never uncover the new.

"You are stating that knowledge is ever in the past, and that thought originating from the past must inevitably cloud the perception of that which may be called truth. However, without the past as memory, we could not recognize this object which we have agreed to call a chair. The word 'chair' reflects a conclusion reached by common consent, and all communication would cease if such conclusions were not taken for granted. Most of our thinking is based on conclusions, on traditions, on the experiences of others, and life would be impossible without the more obvious and inevitable of these conclusions. Surely you don't mean that we should put aside all conclusions, all memories and traditions?"

The ways of tradition inevitably lead to mediocrity, and a mind caught in tradition cannot perceive what is true. Tradition may be one day old, or it may go back for a thousand years. Obviously it would be absurd for an engineer to set aside the engineering knowledge he has gained through the experience of a thousand others; and if one were to try to set aside the memory of where one lived, it would only indicate a neurotic state. But the gathering of facts does not make for the understanding of life. Knowledge is one thing, and understanding another. Knowledge does not lead to understanding; but understanding may enrich knowledge, and knowledge may implement understanding.

"Knowledge is essential and not to be despised. Without knowledge, modern surgery and a hundred other marvels could not exist."

We are not attacking or defending knowledge, but trying to understand the whole problem. Knowledge is only a part of life, not the totality, and when that part assumes all-consuming importance, as it is threatening to do now, then life becomes superficial, a dull routine from which man seeks to escape through every form of diversion and superstition, with disastrous consequences. Mere knowledge, however wide and cunningly put together, will not resolve our human problems; to assume that it will is to invite frustration and misery. Something much more profound is needed. One may know that hate is futile, but to be free of hate is quite another matter. Love is not a question of knowledge.

To go back, positive thinking is no thinking at all; it is merely a modified continuity of what *has* been thought. The outward shape of it may change from time to time, depending on compulsions and pressures, but the core of positive thinking is always tradition. Positive thinking is the process of conformity, and the mind that conforms can

3

never be in a state of discovery.

"But can positive thinking be discarded? Is it not necessary at a certain level of human existence?"

Of course, but that's not the whole issue. We are trying to find out if knowledge may become a hindrance to the understanding of truth. Knowledge is essential, for without it we should have to begin all over again in certain areas of our existence. This is fairly simple and clear. But will accumulated knowledge, however vast, help us to understand truth?

"What *is* truth? Is it a common ground to be trodden by all? Or is it a subjective, individual experience?"

By whatever name it may be called, truth must ever be new, living; but the words 'new' and 'living' are used only to convey a state that is not static, not dead, not a fixed point within the mind of man. Truth must be discovered anew from moment to moment, it is not an experience that can be repeated; it has no continuity, it is a timeless state. The division between the many and the one must cease for truth to be. It is not a state to be achieved, nor a point towards which the mind can evolve, grow. If truth is conceived as a thing to be gained, then the cultivation of knowledge and the accumulations of memory become necessary, giving rise to the *guru* and the follower, the one who knows and the one who does not know.

"Then you are against *gurus* and followers?"

It's not a matter of being against something, but of perceiving that conformity, which is the desire for security, with its fears, prevents the experiencing of the timeless.

"I think I understand what you mean. But is it not immensely difficult to renounce all that one has gathered? Indeed, is it possible?"

To give up in order to gain is no renunciation at all. To see the false as the false, to see the true in the false, and to see the true as the true—it is this that sets the mind free.

SELF-KNOWLEDGE OR SELF-HYPNOSIS?

IT HAD rained all night and most of the morning, and now the sun was going down behind dark, heavy clouds. There was no colour in the

4

sky, but the perfume of the rain-soaked earth filled the air. The frogs had croaked all night long with persistency and rhythm, but with the dawn they became silent. The tree trunks were dark with the long rain, and the leaves, washed clean of the summer's dust, would be rich and green again in a few more days. The lawns too would be greener, the bushes would soon be flowering, and there would be rejoicing. How welcome was the rain after the hot, dusty days! The mountains beyond the hills seemed not too far away, and the breeze blowing from them was cool and pure. There would be more work, more food, and starvation would be a thing of the past.

One of those large brown eagles was making wide circles in the sky, floating on the breeze without a beat of its wings. Hundreds of people on bicycles were going home after a long day in the office. A few talked as they rode, but most of them were silent and evidently tired out. A large group had stopped, with their bicycles resting against their bodies, and were animatedly discussing some issue, while nearby a policeman wearily watched them. On the corner a big new building was going up. The road was full of brown puddles, and the passing cars splashed one with dirty water which left dark marks on one's clothing. A cyclist stopped, bought from a vendor one cigarette, and was on his way again.

A boy came along carrying on his head an old kerosene tin, half-filled with some liquid. He must have been working around that new building which was under construction. He had bright eyes and an extraordinarily cheerful face; he was thin but strongly built, and his skin was very dark, burnt by the sun. He wore a shirt and a loin-cloth, both the colour of the earth, brown with long usage. His head was well-shaped, and there was a certain arrogance in his walk—a boy doing a man's work. As he left the crowd behind, he began to sing, and suddenly the whole atmosphere changed. His voice was ordinary, a boyish voice, lusty and raucous; but the song had rhythm, and he would probably have kept time with his hands, had not one hand been holding the kerosene tin on top of his head. He was aware that some-one was walking behind him, but was too cheerful to be shy, and he was obviously not in any way concerned with the peculiar change that had come about in the atmosphere. There was a blessing in the air, a love that covered everything, a gentleness that was simple, without calculation, a goodness that was ever flowering.

Abruptly the boy stopped singing and turned towards a dilapidated hut that stood some distance back from the road. It would soon be raining again.

The visitor said he had held a government position that was good as far as it went, and as he had had a first-class education both at home and abroad, he could have climbed quite high. He was married, he said, and had a couple of children. Life was fairly enjoyable, for success was assured; he owned the house they were living in, and he had put aside money for the education of his children. He knew Sanskrit, and was familiar with the religious tradition. Things were going along pleasantly enough, he said; but one morning he awoke very early, had his bath, and sat down for meditation before his family or the neighbours were up. Though he had had a restful sleep, he couldn't meditate; and suddenly he felt an overwhelming urge to spend the rest of his life in meditation. There was no hesitancy or doubt about it; he would devote his remaining years to finding whatever there was to be found through meditation, and he told his wife, and his two boys, who were at college, that he was going to become a *sannyasi*. His colleagues were surprised by his decision, but accepted his resignation; and in a few days he had left his home, never to return,

That was twenty-five years ago, he went on. He disciplined himself rigorously; but he found it difficult after a life of ease, and it took him a long time to master completely his thoughts and the passions that were in him. Finally, however, he began to have visions of the Buddha, of Christ and Krishna, visions whose beauty was enthralling, and for days he would live as if in a trance, ever widening the boundaries of his mind and heart, utterly absorbed in that love which is devotion to the Supreme. Everything about him—the villagers, the animals, the trees, the grass—was intensely alive, brilliant in its vitality and loveliness. It had taken him all these years to touch the hem of the Infinite, he said, and it was amazing that he had survived it all.

"I have a number of disciples and followers, as is inevitable in this country," he went on, "and one of them suggested to me that I attend a talk which was to be given by you in this town, where I happened to be for a few days. More to please him than to listen to the speaker, I went to the talk, and I was greatly impressed by what was said in reply to a question on meditation. It was stated that without self-knowledge, which in itself is meditation, all meditation is a process of

6

self-hypnosis, a projection of one's own thought and desire. I have been thinking about all this, and have now come to talk things over with you.

"I see that what you say is perfectly true, and it's a great shock to me to perceive that I have been caught in the images or projections of my own mind. I now realize very profoundly what my meditation has been. For twenty-five years I have been held in a beautiful garden of my own making; the personages, the visions -were the outcome of my particular culture and of the things I have desired, studied and absorbed. I now understand the significance of what I have been doing, and I am more than appalled at having wasted so many precious years."

We remained silent for some time.

"What am I to do now?" he presently continued. "Is there any way out of the prison I have built for myself? I can see that what I have come to in my meditation is a dead-end, though only a few days ago it seemed so full of glorious significance. However much I would like to, I can't go back to all that self-delusion and self-stimulation. I want to tear through these veils of illusion and come upon that which is not put together by the mind. You have no idea what I have been through during the last two days! The structure which I had so carefully and painfully built up over a period of twenty-five years has no meaning any more, and it seems to me that I shall have to start all over again. From where am I to start?"

May it not be that there is no restarting at all, but only the perception of the false as the false, which is the beginning of understanding? If one were to start again, one might be caught in another illusion, perhaps in a different manner. What blinds us is the desire to achieve an end, a result; but if we perceived that the result we desire is still within the self-centred field, then there would be no thought of achievement. Seeing the false as the false, and the true as the true, is wisdom.

"But do I really see that what I have been doing for the last twenty-five years is false? Am I aware of all the implications of what I have regarded as meditation?"

The craving for experience is the beginning of illusion. As you now realize, your visions were but the projections of your background, of your conditioning, and it is these projections that you have experienced. Surely this is not meditation. The beginning of meditation is the understanding of the background, of the self; and without this understanding, what is called meditation, however pleasurable or painful, is merely a form of self-hypnosis. You have practised self-control, mastered thought, and concentrated on the furthering of experience. This is a self-centred occupation, it is not meditation; and to perceive that it is not meditation is the beginning of meditation. To see the truth in the false sets the mind free from the false. Freedom from the false does not come about through the desire to achieve it; it comes when the mind is no longer concerned with success, with the attainment of an end. There must be the cessation of all search, and only then is there a possibility of the coming into being of that which is nameless.

"I do not want to deceive myself again."

Self-deception exists when there is any form of craving or attachment: attachment to a prejudice, to an experience, to a system of thought. Consciously or unconsciously, the experiencer is always seeking greater, deeper, wider experience; and as long as the experiencer exists, there must be delusion in one form or another.

"All this involves time and patience, doesn't it?"

Time and patience may be necessary for the achievement of a goal. An ambitious man, worldly or otherwise, needs time to gain his end. Mind is the product of time, as all thought is its result; and thought working to free itself from time only strengthens its enslavement to time. Time exists only when there is a psychological gap between what *is* and what *should* be, which is called the ideal, the end. To be aware of the falseness of this whole manner of thinking is to be free from it —which does not demand any effort, any practice. Understanding is immediate, it is not of time.

"The meditation I have indulged in can have meaning only when it is seen to be false, and I think I see it to be false. But . . ."

Please don't ask the inevitable question as to what there will be in its place, and so on. When the false has dropped away, there is freedom for that which is not false to come into being. You cannot seek the true through the false; the false is not a stepping-stone to the true. The false must cease wholly, not in comparison to the true. There is no comparison between the false and the true; violence and love cannot be compared. Violence must cease for love to be. The cessation of violence is not a matter of time. The perception of the false as the false is the ending of the false. Let the mind be empty, and not filled

8

with the things of the mind. Then there is only meditation, and not a meditator who is meditating.

"I have been occupied with the meditator, the seeker, the enjoyer, the experiencer, which is myself. I have lived in a pleasant garden of my own creation, and have been a prisoner therein. I now see the falseness of all that—dimly, but I see it."

THE ESCAPE FROM WHAT *Is*

IT WAS a rather nice garden, with open, green lawns and flowering bushes, completely enclosed by wide-spreading trees. There was a road running along one side of it, and one often overheard loud talk, especially in the evenings, when people were making their way home. Otherwise it was very quiet in the garden. The grass was watered morning and evening, and at both times there were a great many birds running up and down the lawn in search of worms. They were so eager in their search, that they would come quite close without any fear when one remained seated under a tree. Two birds, green and gold, with square tails and a long, delicate feather sticking out, came regularly to perch among the rose-bushes. They were exactly the same colour as the tender leaves, and it was almost impossible to see them. They had flat heads and long, narrow eyes, with dark beaks. They would swoop in a curve close to the ground, catch an insect, and return to the swaying branch of a rose-bush. It was a most lovely sight, full of freedom and beauty. One couldn't get near them, they were too shy; but if one sat under the tree without moving too much, one would see them disporting themselves, with the sun on their transparent, golden wings.

Often a big mongoose would emerge from the thick bushes, its red nose high in the air and its sharp eyes watching every movement around it. The first day it seemed very disturbed to see a person sitting under the tree, but it soon got used to the human presence. It would cross the whole length of the garden, unhurriedly, its long tail flat on the ground. Sometimes it would go along the edge of the lawn, close to the bushes, and then it would be much more alert, its nose vibrant and twitching. Once the whole family came out, the big mongoose leading, followed by his smaller wife, and behind her, two little

9

ones, all in a line. The babies stopped once or twice to play; but when the mother, feeling that they weren't immediately behind her, turned her head sharply, they raced forward and fell in line again.

In the moonlight the garden became an enchanted place, the motionless, silent trees casting long, dark shadows across the lawn and among the still bushes. After a great deal of bustle and chatter, the birds had settled down for the night in the dark foliage. There was now hardly anyone on the road, but occasionally one would hear a song in the distance, or the notes of a flute being played by someone on his way to the village. Otherwise the garden was very quiet, full of soft whispers. Not a leaf stirred, and the trees gave shape to the hazy, silver sky.

Imagination has no place in meditation; it must be completely set aside, for the mind caught in imagination can only breed delusions. The mind must be clear, without movement, and in the light of that clarity the timeless is revealed.

He was a very old man with a white beard, and his lean body was scarcely covered by the saffron robe of a *sannyasi.* He was gentle in manner and speech, but his eyes were full of sorrow—the sorrow of vain search. At the age of fifteen he had left his family and renounced the world, and for many years he had wandered all over India, visiting *ashramas,* studying, meditating, endlessly searching. He had lived for a time at the *ashrama* of the religious-political leader who had worked so strenuously for the freedom of India, and had stayed at another in the south, where the chanting was pleasant. In the hall where a saint lived silently, he too, amongst many others, had remained silently searching. There were *ashramas* on the east coast and on the west coast where he had stayed, probing, questioning, discussing. In the far north, among the snows and in the cold caves, he had also been; and he had meditated by the gurgling waters of the sacred river. Living among the ascetics, he had physically suffered, and he had made long pilgrimages to sacred temples. He was well-versed in Sanskrit, and it had delighted him to chant as he walked from place to place.

"I have searched for God in every possible way from the age of fifteen, but I have not found Him, and now I am past seventy. I have come to you as I have gone to others, hoping to find God. I must find Him before I die—unless, indeed, He is just another of the many myths of man."

If one may ask, sir, do you think that the immeasurable can be found by searching for it? By following different paths, through discipline and self-torture, through sacrifice and dedicated service, will the seeker come upon the eternal? Surely, sir, whether the eternal exists or not is unimportant, and the truth of it may be uncovered later; but what is important is to understand why we seek, and what it is that we are seeking. Why do we seek?

"I seek because, without God, life has very little meaning. I seek Him out of sorrow and pain. I seek Him because I want peace. I seek Him because He is the permanent, the changeless; because there is death, and He is deathless. He is order, beauty and goodness, and for this reason I seek Him."

That is, being in agony over the impermanent, we hopefully pursue what we call the permanent. The motive of our search is to find comfort in the ideal of the permanent, and this ideal is born of impermanency, it has grown out of the pain of constant change. The ideal is unreal, whereas the pain is real; but we do not seem to understand the fact of pain, and so we cling to the ideal, to the hope of painlessness. Thus there is born in us the dual state of fact and ideal, with its endless conflict between what *is* and what *should* be. The motive of our search is to escape from impermanency, from sorrow, into what the mind thinks is the state of permanency, of everlasting bliss. But that very thought is impermanent, for it is born of sorrow. The opposite, however exalted, holds the seed of its own opposite. Our search, then, is merely the urge to escape from what *is*.

"Do you mean to say that we must cease to search?"

If we give our undivided attention to the understanding of what *is*, then search, as we know it, may not be necessary at all. When the mind is free from sorrow, what need is there to search for happiness?

"Can the mind ever be free from sorrow?"

To conclude that it can or that it cannot be free is to put an end to all inquiry and understanding. We must give our complete attention to the understanding of sorrow, and we cannot do this if we are trying to escape from sorrow, or if our minds are occupied in seeking the cause of it. There must be total attention, and not oblique concern.

When the mind is no longer seeking, no longer breeding conflict through its wants and cravings, when it is silent with understanding, only then can the immeasurable come into being.

THERE WERE several of us in the room. Two had been in prison for many years for political reasons; they had suffered and sacrificed in gaining freedom for the country, and were well-known. Their names were often in the papers, and while they were modest, that peculiar arrogance of achievement and fame was still in their eyes. They were well-read, and they spoke with the facility that comes from public speaking. Another was a politician, a big man with a sharp glance, who was full of schemes and had an eye on self-advancement. He too had been in prison for the same reason, but now he was in a position of power, and his look was assured and purposeful; he could manipulate ideas and men. There was another who had renounced worldly possessions, and who hungered for the power to do good. Very learned and full of apt quotations, he had a smile that was genuinely kind and pleasant, and he was currently travelling all over the country, talking, persuading, and fasting. There were three or four others who also aspired to climb the political or spiritual ladder of recognition or humility.

"I cannot understand," one of them began, "why you are so much against action. Living is action; without action, life is a process of stagnation. We need dedicated people of action to change the social and religious conditions of this unfortunate country. Surely you are not against reform: the landed people voluntarily giving some of their land to the landless, the educating of the villager, the improving of the village, the breaking up of caste divisions, and so on."

Reform, however necessary, only breeds the need for further reform, and there is no end to it. What is essential is a revolution in man's thinking, not patchwork reform. Without a fundamental change in the mind and heart of man, reform merely puts him to sleep by helping him to be further satisfied. This is fairly obvious, isn't it?

"You mean that we must have no reforms?" another asked, with an intensity that was surprising.

"I think you are misunderstanding him," explained one of the older men. "He means that reform will never bring about the total transformation of man. In fact, reform impedes that total transformation, because it puts man to sleep by giving him temporary satisfaction. By multiplying these gratifying reforms, you will slowly drug your neighbour into contentment."

"But if we strictly limit ourselves to one essential reform—the voluntary giving of land to the landless, let's say—until it is brought about, will that not be beneficial?"

Can you separate one part from the whole field of existence? Can you put a fence around it, concentrate upon it, without affecting the rest of the field?

"To affect the whole field of existence is exactly what we plan to do. When we have achieved one reform, we shall turn to another."

Is the totality of life to be understood through the part? Or is it that the whole must first be perceived and understood, and that only then the parts can be examined and reshaped in relation to the whole? Without comprehending the whole, mere concentration on the part only breeds further confusion and misery.

"Do you mean to say," demanded the intense one, "that we must not act or bring about reforms without first studying the whole process of existence?"

"That's absurd, of course," put in the politician. "We simply haven't time to search out the full meaning of life. That will have to be left to the dreamers, to the *gurus,* to the philosophers. *We* have to deal with everyday existence; we have to act, we have to legislate, we have to govern and bring order out of chaos. We are concerned with dams, with irrigation, with better agriculture; we are occupied with trade, with economics, and we must deal with foreign powers. It is sufficient for us if we can manage to carry on from day to day without some major calamity taking place. We are practical men in positions of responsibility, and we have to act to the best of our ability for the good of the people."

If it may be asked, how do you know what's good for the people? You assume so much. You start with so many conclusions; and when you start with a conclusion, whether your own or that of another, all thinking ceases. The calm assumption that you know, and that the other does not, leads to greater misery than the misery of having only one meal a day; for it is the vanity of conclusions that brings about the exploitation of man. In our eagerness to act for the good of others, we seem to do a great deal of harm.

"Some of us think we really *do* know what's good for the country and its people," explained the politician. "Of course, the opposition also thinks *it* knows; but the opposition is not very strong in this country, fortunately for us, so we shall win and be in a position to try out what we think is good and beneficial."

Every party knows, or thinks it knows, what's good for the people. But what is truly good will not create antagonism, either at home or abroad; it will bring about unity between man and man; what is truly good will be concerned with the totality of man, and not with some superficial benefit that may lead only to greater calamity and misery; it will put an end to the division and the enmity that nationalism and organized religions have created. And is the good so easily found?

"If we have to take into consideration *all* the implications of what is good, we shall get nowhere; we shall not be able to act. Immediate necessities demand immediate action, though that action may bring marginal confusion," replied the politician. "We just haven't time to ponder, to philosophize. Some of us are busy from early in the morning till late at night, and we can't sit back to consider the full meaning of each and every action that we must take. We literally cannot afford the pleasure of deep consideration, and we leave that pleasure to others."

"Sir, you appear to be suggesting," said one of those who had thus far remained silent, "that before we perform what we assume to be a good act, we should think out fully the significance of that act, since, even though seemingly beneficial, such an act may produce greater misery in the future. But is it possible to have such profound insight into our own actions? At the moment of action we may think we have that insight, but later on we may discover our blindness."

At the moment of action, we are enthusiastic, impetuous, we are carried away by an idea, or by the personality and the fire of a leader. All leaders, from the most brutal tyrant to the most religious politician, state that they are acting for the good of man, and they all lead to the grave; but nevertheless we succumb to their influence, and follow them. Haven't you, sir, been influenced by such a leader? He may no longer be living, but you still think and act according to his sanctions, his formulas, his pattern of life; or else you are influenced by a more recent leader. So we go from one leader to another, dropping them when it suits our convenience, or when a better leader turns up with greater promise of some 'good'. In our enthusiasm we bring others into the net of our convictions, and they often remain in that net when we ourselves have moved on to other leaders and other convictions. But what is good is free of influence, compulsion and convenience, and any act which is not good in this sense is bound to breed confusion and misery.

"I think we can all plead guilty to being influenced by a leader, directly or indirectly," acquiesced the last speaker, "but our problem is this. Realizing that we receive many benefits from society and give very little in return, and seeing so much misery everywhere, we feel that we have a responsibility towards society, that we must do something to relieve this unending misery. Most of us, however, feel rather lost, and so we follow someone with a strong personality. His dedicated life, his obvious sincerity, his vital thoughts and acts, influence us greatly, and in various ways we become his followers; under his influence we are soon caught up in action, whether it be for the liberation of the country, or for the betterment of social conditions. The acceptance of authority is ingrained in us, and from this acceptance of authority flows action. What you are telling us is so contrary to all we are accustomed to, that it leaves us no measure by which to judge and to act. I hope you see our difficulty."

Surely, sir, any act based on the authority of a book, however sacred, or on the authority of a person, however noble and saintly, is a thoughtless act which must inevitably bring confusion and sorrow. In this and other countries the leader derives his authority from the interpretation of the so-called sacred books, which he liberally quotes, or from his own experiences, which are conditioned by the past, or from his austere life, which again is based on the pattern of saintly records. So the leader's life is as bound by authority as the life of the follower; both are slaves to the book, and to the experience or knowledge of another. With this background, you want to remake the world. Is that possible? Or must you put aside this whole authoritarian, hierarchical outlook on life, and approach the many problems with a fresh, eager mind? Living and action are not separate, they are an interrelated, unitary process; but now you have separated them, have you not? You regard daily living, with its thoughts and acts, as different from the action which is going to change the world.

"Again, this is so," went on the last speaker. "But how are we to throw off this yoke of authority and tradition, which we have willingly and happily accepted from childhood? It is part of our immemorial tradition, and you come along and tell us to set it all aside and rely on ourselves! From what I have heard and read, you say that the very *Atman* itself is without permanency. So you can see why we are confused."

May it not be that you have never really inquired into the authoritarian way of existence? The very questioning of authority is the end of authority. There is no method or system by which the mind can be set free from authority and tradition; if there were, then the system would become the dominating factor.

Why do you accept authority, in the deeper sense of that word? You accept authority, as the *guru* also does, in order to be safe, to be certain, in order to be comforted, to succeed, to reach the other shore. You and the *guru* are worshippers of success; you are both driven by ambition. Where there is ambition, there is no love; and action without love has no meaning.

"Intellectually I see that what you say is true, but inwardly, emotionally, I don't feel the authenticity of it."

There is no intellectual understanding; either we understand, or we don't. This dividing of ourselves into water-tight compartments is another of our absurdities. It is better to admit to ourselves that we do not understand, than to maintain that there is an intellectual understanding, which only breeds arrogance and self-imposed conflict.

"We have taken too much of your time, but perhaps you will allow us to come again."

"I Want to Find the Source of Joy"

THE SUN was behind the hills, the town was afire with the evening glow, and the sky was full of light and splendour. In the lingering twilight, the children were shouting and playing; there was still plenty of time before their dinner. A discordant temple bell was ringing in the distance, and from the nearby mosque a voice was calling for evening prayers. The parrots were coming back from the outlying woods and fields to the dense trees with their heavy foliage, all along the road. They were making an awful noise before settling down for the night. The crows joined them, with their raucous calling, and there were other birds, all scolding and noisy. It was a secluded part of the town, and the sound of the traffic was drowned by the loud chatter

16

of the birds; but with the coming of darkness they became quieter, and within a few minutes they were silent and ready for the night.

A man came along with what looked like a thick rope around his neck. He was holding one end of it. A group of people were chatting and laughing under a tree, where there were patches of light from an electric lamp above; and the man, walking up to the group, put his rope on the ground. There were frightened screams as everyone started running; for the 'rope' was a big cobra, hissing and swaying its hood. Laughing, the man pushed it with his naked toes, and presently picked it up again, holding it just behind the head. Of course, its fangs had been removed; it was really harmless, but frightening. The man offered to put the snake around my neck, but he was satisfied when I stroked it. It was scaly and cold, with strong, rippling muscles, and eyes that were black and staring—for snakes have no eyelids. We walked a few steps together, and the cobra around his neck was never still, but all movement.

The street-lights made the stars seem dim and far away, but Mars was red and clear. A beggar was walking along with slow, weary steps, hardly moving; he was covered with rags, and his feet were wrapped in torn pieces of canvas, tied together with heavy string. He had a long stick, and was muttering to himself, and he did not look up as we passed. Further along the street there was a smart and expensive hotel, with cars of almost every make drawn up in front of it.

A young professor from one of the universities, rather nervous and with a high-pitched voice and bright eyes, said that he had come a long way to ask a question which was most important to him.

"I have known various joys: the joy of conjugal love, the joy of health, of interest, and of good companionship. Being a professor of literature, I have read widely, and delight in books. But I have found that every joy is fleeting in nature; from the smallest to the greatest, they all pass away in time. Nothing I touch seems to have any permanency, and even literature, the greatest love of my life, is beginning to lose its perennial joy. I feel there must be a permanent source of all joy, but though I have sought for it intensely, I have not found it."

Search is an extraordinarily deceptive phenomenon, is it not? Being dissatisfied with the present, we seek something beyond it. Aching with the present, we probe into the future or the past; and even that which we find is consumed in the present. We never stop to inquire into the full content of the present, but are always pursuing the dreams of the future; or from among the dead memories of the past we select the richest, and give life to it. We cling to that which has been, or reject it in the light of to-morrow, and so the present is slurred over; it is merely a passage, to be gone through as quickly as possible.

"Whether it's in the past or in the future, I want to find the source of joy," he went on. "You know what I mean, sir. I no longer seek the objects from which joy is derived—ideas, books, people, nature—but the source of joy itself, beyond all transiency. If one doesn't find that source, one is everlastingly caught in the sorrow of the impermanent."

Don't you think, sir, that we must understand the significance of that word 'search'? Otherwise we shall be talking at cross-purposes. Why is there this urge to seek, this anxiety to find, this compulsion to attain? Perhaps if we can uncover the motive and see its implications, we shall be able to understand the significance of search.

"My motive is simple and direct: I want to find the permanent source of joy, for every joy I have known has been a passing thing. The urge that is making me seek is the misery of not having anything enduring. I want to get away from this sorrow of uncertainty, and I don't think there's anything abnormal about it. Anyone who is at all thoughtful must be seeking the joy I am seeking. Others may call it by a different name—God, truth, bliss, freedom, Moksha, and so on—but it's essentially the same thing."

Being caught in the pain of impermanency, the mind is driven to seek the permanent, under whatever name; and its very craving for the permanent creates the permanent, which is the opposite of what *is*. So really there is no search, but only the desire to find the comforting satisfaction of the permanent. When the mind becomes aware of being in a constant state of flux, it proceeds to build the opposite of that state, thereby getting caught in the conflict of duality; and then, wanting to escape from this conflict, it pursues still another opposite. So the mind is bound to the wheel of opposites.

"I am aware of this reactionary process of the mind, as you explain it; but should one not seek at all? Life would be a pretty poor thing if there were no discovering."

Do we discover anything new through search? The new is not the opposite of the old, it is not the antithesis of what *is*. If the new is a projection of the old, then it is only a modified continuation of the old.

18

All recognition is based on the past, and what is recognizable is not the new. Search arises from the pain of the present, therefore what is sought is already known. You are seeking comfort, and probably you will find it; but that also will be transient, for the very urge to find is impermanent. All desire for something—for joy, for God, or whatever it be—is transient.

"Do I understand you to mean that, since my search is the outcome of desire, and desire is transient, therefore my search is in vain?"

If you realize the truth of this, then transience itself is joy.

"How am I to realize the truth of it?"

There is no 'how', no method. The method breeds the idea of the permanent. As long as the mind desires to arrive, to gain, to attain, it will be in conflict. Conflict is insensitivity. It is only the sensitive mind that realizes the true. Search is born of conflict, and with the cessation of conflict there is no need to seek. Then there is bliss.

PLEASURE, HABIT AND AUSTERITY

THE ROAD led south of the noisy, sprawling town, with its seemingly endless rows of new buildings. The road was crowded with buses, cars and bullock-carts, and with hundreds of cyclists who were going home from their offices, looking worn out after a long day of routine work which held no interest for them. Many stopped at an open market on the roadside to buy wilted vegetables. As we went through the outskirts of the town, there were rich green trees on both sides of the road, recently washed by the heavy rains. The sun was setting to our right, a huge golden ball above the distant hills. There were many goats among the trees, and the kids were chasing each other. The curving road went past an eleventh-century tower, standing red and lofty amidst Hindu and Mogul ruins. Dotted about here and there were ancient tombs, and a splendid, ruined archway told of a glory that was long ago.

The car was stopped, and we walked along the road. A group of peasants were returning from their work in the fields; all were women, and after a long day of toil, they were singing a lilting song. In that peaceful countryside their voices rang out, clear, resonant and gay. As we approached, they shyly stopped singing, but continued with their song as soon as we had passed.

The evening light was among the gently rolling hills, and the trees were dark against the evening sky. On a huge jutting rock stood the crumbling battlements of an ancient fortress. There was an astonishing beauty covering the land; it was all about us, filling every nook and corner of the earth, and the dark recesses of our hearts and minds. There is only love, not the love of God and the love of man; it is not to be divided. A big owl flew silently across the moon, and a group of the educated villagers were talking loudly, debating whether or not to go to the cinema in the town; they were rowdy, and aggressively occupied half of the road.

It was pleasant in the soft moonlight, and the shadows on the ground were clear and sharp. A lorry came rattling along the road, blowing its threatening horn; but it soon passed, leaving the countryside to the loveliness of the evening, and to the immense solitude.

He was a healthy and thoughtful young man, still in his thirties, and was employed in some government office. He was not too averse to his work, he explained, and everything considered, had a fairly good salary and a promising future. He was married and had a son of four whom he had wanted to bring along, but the boy's mother had insisted that he would be a nuisance.

"I attended one or two of your talks," he said, "and, if I may, I would like to ask a question. I have got into certain bad habits which are bothering me, and which I want to be free of. For several months now I have tried to get rid of them, but without success. What am I to do?"

Let us consider habit itself, and not divide it into good and bad. The cultivation of habit, however good and respectable, only makes the mind dull. What do we mean by habit? Let us think it out, and not depend on mere definition.

"Habit is an oft-repeated act."

It is a momentum of action in a certain direction, whether pleasant or unpleasant, and it may operate consciously or unconsciously, with thought, or thoughtlessly. Is that it?

"Yes, sir, that's right."

Some feel the need of coffee in the morning, and without it they get a headache. The body may not have required it at first, but it has gradually got used to the pleasurable taste and stimulation of coffee, and now it suffers when deprived of it.

"But is coffee a necessity?"

What do you mean by a necessity?

"Good food is necessary to good health."

Surely; but the tongue becomes accustomed to food of a certain kind or flavour, and then the body feels deprived and anxious when it does not get what it's used to. This insistence on food of a particular kind indicates—does it not?—that a habit has been formed, a habit based on pleasure and the memory of it.

"But how can one break a pleasurable habit? To break an unpleasant habit is comparatively easy, but my problem is how to break the pleasant ones."

As I said, we aren't considering pleasant and unpleasant habits, or how to break away from either of them, but we are trying to understand habit itself. We see that habit is formed when there is pleasure and the demand for the continuation of the pleasure. Habit is based on pleasure and the memory of it. An initially unpleasant experience may gradually become a pleasant and 'necessary' habit.

Now, let's go a little further into the matter. What is your problem?

"Amongst other habits, sexual indulgence has become a powerful and consuming habit with me. I have tried to bring it under control by disciplining myself against it, by dieting, practising various exercises, and so on, but in spite of all my resistance the habit has continued."

Perhaps there is no other release in your life, no other driving interest. Probably you are bored with your work, without being aware of it; and religion for you may be only a repetitious ritual, a set of dogmas and beliefs without any meaning at all. If you are inwardly thwarted, frustrated, then sex becomes your only release. To be inwardly alert, to think anew about your work, about the absurdities of society, to find out for yourself the true significance of religion—it is this that will free the mind from being enslaved by any habit.

"I used to be interested in religion and in literature, but I have no leisure for either of them now, because all my time is taken up with my work. I am not really unhappy in it, but I realize that earning a livelihood isn't everything, and it may be that, as you say, if I can find time for wider and deeper interests, it will help to break down the habit which is bothering me."

As we said, habit is the repetition of a pleasurable act brought about by the stimulating memories and images which the mind evokes. The glandular secretions and their results, as in the case of hunger, are not a habit, they are the normal process of the physical organism; but when the mind indulges in sensation, stimulated by thoughts and pictures, then surely the formation of habit is set going. Food is necessary, but the demand for a particular taste in food is based on habit. Finding pleasure in certain thoughts and acts, subtle or crude, the mind insists on their continuance, thereby breeding habit. A repetitive act, like brushing one's teeth in the morning, becomes a habit when attention is not given to it. Attention frees the mind from habit.

"Are you implying that we must get rid of all pleasure?"

No, sir. We are not trying to get rid of anything, or to acquire anything; we are trying to understand the full implication of habit; and we have to understand, too, the problems of pleasure. Many *sannyasis, yogis,* saints, have denied themselves pleasure; they have tortured themselves and forced the mind to resist, to be insensitive to pleasure in every form. It is a pleasure to see the beauty of a tree, of a cloud, of moonlight on the water, or of a human being; and to deny that pleasure is to deny beauty.

On the other hand, there are people who reject the ugly and cling to the beautiful. They want to remain in the lovely garden of their own making, and shut out the noise, the smell and the brutality that exist beyond the wall. Very often they succeed in this; but you cannot shut out the ugly and hold to the beautiful without becoming dull, insensitive. You must be sensitive to sorrow as well as to joy, and not eschew the one and seek out the other. Life is both death and love. To love is to be vulnerable, sensitive, and habit breeds insensitivity; it destroys love.

"I am beginning to feel the beauty of what you are saying. It is true that I have made myself dull and stupid. I used to love to go into the woods, to listen to the birds, to observe the faces of people in the streets, and I now see what I have allowed habit to do to me. But what is love?"

Love is not mere pleasure, a thing of memory; it's a state of intense vulnerability and beauty, which is denied when the mind builds walls of self-centred activity. Love is life, and so it is also death. To deny death and cling to life is to deny love.

"I am really beginning to have an insight into all this, and into myself. Without love, life does become mechanical and habit-ridden. The work I do in the office is largely mechanical, and so indeed is the rest of my life; I am caught in a vast wheel of routine and boredom. I have been asleep, and now I must wake up."

The very realization that you have been asleep is already an awakened state; there is no need of volition.

Now, let's go a little further into the matter. There is no beauty without austerity, is there?

"That I don't understand, sir."

Austerity does not lie in any outward symbol or act: wearing a loincloth or a monk's robe, taking only one meal a day, or living the life of a hermit. Such disciplined simplicity, however rigorous, is not austerity; it is merely an outward show without an inner reality. Austerity is the simplicity of inward aloneness, the simplicity of a mind that is purged of all conflict, that is not caught in the fire of desire, even the desire for the highest. Without this austerity, there can be no love; and beauty is of love.

"WON'T YOU JOIN OUR ANIMAL-WELFARE SOCIETY?"

THE SUN was very clear in the sky, and there was a cool breeze from the sea. It was still fairly early in the morning; there were but few people in the streets, and the heavy traffic had not yet begun. Fortunately, it wasn't going to be too hot a day; but there was dust everywhere, fine and penetrating, for there had been no rain during the long, hot summer. In the small, well-kept park, dust lay heavily on the trees; but under the trees, and among the bushes, there was a stream of cool, fresh water, brought down from a lake in the distant mountains. On a bench by the stream it was pleasant and peaceful, and there was plenty of shade. Later in the day, the park would be crowded with children and their nurses, and with people who worked in offices. The sound of running water among the bushes was friendly and welcoming, and many birds fluttered on the edge of the stream, bathing and chirping happily. Big peacocks wandered in and out of the bushes, stately and unafraid. In deep pools of clear water there were large goldfish, and the children came every day to watch and feed them, and to take delight in the many white geese which swam about in a shallow pool.

Leaving the little park, we drove along a noisy, dusty road to the foot of a rocky hill, and walked up a steep path to an entrance which opened into the sacred precincts of an ancient temple. To the west could be seen an expanse of the blue sea, famous for its historic naval battle, and to the east were the low-lying hills, barren and harsh in the autumnal air, but full of silent and happy memories. To the north towered the higher mountains, overlooking the hills and the hot valley. The ancient temple on the rocky hill stood in ruins, destroyed by the brutal violence of man. Its broken marble columns, washed by the rains of many centuries, seemed almost transparent—light, fading, and stately. The temple was still a perfect thing, to be touched and silently gazed upon. A small yellow flower, bright in the morning light, grew in a crevice at the foot of a splendid column. To sit in the shadow of one of those columns, looking at the silent hills and the distant sea, was to experience something beyond the calculations of the mind.

One morning, climbing the rocky hill, we found a large crowd around the temple. There were huge camera booms, reflectors and other paraphernalia, all bearing the trade-mark of a well-known cinema company, and green, canvas-back chairs with names printed upon them. Electric cables were lying about on the ground, directors and technicians were shouting at each other, and the principal actors were preening themselves and being fussed over by the dressers. Two men, wearing the robes of orthodox priests, were waiting for their call, and gaily-dressed women were chatting and giggling. They were shooting a picture!

We sat in a small room, and through an open window the green lawn, sparkling in the morning sun, threw a soft, green light on the white ceiling. Wearing expensive jewels, well-made sandals with high heels, and a *sari* that must have cost a good bit of money, she explained that she was one of the chief workers in an organization dedicated to animal welfare. Man was appallingly cruel to animals, beating them, twisting their tails, goading them with sticks that had a nail at the end, and otherwise perpetrating upon them unspeakable horrors. They must be protected by legislation, and to this end, public opinion, which is so indifferent, must be aroused through propaganda, and so on.

"I have come to ask if you will help in this important work. Other prominent public figures have come forward to offer their help, and it would be fitting if you also joined us."

Do you mean that I should join your society?

"It would be a great help if you did. Will you?"

Do you think that organizations against the cruelty of man will bring love into being? Through legislation, can you bring about the brotherhood of man?

"If we don't work for what is good, how else can it be brought about? The good doesn't come into being through our withdrawal from society; on the contrary, we must all work together, from the greatest to the least among us, to bring it about."

Of course we must work together, that is most natural; but co-operation isn't a matter of following a blue-print laid down by the State, by the leader of a party or a group, or by any other authority. To work together through fear or through greed for reward is not co-operation. Co-operation comes naturally and easily when we love what we are doing; and then co-operation is a delight. But to love, there must first be the putting aside of ambition, greed and envy. Isn't this so?

"To put aside personal ambition will take centuries, and in the meantime the poor animals suffer."

There is no meantime, there is only now. You do want man to love animals and his fellow human beings, do you not? You do want to put an end to cruelty, not at some future time, but now. If you think in terms of the future, love has no reality. If one may ask, which is the true beginning of any action: is it love, or the capacity to organize?

"Why do you separate the two?"

Is there separation implied in the question just asked? If action arises from seeing the necessity of a certain work, and from having the capacity to organize it, such action leads in a direction quite different from that of action which is the outcome of love, and in which also there is the capacity to organize. When action springs from frustration, or from the desire for power, however excellent that action may be in itself, its effects are bound to be confusing and wrought with sorrow. The action of love is not fragmentary, contradictory, or separative; it has a total, integrated effect.

"Why are you raising this issue? I came to ask if you would kindly help us in our work, and you are questioning the source of action. What for?"

If one may ask, what is the source of your own interest in bringing about an organization which will help the animals? Why are you so active?

"I think that's fairly obvious. I see how appallingly the poor animals are treated, and I want to help, through legislation and other means, to put an end to this cruelty. I don't know if I have any motive other than this. Perhaps I have."

Isn't it important to find out? Then you may be able to help the animals and man in a greater and deeper sense. Are you organizing this movement out of the desire to be somebody, to fulfil your ambition, or to escape from a sense of frustration?

"You are very serious; you want to go to the root of things, don't you? I might as well be frank. In a way I am very ambitious. I do want to be known as a reformer; I want to be a success, and not a miserable failure. Everyone is struggling up the ladder of success and fame; I think it is normal and human. Why do you object to it?"

I am not objecting to it. I am only pointing out that if your motive is not that of really helping the animals, then you are using them as a means to your self-aggrandizement, which is what the bullock-cart driver is doing. He does it in a crude, brutal way, whereas you and others are more subtle and cunning about it, that is all. You are not stopping cruelty as long as your efforts to stop it are profitable to yourself. If by helping the animals you could not fulfil your ambition, or escape from your frustration and sorrow, you would then turn to some other means of fulfilment. All this indicates—doesn't it?—that you are not interested in animals at all, except as a means to your own personal gain.

"But everybody is doing that in one way or another, aren't they? And why shouldn't I?"

Of course, that is what the vast majority of people are doing. From the biggest politician to the village manipulator, from the highest prelate to the local priest, from the greatest social reformer to the worn-out social worker, each one is using the country, the poor, or the name of God, as a means of fulfilling his ideas, his hopes, his Utopias. *He* is the centre, *his* is the power and the glory, but always in the name of the people, in the name of the holy, in the name of the down-trodden. It is for this reason that there is such a frightening and sorrowful mess in the world. These are not the people who will bring peace to the world, who will stop exploitation, who will put an end to cruelty. On the contrary, they are responsible for even greater confusion and misery.

"I see the truth of this, all right, as you explain it; but there is pleasure in exercising power, and I, like others, succumb to it."

Can't we leave others out of our discussion? When you compare yourself with others, it is to justify or condemn what you do, and then you are not thinking at all. You are defending yourself by taking a stand, and that way we shall get nowhere.

Now, as a human being who is somewhat aware of the significance of all that we have talked about this morning, don't you feel there may be a different approach to all this cruelty, to man's ambition, and so on?

"Sir, I have heard a great deal about you from my father, and I came, partly out of curiosity, and partly because I thought that you might join us if I could be sufficiently persuasive. But I was wrong.

"May I ask: how am I to forget myself, outwardly and inwardly, and really love? After all, being a Brahman, and all that, I have the religious life in my blood; but I have wandered so far from the religious outlook that I don't think I can ever get back to it again. What am I to do? Perhaps I am not asking this question in all seriousness, and I shall probably continue my superficial life; but can you not tell me something that will remain in me like a seed and germinate in spite of me?"

The religious life is not a matter of revival; you cannot put new life into what is past and gone. Let the past be buried, don't try to revive it. Be aware that you are interested in yourself, and that your activities are self-centred. Don't pretend, don't deceive yourself. Be aware of the fact that you are ambitious, that you are seeking power, position, prestige, that you want to be important. Don't justify it to yourself or to another. Be simple and direct about what you are. Then love may come unasked, when you are not seeking it. Love alone can purge the cunning pursuits from the hidden recesses of the mind. Love is the only way out of man's confusion and sorrow, not the efficient organizations that he puts together.

"But how can one individual, even though he may love, affect the course of events without collective organization and action? To put a stop to cruelty will require the co-operation of a great many people. How can this be achieved?"

If you really feel that love is the only true source of action, you will talk to others about it, and you will then gather together a few who have a similar feeling. The few may grow into the many, but that is not your concern. You are concerned with love and its total action. It is only this total action on the part of each individual that will bring a wholly different world into being.

IT WAS an enchanting walk. The path from the house lay through the vineyard, and the grapes were just beginning to ripen; they were rich and full, and would yield a great deal of red wine. The vineyard was well-tended, and there were no weeds. Next came the beautifully-kept tobacco patch, long and wide. After the rain, the plants were beginning to blossom with pink flowers, neat and tidy; their faint smell of fresh tobacco, so different from the sickening smell of burnt tobacco, would become stronger in the hot sun. The long stem on which the flowers grew would presently be cut off to make the pale, silvery-green tobacco leaves, already quite large, grow still larger and richer by the time they were picked. Then they would be gathered together, classified, tied on long strings, and strung up in the long building behind the house, to dry evenly where the sun wouldn't touch them, but where there would be the evening breeze. Men with oxen were working in that tobacco patch even then, drawing a furrow between the long, straight rows of plants, to destroy the weeds. The soil had been carefully prepared and heavily manured, and weeds grew in it as richly as did the tobacco plants; but after all those weeks, there was not a single weed to be seen.

The path went on through an orchard of peach, pear, plum, greengage, nectarine and other trees, all laden with ripening fruit. In the evening there was a sweet scent in the air, and during the day, the hum of many bees. Beyond the orchard, the path led down a long slope, deep into thick, sheltering woods. Here the earth was soft under the feet with the dead leaves of many summers. It was very cool under the trees, for the sun had little chance to penetrate their thick foliage; the soil was always damp and sweet-smelling, giving off the scent of rich humus. There were quantities of mushrooms, most of them the inedible variety. Here and there could be found the kind that can be eaten, but you had to look for them; they were more retiring, generally hidden under a leaf of the same colour. The peasants would come early to pick them for the market, or for their own use.

There were hardly any birds in those woods, which spread for miles over the gently rolling hills. It was very quiet; there was not even the stirring of a breeze among the leaves. But there was always a movement of some kind in those woods, and that movement was part of the immense silence; it was not disturbing, and it seemed to add to the stillness of the mind. The trees, the insects, the spreading ferns, were not separate, something seen from the outside; they were part of that quietude, within and without. Even the muffled roar of a distant train was contained in that quietness. There was complete absence of resistance, and the bark of a dog, insistent and penetrating, seemed to heighten the stillness.

Beyond the woods was the lovely, curving river. It was not too wide or impressive, but wide enough to give space for the keen eye to see people on the opposite bank. All along both banks there were trees, mostly poplars, tall and stately, with their leaves aquiver in the breeze. The water was deep and cool, and always flowing. It was a beautiful thing to watch, so alive and rich. A lonely fisherman was sitting on a stool, with a picnic basket beside him and a newspaper on his knee. The river brought contentment and peace, though the fish seemed to avoid the bait. The river would always be there, though there would be wars and men would die; it would always be nourishing the earth and men. Far away were the snow-covered mountains, and on a clear evening, when the setting sun was upon them, their lofty peaks could be seen like sunlit clouds.

Three or four of us were in the room, and just beyond the window was a wide, sparkling lawn. The sky was pale blue, with heavy, billowy clouds.

"Is it ever really possible," asked the man, "for the mind to free itself from its conditioning? If so, what is the state of a mind that has unconditioned itself? I have heard your talks over a period of several years, and have given a great deal of thought to the matter, yet my mind doesn't seem able to break away from the traditions and ideas that were implanted during childhood. I know that I am as conditioned as any other person. From childhood we are taught to conform—taught brutally, or with affection and gentle suggestions—until conforming becomes instinctive, and the mind is afraid of the insecurity of *not* conforming.

"I have a friend who grew up in a Catholic environment," he went on, "and of course she was told of sin, hell-fire, the comforting joys of heaven, and all the rest of it. Upon reaching maturity, and after a great deal of reflection, she threw off the Catholic structure of thought;

yet even now, in middle life, she finds herself influenced by the idea of hell, with its contagious fears. Though my background is superficially quite different, I, like her, am also afraid of not conforming. I see the absurdity of conforming, but I can't shake it off; and even if I could, I should probably be doing the same thing in another way—merely conforming to a new pattern."

"That's also my difficulty," added one of the ladies. "I seè very clearly the many ways in which I am bound by tradition; but can I break away from my present bondage without being caught in a new one? There are people who drift from one religious organization to another, always seeking, never satisfied; and when at last they *are* satisfied, they become frightful bores. That's probably what will happen to me if I try to break away from my present conditioning: without knowing it, I shall be dragged into another pattern of life."

"As a matter of fact," went on the man, "most of us have never thought very deeply about how our mind is almost entirely shaped by the society and the culture in which we have grown up. We are unaware of our conditioning and just carry on, struggling, achieving, or being frustrated within the pattern of a given society. That's the lot of almost all of us, including the political and religious leaders. Unfortunately for me, perhaps, I came to hear several of your talks, and then the pain of questioning began. For some time I did not think about this matter very deeply, but suddenly I find myself becoming serious. I have been experimenting, and am now aware of many things in myself which I had never noticed before. If I may continue without everyone feeling that I am talking too much, I would like to go into this question of conditioning a little further."

When the others had assured him that they too were deeply interested in this subject, he went on.

"After having heard or read most of the things you have said, I realized how conditioned I am; and I likewise saw that one must be free from conditioning—not only from the conditioning of the superficial mind, but also from that of the unconscious. I perceived the absolute necessity of it. But what is actually taking place is this: the conditioning I received in my youth continues, and at the same time there is a strong desire to uncondition myself. So my mind is caught in this conflict between the conditioning of which I am aware, and the urge to be free from it. That's my actual position right now. How shall I proceed from there?"

30

Does not the urge of the mind to free itself from its conditioning set going another pattern of resistance and conditioning? Having become aware of the pattern or mould in which you have grown up, you want to be free from it; but will not this desire to be free condition the mind again in a different manner? The old pattern insists that you conform to authority, and now you are developing a new one which maintains that you must *not* conform; so you have two patterns, one in conflict with the other. As long as there is this inner contradiction, further conditioning takes place.

"I know that the old pattern is quite absurd and dead, and that there must be freedom from it, otherwise my mind will go on in the same stupid way."

Let's be patient and go into it more. The old pattern has told you to conform, and for various reasons—fear of insecurity, and so on—you have conformed. Now, for reasons of a different kind, but in which there is still fear and the desire for security, you feel you must *not* conform. That's so, isn't it?

"Yes, that's so, more or less. But the old is stupid, and I must be free from stupidity."

May I point out, sir, that you are not listening. You go on insisting that the old is bad, and you must have the new. But having the new is not the problem at all.

"That's my problem, sir."

Is it? You think so, but let's see. Please don't carry on with your own thoughts about the problem, but just listen, will you?

"I will try."

One conforms instinctively for various reasons: out of attachment, fear, the desire for reward, and so on. That is one's first response. Then somebody comes along and says that one must be free from conditioning, and there arises the urge *not* to conform. Do you follow?

"Yes, sir, that's clear."

Now, is there any essential difference between the desire to conform, and the craving to be free of conformity?

"It seems as if there should be, but I really don't know. What do you say, sir?"

It is not for me to tell you, and for you to accept. Must you not find out for yourself whether there is any fundamental difference between these two seemingly opposing desires?"

"How am I to find out?"

By neither condemning the one nor eagerly pursuing the other. What is the state of the mind that is hungering after freedom from conformity, and rejecting conformity? Please don't answer me, but feel it out, actually experience that state. Words are necessary for communication, but the word is not the actual experience. Unless you really experience and understand that state, your efforts to be free will only bring about the formation of other patterns. Isn't that so?

"I don't quite understand."

Surely, not to put an end completely to the mechanism that produces patterns, moulds, whether positive or negative, is to continue in a modified pattern or conditioning.

"I can understand this verbally, but I don't really *feel* it."

To a hungry man, the mere description of food is valueless; he wants to eat.

There is the urge that makes for conformity, and the urge to be free. However dissimilar these two urges may seem to be, are they not fundamentally similar? And if they are fundamentally similar, then your pursuit of freedom is vain, for you will only move from one pattern to another, endlessly. There is no noble or better conditioning; all conditioning is pain. The desire to be, or not to be, breeds conditioning, and it is this desire that has to be understood.

THE VOID WITHIN

SHE WAS carrying a large basket on her head, holding it in place with one hand; it must have been quite heavy, but the swing of her walk was not altered by the weight. She was beautifully poised, her walk easy and rhythmical. On her arm were large metal bangles which made a slight tinkling sound, and on her feet were old, worn-out sandals. Her *sari* was torn and dirty with long use. She generally had several companions with her, all of them carrying baskets, but that morning she was alone on the rough road. The sun wasn't too hot yet, and high up in the blue sky some vultures were moving in wide circles without a flutter of their wings. The river ran silently by the road. It was a very peaceful morning, and that solitary woman with the large basket on her head seemed to be the focus of beauty and grace; all things seemed to be pointing to her and accepting her as part of their own being. She was not a separate entity, but part of you and me, and of that tamarind tree. She wasn't walking in front of me, but I was walking with that basket on my head. It wasn't an illusion, a thought-out, wished-for, and cultivated identification, which would be ugly beyond measure, but an experience that was natural and immediate. The few steps that separated us had vanished; time, memory, and the wide distance that thought breeds, had totally disappeared. There was only that woman, not I looking at her. And it was a long way to the town, where she would sell the contents of her basket. Towards evening she would come back along that road and cross the little bamboo bridge on her way to her village, only to appear again the next morning with her basket full.

He was very serious, and no longer young, but he had a pleasant smile and was in good health. Sitting cross-legged on the floor, he explained in somewhat halting English, of which he was rather shy, that he had been to college and taken his M.A., but had not spoken English for so many years that he had almost forgotten it. He had read a great deal of Sanskrit literature, and Sanskrit words were frequently on his lips. He had come, he said, to ask several questions about the inward void, the emptiness of the mind. Then he began to chant in Sanskrit, and the room was instantly filled with a deep resonance, pure and penetrating. He went on chanting for some time, and it was a delight to listen. His face shone with the meaning he was giving to each word, and with the love he felt for what the word contained. He was devoid of any artifice, and was much too serious to put on a pose.

"I am very happy to have chanted those *slokas* in your presence. To me they have great significance and beauty; I have meditated upon them for many years, and they have been to me a source of guidance and strength. I have trained myself not to be easily moved, but these *slokas* bring tears to my eyes. The very sound of the words, with their rich meaning, fills my heart, and then life is not a travail and a misery. Like every other human being, I have known sorrow; there has been death and the ache of life. I had a wife who died before I left the comforts of my father's house, and now I know the meaning of voluntary poverty. I am telling you all this merely by way of explanation. I am not frustrated, lonely, or anything of that kind. My heart takes delight in many things; but my father used to tell me something about your talks, and an acquaintance has urged me to see you; and so here I am.

"I want you to speak to me of the immeasurable void," he went on. "I have had a feeling of that void, and I think I have touched the hem of it in my wanderings and meditations." Then he quoted a *sloka* to explain and to support his experience. If it may be pointed out, the authority of another, however great, is no proof of the truth of your experience. Truth needs no proof by action, nor does it depend on any authority; so let's put aside all authority and tradition, and try to find out the truth of this matter for ourselves.

"That would be very difficult for me, for I am steeped in tradition— not in the tradition of the world, but in the teachings of the *Gita*, the *Upanishads*, and so on. Is it right for me to let all that go? Would that not be ingratitude on my part?"

Neither gratitude nor ingratitude are in any way involved; we are concerned with discovering the truth or the falseness of that void of which you have spoken. If you walk on the path of authority and tradition, which is knowledge, you will experience only what you desire to experience, helped on by authority and tradition. It will not be a discovery; it will already be known, a thing to be recognized and experienced. Authority and tradition may be wrong, they may be a comforting illusion. To discover whether that void is true or false, whether it exists or is merely another invention of the mind, the mind must be free from the net of authority and tradition.

"Can the mind ever free itself from this net?"

The mind cannot free itself, for any effort on its part to be free only weaves another net in which it will again be caught. Freedom is not an opposite; to be free is not to be free *from* something, it's not a state of release from bondage. The urge to be free breeds its own bondage. Freedom is a state of being which is not the outcome of the desire to be free. When the mind understands this, and sees the falseness of authority and tradition, then only does the false wither away.

"It may be that I have been induced to feel certain things by my reading, and by the thoughts based on such reading; but apart from all that, I have vaguely felt from childhood, as in a dream, the existence of this void. There has always been an intimation of it, a nostalgic feeling for it; and as I grew older, my reading of various religious books only strengthened this feeling, giving it more vitality and purpose. But I begin to realize what you mean. I have depended almost entirely on the description of the experiences of others, as given in the sacred Scriptures. This dependence I can throw off, since I now see the necessity of doing so; but can I revive that original, uncontaminated feeling for that which is beyond words?"

What is revived is not the living, the new; it is a memory, a dead thing, and you cannot put life into the dead. To revive and live on memory is to be a slave to stimulation, and a mind that depends on stimulation, conscious or unconscious, will inevitably become dull and insensitive. Revival is the perpetuation of confusion; to turn to the dead past in the moment of a living crisis is to seek a pattern of life which has its roots in decay. What you experienced as a youth, or only yesterday, is over and gone; and if you cling to the past, you prevent the quickening experience of the new.

"As I think you will realize, sir, I am really in earnest, and for me it has become an urgent necessity to understand and to *be* of that void. What am I to do?"

One has to empty the mind of the known; all the knowledge that one has gathered must cease to have any influence on the living mind. Knowledge is ever of the past, it is the very process of the past, and the mind must be free from this process. Recognition is part of the process of knowledge, isn't it?

"How is that?"

To recognize something, you must have known or experienced it previously, and this experience is stored up as knowledge, memory. Recognition comes out of the past. You may have experienced, once upon a time, this void, and having once experienced it, you now crave for it. The original experience came about without your pursuing it; but now you are pursuing it, and the thing that you are seeking is not the void, but the renewal of an old memory. If it is to happen again, all remembrance of it, all knowledge of it, must disappear. All search for it must cease, for search is based on the desire to experience.

"Do you really mean that I must not search it out? This seems incredible!"

The motive of search is of greater significance than the search itself. The motive pervades, guides and shapes the search. The motive of your search is the desire to experience the unknowable, to know the bliss and the immensity of it. This desire has brought into being the experiencer who craves for experience. The experiencer is searching for greater, wider and more significant experience. All other experiences having lost their taste, the experiencer now longs for the void; so there is the experiencer, and the thing to be experienced. Thus conflict is set going between the two, between the pursuer and the pursued.

"This I understand very well, because it is exactly the state I am in. I now see that I am caught in a net of my own making."

As every seeker is, and not just the seeker after truth, God, the void, and so on. Every ambitious or covetous man who is pursuing power, position, prestige, every idealist, every worshipper of the State, every builder of a perfect Utopia—they are all caught in the same net. But if once you understand the total significance of search, will you continue to seek the void?

"I perceive the inward meaning of your question, and I have already stopped seeking."

If this be a fact, then what is the state of the mind that is not seeking?

"I do not know; the whole thing is so new to me that I shall have to gather myself and observe. May I have a few minutes before we go any further?"

After a pause, he continued.

"I perceive how extraordinarily subtle it is; how difficult it is for the experiencer, the watcher, not to step in. It seems almost impossible for thought not to create the thinker; but as long as there is a thinker, an experiencer, there must obviously be separation from, and conflict with, that which is to be experienced. And you are asking, aren't you, what is the state of the mind when there is no conflict?"

Conflict exists when desire assumes the form of the experiencer and pursues that which is to be experienced; for that which is to be experienced is also put together by desire.

"Please be patient with me, and let me understand what you are saying. Desire not only builds the experiencer, the watcher, but also brings into being that which is to be experienced, the watched. So desire is the cause of the division between the experiencer and the thing to be experienced, and it is this division that sustains conflict. Now, you are asking, what is the state of the mind which is no longer in conflict, which is not driven by desire? But can this question be answered without the watcher who is watching the experience of desirelessness?"

When you are conscious of your humility, has not humility ceased? Is there virtue when you deliberately practise virtue? Such practice is the strengthening of self-centered activity, which puts an end to virtue.

The moment you are aware that you are happy, you cease to be happy. What is the state of the mind which is not caught in the conflict of desire? The urge to find out is part of the desire which has brought into being the experiencer and the thing to be experienced, is it not?

"That's so. Your question was a trap for me, but I am thankful you asked it. I am seeing more of the intricate subtleties of desire."

It was not a trap, but a natural and inevitable question which you would have asked yourself in the course of your inquiry. If the mind is not extremely alert, aware, it is soon caught again in the net of its own desire.

"One final question: is it really possible for the mind to be totally free of the desire for experience, which sustains this division between the experiencer and the thing to be experienced?"

Find out, sir. When the mind is entirely free of this structure of desire, is the mind then different from the void?

THE PROBLEM OF SEARCH

IT WAS very early in the morning of a sunlit day, limpid and clear, and the restless sea was quiet, gently lapping the white shore. There was hardly any movement of the vast waters, which were intensely blue, as though some artificial colour had been added. There was a sparkle in the sea, and a gaiety; it was bluer than the blue sky, and it was old and full of joy. Last week the waters had been violent and threatening, with a strong current that would have carried one far out; but now they were all but still, with only a whisper of movement. The wind had exhausted itself after days of heavy blowing, and there wasn't even a breeze. The smoke of a steamer far out at sea was going almost straight up in the cloudless sky. It was so quiet that one could hear the sound of a train, still several miles away, as it came along the low cliff overlooking the sea. The faint rumble grew into a roar, and soon the earth shook as the long freight train, a hundred steel cars pulled by a spanking new diesel, passed swiftly overhead. The driver waved his hand and smiled. Soon the train was out of sight, and once again there was quiet by the blue sea. Miles to the north, one could just see rows of carefully-planted palm trees, with green lawns, where the town came down to the edge of the sea; but here it was very peaceful. There were hundreds of sea-gulls on the beach. One evidently had a broken wing, for it was standing apart, its wing hanging down; further along, a dead gull was almost covered by the shifting sands. A large dog came along, a lovely creature in the sun, and the whole flock of birds flew out to sea, made a wide half-circle, and landed on the sand again, some distance behind the dog. With a frightened cry, the injured gull moved towards the water, dragging its wing; the dog saw it, but paying no attention, went on its way, chasing the small crabs that came out of the wet sands.

A clerk in some office, he was grave and very earnest, with bright, serious eyes and a ready smile. Prices had gone up, he said, and living had become so expensive that it was difficult to make ends meet. Although still quite young, in his thirties, he was anxious about the future, for he had responsibilities—no children, he explained, but a wife and an old mother to provide for.

"What is the purpose of life, of this monotonous, routine existence?" he suddenly asked. "I have always been seeking something or other: seeking a job when I got through college, seeking pleasure with my wife, seeking to bring about a better world by joining the Communist Party—which I soon left, incidentally, because it's just an organized religion, like any other; and now I am seeking God. By nature I am not a pessimist, but everything in life has saddened me. We seek and seek, and we never seem to find. I have read the books that most educated people read, but intellectual stimulation soon becomes wearisome. I must find, and my life is beginning to shorten. I want to talk most seriously with you, for I feel that you may be of help in my search."

Can we go slowly and patiently into this movement called search? There are those who assert that they have sought and found, and being satisfied with what they have found, they have their reward. You say you are seeking. Do you know why you are seeking, and what it is you seek?

"Like everyone else, I have sought many things, most of which have passed away; but, like some disease that has no cure, the search goes on."

Before we go into the whole question of what it is we seek, let's find out what we mean by that word 'seeking'. What is the state of the mind that is seeking?

"It is a state of effort in which the mind is trying to get away from a painful or conflicting situation, and to find a pleasurable, comforting one."

Is such a mind really seeking? What the mind seeks it will find, but what it finds will be its own projection. Is there true search, if search is the outcome of a motive? Must all search have a motive, or is there a search which has no motive whatsoever? Can the mind exist without the movement of search? Is search as we know it merely another means by which the mind escapes from itself? If so, what is it that is driving the mind to escape? Without understanding the full content of the mind that is seeking, search has little significance.

"I am afraid, sir, all this is a bit too much for me. Could you make it simpler?"

Let's begin with the process we know. Why do you seek, and what are you seeking?

"One is seeking so many things: happiness, security, comfort, permanency, God, a society which is not everlastingly at war with itself, and so on."

The state you are actually in, and the end you are seeking, are both creations of the mind, are they not?

"Please, sir, don't make it too difficult. I know I suffer, and I want to find a way out of it, I want to move towards a state in which there will be no sorrow."

But the end you are seeking is still the projection of a mind that doesn't want to be disturbed; isn't that so? And there may be no such thing, it may be a myth.

"If that is a myth, then there must be something else which is real, and which I must find."

We are trying to understand, aren't we?, the total significance of search, not how to find the real. We may come upon that presently. For the moment we are concerned with what we mean when we say we are seeking, so let's inquire into the whole implication of that word.

Being unhappy, you are seeking happiness, are you not? One man seeks happiness in power, position, prestige, another in wealth or knowledge, another in God, another in the ideal State, the perfect Utopia, and so on. As a man who is ambitious in the worldly sense pursues the path of his fulfilment, in which there is ruthlessness, frustration, fear, perhaps covered over with sweet-sounding words, so you also are seeking to fulfil your desire, even though it be for the highest; and when you already know what the end is, is there search?

"Surely, sir, God or bliss cannot be known beforehand; it must be sought out."

How can you seek out that which you do not know? You know, or think you know, what God is, and you know according to your conditioning, or according to your own experience, which is based on your conditioning; so, having formulated what God is, you proceed to 'discover' that which your mind has projected. This is obviously not search; you are merely pursuing what you already know. Search ceases when you know, because knowing is a process of recognition, and to recognize is an action of the past, of the known.

"But I am really seeking God, by whatever name He may be called."

You are seeking God, as others are seeking happiness through drink, through the acquisition of power, and so on. These are all well-known and well-established motives. Motive brings about the desired end. But is there search when there is a motive?

"I think I am beginning to see what you mean. Please go on, sir."

If you are really earnest, the moment you perceive that in this whole pattern of so-called search, there is no search at all, you abandon it. But the cause of your search still remains. You may set aside pattern A, which is the search after that which the mind has projected; but then you will turn to pattern B, which is the idea that you must not pursue pattern A; and if it is not pattern B, it will be pattern C, N, or Z. The core of your mind has not understood the whole problem of seeking, and that is why it moves from one pattern to another, from one ideal to another, from one *guru* or leader to another. It is ever moving in the net of the known.

Now, can the mind remain without seeking? *Is* there the mind, the seeker, when this movement of search is not? The mind swings from one movement of search to another, ever groping, ever seeking, ever caught in the net of experience. This movement is always towards the 'more': more stimulation, more experience, wider and deeper knowledge. The hunter is ever projecting the hunted. Does the mind seek, once it is aware of the significance of this whole process of seeking? And when the mind is not seeking, is there an experiencer to experience?

"What do you mean by the experiencer?"

As long as there is a seeker and a thing sought, there must be the experiencer, the one who recognizes, and this is the core of the mind's self-centred movement. From this centre, all activities take place, whether noble or ignoble: the desire for wealth and power, the compulsion to be content with what *is*, the urge to seek God, to bring about reforms, and so on.

"I see in myself the truth of what you are saying. I have approached the whole thing wrongly."

Does this mean you are going to approach it 'rightly'? Or are you aware that *any* approach to the problem, 'right' or 'wrong', is self-centred activity, which only strengthens, subtly or grossly, the experiencer?

"How cunning the mind is, how quick and subtle in its movement to maintain itself! I see that very clearly."

When the mind ceases to seek because it has understood the total significance of search, do not the limitations which it has imposed upon itself fall away? And is the mind not then the immeasurable, the unknown?

PSYCHOLOGICAL REVOLUTION

THERE WAS a great bustle and ado before the train started. The long carriages were very crowded, full of people and full of smoke, every face hidden behind a newspaper; but luckily there were still one or two seats vacant. The train was electric, and soon it was out of the suburbs and gathering speed in the open country, passing the cars and buses on the highway which ran parallel to the tracks. It was beautiful country, green, rolling hills and ancient, historic towns. The sun was bright and gentle, for it was early spring, and the fruit trees were just beginning to show pink and white blossoms. The whole countryside was green, fresh and young, with tender leaves sparkling and dancing in the sun. It was a heavenly day, but the carriage was full of weary people, and the air was thick with tobacco smoke. A little girl and her mother sat just across the aisle, and the mother was explaining to her that she must not stare at strangers; but the child paid no attention, and presently we smiled at each other. From then on she was at ease, looking up often to see if she was being looked at, and smiling when our eyes met. Presently she fell asleep, curled up on the seat, and the mother covered her with a coat.

It must be lovely to walk along that path through the fields, amidst so much beauty and clarity. People waved as we roared along beside the well-paved road. Big white bullocks were slowly pulling carts laden with manure, and some of the men who were driving them must have been singing, for their mouths were open, and one could see by their faces that they were enjoying themselves in that fresh morning air. There were men and women in the fields, digging, planting, sowing.

I wandered up the long aisle, with seats on both sides, towards the head of the train. Walking through the dining car and past the kitchen, I pushed open a door and entered the luggage van. No one stopped me. The many pieces of luggage were neatly arranged in racks, their labels fluttering in the draught. I went through another door, and there were the two engine-drivers, completely surrounded by large, wide windows which gave an unobstructed view all around of the lovely countryside. One of the men was manipulating the handle which controlled the current, and in front of him were the various meters. The other, who was watching and leisurely smoking, offered his seat, and taking a stool, sat directly behind me. He was very insistent that I sit there, and began to ask innumerable questions. In the middle of his questioning he would stop to point out the castles on the hill-tops, some of them in ruins, and others still well-preserved. He explained what those brilliant red and green lights meant, and would pull out his watch to see if we were on schedule at each station. We were doing between 100 and 110 kilometers, round the curves, up the gentle slopes, over the bridges, and on the long, straight runs; but we never went beyond 110. "If you got off at the station we just passed and took another train," he said, "you would go to the town named after a famous saint." Crashing over the switches, we went hurtling past stations with names that came down from ancient days. We were now running along the shores of a blue, misty lake, and could just see the towns on the other side. There had been a famous battle in this area, on whose outcome the fate of a whole people had depended. Soon we had passed the lake, and climbing out of the valley, and around the curving hills, we left behind us the olive and the cypress, and found ourselves in a more rugged country. The man behind me announced the name of the muddy river as we ran beside it, and it looked so small and gentle for such a famous stream. The other man, who had removed his hand from the throttle only once or twice during the two-and-a-half-hour journey, apologized on behalf of them both for not being able to speak English. "But what does it matter," he said, "since you understand our beautiful language?"

42

We were coming now to the outskirts of the big town, and the blue sky was obscured by its smoke.

There were several of us in that small room overlooking the beautiful lake, and it was quiet, though the birds were pleasantly noisy. Among the group was a big man, full of health and vigour, with sharp but gentle eyes, and slow, deliberate speech. As he was eager to talk, the others remained silent, but they would join in when they felt it to be necessary.

"I have been in politics for many years, and have really worked for what I genuinely thought was the good of the country. That doesn't mean that I didn't seek power and position. I *did* seek it; I fought others for it, and as you may know, I have achieved it. I first heard you many years ago, and though some of the things you said hit home, your whole approach to life was for me only of momentary interest; it never took deep root. However, through the passing years, with all their struggle and pain, something has been maturing in me, and recently I have been attending your talks and discussions whenever I could. I now fully realize that what you are saying is the only way out of our confusing difficulties. I have been all over Europe and America, and for a time looked to Russia for a solution. I was an active worker in the Communist Party, and with good and serious intent co-operated with its religious-political leaders. But now I am resigning from everything. It has all become corrupt and ineffectual, though in certain directions good progress was made. Having thought a great deal about these matters, I now want to examine the whole thing afresh, and I feel I am ready for something new and clear."

To examine, one must not start with a conclusion, with a party loyalty or a bias; there must be no desire for success, no demand for immediate action. If one is involved in any of these things, true examination is utterly impossible. To examine afresh the whole issue of existence, the mind must be stripped clean of any personal motive, of any sense of frustration, of any seeking of power, whether for oneself or for one's group, which is the same thing. That is so, isn't it, sir?

"Please don't call me 'sir'! Of course, that is the only way to examine and to understand anything, but I don't know if I am capable of it."

Capacity comes with direct and immediate application. To examine the many complex issues of existence, we must start without being committed to any philosophy, to any ideology, to any system of thought or pattern of action. The capacity to comprehend is not a matter of time; it is an immediate perception, is it not?

"If I perceive something to be poisonous, to avoid it is no problem; I simply don't touch it. Similarly, if I see that any kind of conclusion prevents the complete examination of the problems of life, then all conclusions, personal and collective, fall away; I don't have to struggle to be free of them. Is that it?"

Yes; but a clear statement of a fact is not the actual fact. To be really free from conclusions is quite another matter. Once we perceive that bias of any kind hinders complete examination, we may proceed to look without bias. But out of habit, the mind tends to fall back on authority, on deep-rooted tradition; and to be so aware of this tendency that it does not interfere with the process of examination is also necessary. With this understanding, shall we proceed?

Now, what is man's most fundamental need?

"Food, clothing and shelter; but to bring about an equitable distribution of these basic necessities becomes a problem, because man is by nature greedy and exclusive."

You mean that he is encouraged and educated by society to be what he is? Now, another kind of society, through legislation and other forms of compulsion, may be able to force him *not* to be greedy and exclusive; but this only sets up a counter-reaction, and so there is a conflict between the individual, and the ideal established by the State, or by a powerful religious-political group. To bring about an equitable distribution of food, clothing and shelter, a totally different kind of social organization is necessary, is it not? Separate nationalities and their sovereign governments, power blocks and conflicting economic structures, as well as the caste system and organized religions—each of these proclaims its way to be the only true way. All these must cease to be, which means that the whole hierarchical, authoritarian attitude towards life must come to an end.

"I can see that this is the only real revolution."

It is a complete psychological revolution, and such a revolution is essential if man throughout the world is not to be in want of the basic physical necessities. The earth is ours, it is not English, Russian or American, nor does it belong to any ideological group. We are human beings, not Hindus, Buddhists, Christians or Moslems. All these divisions have to go, including the latest, the Communist, if we are to bring about a totally different economic-social structure. It must start with you and me.

"Can I act politically to help bring about such a revolution?"

If one may ask, what do you mean when you talk about acting politically? Is political action, whatever that may be, separate from the total action of man, or is it part of it?

"By political action, I mean action at the governmental level: legislative, economic, administrative, and so on."

Surely, if political action is separate from the total action of man, if it does not take into consideration his whole being, his psychological as well as his physical state, then it is mischievous, bringing further confusion and misery; and this is exactly what is taking place in the world at the present time. Cannot man, with all his problems, act as a complete human being, and not as a political entity, separated from his psychological or 'spiritual' state? A tree is the root, the trunk, the branch, the leaf and the flower. Any action which is not comprehensive, total, must inevitably lead to sorrow. There is only total human action, not political action, religious action, or Indian action. Action which is separative, fragmentary, always leads to conflict both within and without.

"This means that political action is impossible, doesn't it?"

Not at all. The comprehension of total action surely does not prevent political, educational or religious activity. These are not separate activities, they are all part of a unitary process which will express itself in different directions. What is important is this unitary process, and not a separate political action, however apparently beneficial.

"I think I see what you mean. If I have this total understanding of man, or of myself, my attention may be turned in different directions, as necessary, but all my actions will be in direct relation to the whole. Action which is separative, departmentalized, can only produce chaotic results, as I am beginning to realize. Seeing all this, not as a politician, but as a human being, my outlook on life utterly changes; I am no longer of any country, of any party, of any particular religion. I need to know God, as I need to have food, clothing and shelter; but if I seek the one apart from the other, my search will only lead to various forms of disaster and confusion. Yes, I see this is so. Politics, religion and education are all intimately related to each other.

"All right, sir, I am no longer a politician, with a political bias in

45

action. As a human being, not as a Communist, a Hindu or a Christian, I want to educate my son. Can we consider this problem?"

Integrated life and action is education. Integration does not come about through conformity to a pattern, either one's own, or that of another. It comes into being through understanding the many influences that impinge on the mind; through being aware of them without being caught in them. The parents and society are conditioning the child by suggestion, by subtle, unexpressed desires and compulsions, and by the constant reiteration of certain dogmas and beliefs. To help the child to be aware of all these influences, with their inward, psychological significance, to help him understand the ways of authority and not be caught in the net of society, is education.

Education is not merely a matter of imparting a technique which will equip the boy to get a job, but it is to help him discover what it is he loves to do. This love cannot exist if he is seeking success, fame or power; and to help the child understand this is education.

Self-knowledge is education. In education there is neither the teacher nor the taught, there is only learning; the educator is learning, as the student is. Freedom has no beginning and no ending; to understand this is education.

Each of these points has to be carefully gone into, and we haven't the time now to consider too many details.

"I think I understand, in a general sense, what you mean by education. But where are the people who will teach in this new way? Such educators simply don't exist."

For how many years did you say you worked in the political field?

"For more years than I care to remember. I am afraid it was well over twenty."

Surely, to educate the educator, one must work for it as arduously as you worked in politics—only it is a much more strenuous task which demands deep psychological insight. Unfortunately, no one seems to care about right education, yet it is far more important than any other single factor in bringing about a fundamental social transformation.

"Most of us, especially the politicians, are so concerned with immediate results, that we think only in short terms, and have no long-range view of things.

"Now, may I ask one more question? In all that we have been talking about, where does inheritance come in?"

What do you mean by inheritance? Are you referring to the inheritance of property, or to psychological inheritance?

"I was thinking of the inheritance of property. To tell you the truth, I have never thought about the other."

Psychological inheritance is as conditioning as the inheritance of property; both limit and hold the mind in a particular pattern of society, which prevents a fundamental transformation of society. If our concern is to bring about a wholly different culture, a culture not based on ambition and acquisitiveness, then psychological inheritance becomes a hindrance.

"What exactly do you mean by psychological inheritance?"

The imprint of the past on the young mind; the conscious and unconscious conditioning of the student to obey, to conform. The Communists are now doing this very efficiently, as the Catholics have for generations. Other religious sects are also doing it, but not so purposefully or effectively. Parents and society are shaping the minds of the children through tradition, belief, dogma, conclusion, opinion, and this psychological inheritance prevents the coming into being of a new social order.

"I can see that; but to put a stop to this form of inheritance is almost an impossibility, isn't it?"

If you really see the necessity of putting a stop to this form of inheritance, then will you not give immense attention to bringing about the right kind of education for your son?

"Again, most of us are so caught up in our own preoccupations and fears, that we don't go into these matters very deeply, if at all. We are a generation of double-talkers and word-slingers. The inheritance of property is another difficult problem. We all want to own something, a piece of earth, however small, or another human being; and if it is not that, then we want to own ideologies or beliefs. We are incorrigible in our pursuit of possessions."

But when you realize very deeply that inheriting property is as destructive as psychological inheritance, then you will set about helping your children to be free from both forms of inheritance. You will educate them to be completely self-sufficient, not to depend on your own or other people's favour, to love their work, and to have confidence in their capacity to work without ambition, without worshipping success; you will teach them to have the feeling of co-operative responsibility, and therefore to know when *not* to co-operate. Then there is no need for your children to inherit your property. They are free human beings from the very beginning, and not slaves, either to the family or to society.

"This is an ideal which I am afraid can never be realized."

It is *not* an ideal, it is not something to be achieved in the never-never land of some far-distant Utopia. Understanding is now, not in the future. Understanding is action. Understanding doesn't come first, and action later; action and realization are inseparable. In the very moment of seeing a cobra, there is action. If the truth of all that we have been talking about this morning is seen, then action is inherent in that perception. But we are so caught up in words, in the stimulating things of the intellect, that words and intellect become a hindrance to action. So-called intellectual understanding is only the hearing of verbal explanations, or the listening to ideas, and such understanding has no significance, as the mere description of food has no point to a hungry man. Either you understand, or you don't. Understanding is a total process, it is not separated from action, nor is it the result of time.

There Is No Thinker, Only Conditioned Thinking

THE RAINS had washed the skies clean; the haze that had hung about was gone, and the sky was clear and intensely blue. The shadows were sharp and deep, and high on the hill a column of smoke was going straight up. They were burning something up there, and you could hear their voices. The little house was on a slope, but well-sheltered, with a small garden of its own to which loving care had been given. But this morning it was part of the whole of existence, and the wall around the garden seemed so unnecessary. Creepers grew on that wall, hiding the rocks, but here and there they were exposed; they were beautiful rocks, washed by many rains, and they had a growth of green-grey moss on them. Beyond the wall was a bit of wilderness, and somehow that wilderness was part of the garden. From the garden gate a path led to the village, where there was a dilapidated old church with a graveyard behind it. Very few came to the church, even on Sundays, mostly the old; and during the week no one came, for the village had other amusements. A small diesel locomotive with two carriages, cream and red, went to the larger town twice a day. The train was almost

48

always filled with a cheerful, chattering crowd. Beyond the village another path led round to the right, gently going up the hill. On that path you would meet an occasional peasant carrying something, and with a grunt he would pass you by. On the other side of the hill, the path led down into a dense wood where the sun never penetrated; and going from the brilliant sunlight into the cool shadow of the wood was like a secret blessing. Nobody seemed to pass that way, and the wood was deserted. The dark green of the thick foliage was refreshing to the eyes and to the mind. One sat there in complete silence. Even the breeze was still; not a leaf moved, and there was that strange quietness which comes in places not frequented by human beings. A dog barked in the distance, and a brown deer crossed the path with easy leisure.

He was an elderly man, pious, and eager for sympathy and blessing. He explained that he had been going regularly for several years to a certain teacher in the north to listen to his explanatory discourses on the Scriptures, and was now on his way to join his family in the south.

"A friend told me that you were giving a series of talks here, and I stayed over to attend them. I have been listening with close attention to all that you have been saying, and I am aware of what you think of guides and of authority. I do not entirely agree with you, for we human beings need help from those who can offer it, and the fact that one eagerly accepts such help does not make one a follower."

Surely, the desire for guidance makes for conformity, and a mind that conforms is incapable of finding the true.

"But I am not conforming. I am not credulous, nor do I follow blindly; on the contrary, I use my mind, I question all that's said by this teacher I go to."

To look for light from another, without self-knowledge, is to follow blindly. All following is blind.

"I do not think I am capable of penetrating the deeper layers of the self, and so I seek help. My coming to you for help does not make me your follower."

If it may be pointed out, sir, the setting up of authority is a complex affair. Following another is merely an effect of a deeper cause, and without understanding that cause, whether one outwardly follows or not has very little meaning. The desire to arrive, to reach the other shore, is the beginning of our human search. We crave success, permanency, comfort, love, an enduring state of peace, and unless the

49

mind is free of this desire, there must be following in direct or devious ways. Following is merely a symptom of a deep longing for security.

"I do want to reach the other shore, as you put it, and I will take any boat that will carry me across the river. To me the boat is not important, but the other shore is."

It is not the other shore that is important, but the river, and the bank you are on. The river is life, it is everyday living, with its extraordinary beauty, its joy and delight, its ugliness, pain and sorrow. Life is a vast complex of all these things, it is not just a passage to be got through somehow, and you must understand it, and not have your eyes on the other shore. You *are* this life of envy, violence, passing love, ambition, frustration, fear; and you are also the longing to escape from it all to what you call the other shore, the permanent, the soul, the *Atman,* God, and so on. Without understanding this life, without being free of envy, with its pleasures and pains, the other shore is only a myth, an illusion, an ideal invented by a frightened mind in its search for security. A right foundation must be laid, otherwise the house, however noble, will not stand.

"I am already frightened, and you add to my fear, you do not take it away. My friend told me that you are not easy to understand, and I can see why you are not. But I think I'm in earnest, and I do want something more than mere illusion. I quite agree that one must lay the right foundation; but to perceive for oneself what is true and what is false is another matter."

Not at all, sir. The conflict of envy, with its pleasure and pain, inevitably breeds confusion, both outwardly and within. It is only when there is freedom from this confusion that the mind can discover what is true. All the activities of a confused mind only lead to further confusion.

"How am I to be free from confusion?"

The 'how' implies gradual freedom; but confusion cannot be cleared up bit by bit, while the rest of the mind remains confused, for that part which is cleared up soon becomes confused again. The question of how to clear up this confusion arises only when your mind is still concerned with the other shore. You do not see the full significance of greed, or violence, or whatever it is; you only want to get rid of it in order to arrive at something else. If you were wholly concerned with envy, and its resultant misery, you would never ask how to get rid of it. The understanding of envy is a total action, whereas the 'how' implies

50

a gradual achievement of freedom, which is only the action of confusion.

"What do you mean by total action?"

To understand total action, we must explore the division between the thinker and his thought.

"Is there not a watcher who is above both the thinker and his thought? I feel there is. For one blissful moment, I have experienced that state."

Such experiences are the result of a mind that has been shaped by tradition, by a thousand influences. The religious visions of a Christian will be quite different from those of a Hindu or a Moslem, since all are essentially based on the mind's particular conditioning. The criterion of truth is not experience, but that state in which neither the experiencer nor the experience any longer exists.

"You mean the state of *samadhi?*"

No, sir; in using that word, you are merely quoting the description of another's experience.

"But is there not a watcher beyond and above the thinker and his thought? I most definitely feel that there is."

To start with a conclusion puts a stop to all thinking, doesn't it?

"But this is not a conclusion, sir. I know, I have felt the truth of it."

He who says he knows does not know. What you know or feel to be true is what you have been taught; another, who happens to have been taught differently by his society, by his culture, will assert with equal confidence that his knowledge and experience show him that there is no ultimate watcher. Both of you, the believer and the non-believer, are in the same category, are you not? You both start with a conclusion, and with experiences based on your conditioning, don't you?

"When you put it that way, it does seem to put me in the wrong, but I am still not convinced."

I am not trying to put you in the wrong, or to convince you of anything; I am only pointing out certain things for you to examine.

"After considerable reading and study, I imagined I had thought out pretty thoroughly this question of the watcher and the watched. It seems to me that as the eye sees the flower, and the mind watches through the eye, so, behind the mind, there must be an entity who is aware of the whole process, that is, of the mind, the eye, and the flower."

Let us inquire into it without assertiveness, without haste or dogmatism. How does thinking arise? There is perception, contact, sensation, and then thought, based on memory, says, "That is a rose." Thought creates the thinker; it is the thinking process that brings the thinker into being. Thought comes first, and later the thinker; it is not the other way round. If we do not see this to be a fact, we shall be led into all kinds of confusion.

"But there is a division, a gap, narrow or wide, between the thinker and his thought; and does this not indicate that the thinker came into being first?"

Let's see. Perceiving itself to be impermanent, insecure, and desiring permanency, security, thought brings into being the thinker, and then pushes the thinker on to higher and higher levels of permanency. So there is seemingly an unbridgeable gap between the thinker and his thought, between the watcher and the watched; but this whole process is still within the area of thought, is it not?

"Do you mean to say, sir, that the watcher has no reality, that he is as impermanent as thought? I can hardly believe this."

You may call him the soul, the *Atman,* or by what name you will, but the watcher is still the product of thought. As long as thought is related in some way to the watcher, or the watcher is controlling, shaping thought, he is still within the field of thought, within the process of time.

"How my mind objects to this! Yet, in spite of myself, I am beginning to see it to be a fact; and if it is a fact, then there's only a process of thinking, and no thinker."

That is so, isn't it? Thought has bred the watcher, the thinker, the conscious or unconscious censor who is everlastingly judging, condemning, comparing. It is this watcher who is ever in conflict with his thoughts, ever making an effort to guide them.

"Please go a little slower; I really want to feel my way through this. You are indicating—aren't you?—that every form of effort, noble or ignoble, is the result of this artificial, illusory division between the thinker and his thoughts. But are you trying to eliminate effort? Isn't effort necessary to all change?"

We shall go into that presently. We have seen that there's only thinking, which has put together the thinker, the watcher, the censor, the controller. Between the watcher and the watched there is the conflict of effort made by the one to overcome or at least to change the other. This effort is vain, it can never produce a fundamental change in thought, because the thinker, the censor, is himself part of that which he wishes to change. One part of the mind cannot possibly transform another part, which is but a continuity of itself. One desire may, and often does, overcome another desire. But the desire that is dominant breeds still another desire, which in its turn becomes the loser or the gainer, and so the conflict of duality is set going. There's no end to this process.

"It seems to me you are saying that only through the elimination of conflict is there a possibility of fundamental change. I don't quite follow this. Would you kindly go into it a little further?"

The thinker and his thought are a unitary process, neither has an independent continuance; the watcher and the watched are inseparable. All the qualities of the watcher are contained in his thinking; if there's no thinking, there's no watcher, no thinker. This is a fact, is it not?

"Yes, so far I have understood."

If understanding is merely verbal, intellectual, it is of little significance. There must be an actual experiencing of the thinker and his thought as one, an integration of the two. Then there's only the process of thinking.

"What do you mean by the process of thinking?"

The way or direction in which thought has been set going: personal or impersonal, individualistic or collective, religious or worldly, Hindu or Christian, Buddhist or Moslem, and so on. There is no thinker who is a Moslem, but only thinking which has been given a Moslem conditioning. Thinking is the outcome of its own conditioning. The process or way of thinking must inevitably create conflict, and when effort is made to overcome this conflict through various means, it only builds up other forms of resistance and conflict.

"That's clear, at least I think so."

This way of thinking must wholly cease, for it breeds confusion and misery. There's no better or nobler way of thinking. All thinking is conditioned.

"You seem to imply that only when thought ceases is there a radical change. But is this so?"

Thought is conditioned. The mind, being the storehouse of experiences, memories, from which thought arises, is itself conditioned; and any movement of the mind, in any direction, produces its own limited results. When the mind makes an effort to transform itself, it merely

53

builds another pattern, different perhaps, but still a pattern. Every effort of the mind to free itself is the continuance of thought; it may be at a higher level, but it is still within its own circle, the circle of thought, of time.

"Yes, sir, I am beginning to understand. Please proceed."

Any movement of any kind on the part of the mind only gives strength to the continuance of thought, with its envious, ambitious, acquisitive pursuits. When the mind is totally aware of this fact, as it is totally aware of a poisonous snake, then you will see that the movement of thought comes to an end. Then only is there a total revolution, not the continuance of the old in a different form. This state is not to be described; he who describes it is not aware of it.

"I really feel that I have understood, not just your words, but the total implication of what you have been saying. Whether I have understood or not will show in my daily life."

"Why Should It Happen to Us?"

Something went off with an explosive bang. It was half-past four in the morning, and still very dark. It wouldn't be dawn for an hour or more. The birds were still asleep in the trees, and the violent noise didn't seem to have disturbed them, but they would commence their quarrelsome chatter just as soon as it began to get light. There was a slight ground mist, but the stars were very clear. After the first explosion, several others followed in the distance; there was a period of quiet, and then fireworks began going off all over the place. The festive day had begun. That morning, the birds didn't carry on with their chatter as long as usual, but cut it short and rapidly scattered, for those violent sounds were frightening; but towards evening they would assemble again in the same trees, to tell each other noisily of their daily doings. The sun was now touching the tree-tops, and they were aglow with soft light; lovely in their quietude, they were giving shape to the sky. The single rose in the garden was heavy with dew. Though it was already noisy with fireworks, the town was slow and leisurely about waking up, for it was one of the great holidays of the year; there would be feasting and rejoicing, and both rich and poor would be giving things to each other.

As it grew dark that evening, the people began to assemble on the banks of the river. They were gently setting afloat on the water small, burnt-clay saucers full of oil, with a wick burning. They would say a prayer and let the lights go floating off down the river. Soon there were thousands of these points of light on the dark, still water. It was an astonishing sight to behold, the eager faces lit by the little flames, and the river a miracle of light. The heavens with their myriad stars looked down on this river of light, and the earth was silent with the love of the people.

There were five of us in that sunlit room: a man and his wife, and two other men. All of them were young. The wife seemed sad and forlorn, and the husband also was grave, not given to smiles. The two young men sat shyly silent and let the others begin, but they would doubtless speak when the occasion arose and when their shyness had worn off a bit.

"But why should it happen to us?" she asked. There was resentment and anger in her voice, but tears were beginning to fill her eyes and trickle down her cheeks. "We had been good to our son; he was so gay and mischievous, always ready to laugh, and we loved him. We had brought him up so carefully, and had planned a rich life for him . . ." Unable to go on talking, she stopped and waited till she was a little calmer. "Excuse me for being so upset in front of you," she presently continued, "but it has all been too much for me. He was playing and shouting, and a few days later he was gone forever. It is very cruel, and why should it happen to us? We have led a decent life; we love each other, and we loved our boy even more. But he is gone now, and our life has become an empty thing—my husband in his office, and I in my house. It has all become so ugly and meaningless." She would have gone on and on in her bitterness, but her husband gently stopped her. She was sobbing now, without any restraint, and presently was silent.

This happens to all of us, doesn't it? When you ask why it should happen to you, you really don't mean that it should happen only to others and not to you. You share sorrow with the rest.

"But what have we done to deserve it? What is our karma? Why didn't he live? I would gladly have given my life for him."

Will any explanation, any cunning argument or rationalized belief, fill that aching void?

"I naturally want to be comforted, but not by mere words, and not by some future hope. As a result, I just can't find any comfort. My husband has tried to comfort me with the belief in reincarnation, but to no avail. And he too is suffering; even though he believes in reincarnation, sorrow is there. We are both caught up in it and twisted by it. It's like some frightening, hideous nightmare." Again her husband interfered to calm her rising feelings.

"I will be quiet and thoughtful, and I am sorry."

"Sir, we know so little of life, of death, so little of our own sorrow," said her husband. "Since this event I seem to have suddenly matured, and can now ask serious questions. Before, life was gay, and we were constantly laughing; but most of the things that made us happy seem now so silly, so trivial. It has been like a wind-storm that uproots trees and puts sand in one's food. Nothing will ever be the same again. Suddenly I find myself being dreadfully serious, wanting to know what it is all about, and since our son's death I have read more religious and philosophical books than I read in all my earlier life; but when there's pain, mere words are not easy to accept. I know how easily belief becomes a slow poison. Belief dulls the sharp edge of thought, but it also dulls the pain, and without it the mind would become an open, sensitive wound. We came to hear you last evening. You gave us no comfort, which I see is right; but we still want to heal our wounds. Can you help us?"

"The wound we all have," put in one of the other two, "is not to be healed by words, by a comforting phrase. We have come here, not to collect another belief, but to search out the cause of our pain."

Do you think that merely knowing the cause will free you from pain?

"If once I know what causes my inward pain, I can put an end to it. I won't eat something when I know it will poison me."

Do you think it is such an easy matter to wipe away the inward wound? Let's go into it patiently, carefully. What is our problem?

"My problem," the wife replied, "is simple and clear. Why was my son taken away from me? What was the cause of it?"

Will any explanation satisfy you, however comforting it may be for the moment? Haven't you to find out the truth of the matter for yourself?

"How am I to set about it?" demanded the wife.

"That's also one of my problems," said one of the other two. "How am I to find out what's true in this bewildering confusion which is the 'me'?"

56

"Was it our karma to suffer, to lose the one we most loved?" asked the husband.

"Perhaps I might be able to bear the pain of my son's death," added the wife, "if I could just have the comfort of knowing why he was taken away."

Comfort is one thing, and truth another; they lead away from each other. If you seek comfort, you may find it in an explanation, a drug or a belief; but it will be temporary, and sooner or later you will have to begin over again. And *is* there such a thing as comfort? It may be that you will first have to see this fact: that a mind which seeks comfort, security, will always be in sorrow. A satisfactory explanation, or a comforting belief, can put you soothingly to sleep; but is that what you want? Will that wipe away your sorrow? Is sorrow to be got rid of by inducing sleep?

"I suppose what I really want," went on the wife, "is to get back into the happy state I once knew—to have again the joy and the pleasure of it. As I can't do that, I am torn with sorrow, and therefore seek comfort."

Do you mean that you don't want to face the fact which you think causes sorrow, and so you try to escape from it?

"Why shouldn't I be comforted?"

But can you find lasting comfort? There may be no such thing. In seeking comfort, what we want is a state in which there will be no psychological disturbance whatsoever. And *is* there such a state? One may put together, by various means, a state of comfort, but life soon comes knocking at the door. This knocking at the door, this awakening, is called sorrow.

"As you point this out, I see that it is so. But what am I to do?" insisted the wife.

There is nothing to do but realize the truth of this fact, that a mind which seeks comfort, security, will always be subject to sorrow. This realization is its own action. When a man realizes he's a prisoner, he doesn't ask what to do, but a whole series of actions, or inactions, come into being. From realization itself there is action.

"But, sir," put in the husband, "our wounds are real, and can we not heal them? Is there no healing process at all, but only a state of bitter hopelessness?"

The mind can cultivate any state it desires, but to find out the truth

57

of this whole situation is quite another matter. Now, what is it that you are after?

"No man in his senses would want to cultivate bitterness. There is certainly a philosophy of hopelessness, but I have no intention of pursuing that path. I do want to find out, however, what is the cause, the karma of our sorrow."

Do you two also wish to go into this matter?

"We most certainly do, sir. We have our own problems pertaining to the whole process of karma, and it would help us too if we could all consider it together."

What is the root-meaning of the word 'karma'?

"The root-meaning of that word is 'to act'," replied the husband, and the others nodded in agreement. "Karma, as it is generally—and I think wrongly—understood, is action as a determining cause. The future is fixed by past action; as you sow, so shall you reap. I have done something in the past for which I shall pay, or from which I shall gain. If my son dies young, it is due to some cause hidden in a past life. There are many variations on this one general formula."

All things arise and have their being through the chain of causes and effects, do they not?

"That seems to be a fact," replied one of the other two. "I am here in this world because of my father and mother, and through other previous causes. I am a result of causes which stretch back infinitely into the past. Both thought and action are the result of various causes."

Is effect separate from cause? Is there a gap, short or long, an interval of time between them? Is the cause fixed as well as the effect? If cause and effect are static, then the future is already established; and if this is so, there's no freedom for man, he's ever caught in a predeterminate groove. But this is *not* so, as you can observe in everyday happenings, where circumstances are continuously influencing the course of actions. There is always a movement of change going on, whether immediate or gradual.

"Yes, sir, I see that; and it is an immense relief to me, who have been brought up in the one-cause and one-effect conditioning, to realize that we need not be slaves to the past."

The mind need not be held by its conditioning. The effect of a cause is not bound to follow the cause, it may be wiped away. There's no everlasting hell. Cause and effect are not static, fixed; what was the effect becomes the cause of still another effect. To-day is shaped by yesterday, and to-morrow by to-day. That is true, is it not? So cause and effect are not separate, they are a unitary process. A wrong means cannot be used to a right end, because the means is the end; the one contains the other. The seed contains the total tree. If one really feels the truth of this, then thought is action, there is no thinking first followed by action, with the inevitable problem of how to build a bridge between them. The total awareness of cause and effect as an indivisible unit puts an end to the maker of effort, the 'I' who's everlastingly becoming something through some means.

"Are you not giving your own meaning to karma?" asked the husband.

Either it is true, or it is false. What is true needs no interpretation, and what is interpreted is not true. The interpreter becomes a traitor, for he is merely offering his opinion, and opinion is not truth.

"The books say that each one of us starts this life with a certain amount of accumulated karma which has to be worked out," went on the husband. "We are told that it is in the working out of this accumulated karma, whether in one life or through several lives, that there is the operation of free will. Is this so?"

What do *you* think, apart from the authority of the books?

"I don't feel able to think it out for myself."

Let's consider the matter together. One's life in this present existence does start with a certain amount of conditioning, karma; every child is influenced by his environment to think within a certain pattern, and his future tends to be determined by this pattern. Either he follows, with a certain latitude, the dictates of the pattern, or he totally breaks away from it. In the latter case, that part of the mind which makes the effort to break away is also a result of conditioning, of karma; so in breaking away from one pattern, the mind creates another, in which it is again caught.

"In that case, how can the mind ever be free? I see very clearly that the part of the mind that wishes to be free from the pattern, and the part that is caught in it, are both held, as it were, in a frame; the former thinks it is different from the latter, but essentially they have the same quality in that neither is totally free. Then what is freedom?"

"Most people," put in one of the young men, "assert that there is a super-soul, the *Atman*, which will act upon our conditioning and wipe it away through devotion and good works, and through concentration on the Supreme."

But the entity who is devoted, who does good works, is himself conditioned; and the Supreme on which he concentrates is a projection of his conditioning, is it not?

"I see that," said the husband eagerly. "Our gods, our religious concepts, our ideals, are all within the pattern of our conditioning. Now that you point it out, it seems so obvious and factual. But then there's no hope for man."

To jump to a conclusion, and to start thinking from that conclusion, prevents understanding and any further discovery.

When the totality of the mind realizes that it's held within a pattern, what takes place?

"I don't quite understand your question, sir."

Do you realize that the totality of your mind is conditioned, including the part that is supposed to be the super-soul, the *Atman?* Do you feel it, know it to be a fact, or are you merely accepting a verbal explanation? What is actually taking place?

"I cannot definitely say, for I have never thought out this matter to the end."

When the mind realizes the totality of its own conditioning—which it cannot do as long as it is merely pursuing its own comfort, or lazily taking the easy course—then all its movements come to an end; it is completely still, without any desire, without any compulsion, without any motive. Only then is there freedom.

"But we have to live in this world, and whatever we do, from earning a livelihood to the most subtle inquiry of the mind, has some motive or other. Is there ever action without motive?"

Don't you think there is? The action of love has no motive, and every other action has.

Life, Death and Survival

It was a magnificent old tamarind tree, full of fruit, and with tender new leaves. Growing by a deep river, it was well-watered, and it gave just the right amount of shade for animals and men. There was always some kind of bustle and noise going on under it, loud talking, or a calf calling for its mother. It was beautifully proportioned, and against the blue sky its shape was splendid. It had ageless vitality. It must have witnessed many things as through countless summers it watched the river and the goings-on along its banks. It was an interesting river, wide and holy, and pilgrims came from all parts of the country to bathe in its sacred waters. There were boats on it, moving silently, with dark, square sails. When the moon rose, full and almost red, making a silvery path on the dancing waters, there would be rejoicing in the neighbouring village, and in the village across the river. On holy days the villagers came down to the water's edge, singing joyous, lilting songs. Bringing their food, with much chattering and laughter, they would bathe in the river; then they would put a garland at the foot of the great tree, and red and yellow ashes around its trunk, for it too was sacred, as all trees are. When at last the chatter and shouting had ceased, and everyone had gone home, a lamp or two would remain burning, left by some pious villager; these lamps consisted of a home-made wick in a little terra-cotta saucer of oil which the villager could ill afford. Then the tree was supreme; all things were of it: the earth, the river, the people and the stars. Presently it would withdraw into itself, to slumber till touched by the first rays of the morning sun.

Often they would bring a dead body to the edge of the river. Sweeping the ground close to the water, they would first put down heavy logs as a foundation for the pyre, and then build it up with lighter wood; and on the top they would place the body, covered with a new white cloth. The nearest relative would then put a burning torch to the pyre, and huge flames would leap up in the darkness, lighting the water and the silent faces of the mourners and friends who sat around the fire. The tree would gather some of the light, and give its peace to the dancing flames. It took several hours for the body to be consumed, but they would all sit around till there was nothing left except bright embers and little tongues of flame. In the midst of this enormous silence, a baby would suddenly begin to cry, and a new day would have begun.

He had been a fairly well-known man. He lay dying in the small house behind the wall, and the little garden, once cared for, was now neglected. He was surrounded by his wife and children, and by other near relatives. It might be some months, or even longer, before he passed away, but they were all around him, and the room was heavy with grief. As I came in he asked them all to go away, and they reluctantly left, except a little boy who was playing with some toys on the floor. When they had gone out, he waved me to a chair, and we sat for some time without saying a word, while the noises of the household and the street crowded into the room.

He spoke with difficulty.

"You know, I have thought a great deal for a number of years about living, and even more about dying, for I have had a protracted illness. Death seems such a strange thing. I have read various books dealing with this problem, but they were all rather superficial."

Aren't all conclusions superficial?

"I am not so sure. If one could arrive at certain conclusions that were deeply satisfying, they would have some significance. What's wrong with arriving at conclusions, so long as they are satisfying?"

There's nothing wrong with it, but doesn't it trace a deceptive horizon? The mind has the power to create every form of illusion, and to be caught in it seems so unnecessary and immature.

"I have lived a fairly rich life, and have followed what I thought to be my duty; but of course I am human. Anyway, that life is all over now, and here I am, a useless thing; but fortunately my mind has not yet been affected. I have read much, and I am still as eager as ever to know what happens after death. Do I continue, or is there nothing left when the body dies?"

Sir, if one may ask, why are you so concerned to know what happens after death?

"Doesn't everyone want to know?"

Probably they do; but if we don't know what living is, can we ever know what death is? Living and dying may be the same thing, and the fact that we have separated them may be the source of great sorrow.

"I am aware of what you have said about all this in your talks, but still I want to know. Won't you please tell me what happens after death? I won't repeat it to anyone."

Why are you struggling so hard to know? Why don't you allow the whole ocean of life and death to be, without poking a finger into it?

"I don't want to die," he said, his hand holding my wrist. "I have always been afraid of death; and though I have tried to console myself with rationalizations and beliefs, they have only acted as a thin veneer over this deep agony of fear. All my reading about death has been an effort to escape from this fear, to find a way out of it, and it is for the same reason that I am begging to know now."

Will any escape free the mind from fear? Does not the very act of escaping breed fear?

"But you can tell me, and what you say will be true. This truth will liberate me . . ."

We sat silently for a while. Presently he spoke again.

"That silence was more healing than all my anxious questioning. I wish I could remain in it and quietly pass away, but my mind won't let me. My mind has become the hunter as well as the hunted; I am tortured. I have acute physical pain, but it's nothing compared to what's going on in my mind. Is there an identified continuity after death? This 'me' which has enjoyed, suffered, known—will it continue?"

What is this 'me' that your mind clings to, and that you want to be continued? Please don't answer, but quietly listen, will you? The 'me' exists only through identification with property, with a name, with the family, with failures and successes, with all the things you have been and want to be. You are that with which you have identified yourself; you are made up of all that, and without it, you are not. It is this identification with people, property and ideas, that you want to be continued, even beyond death; and is it a living thing? Or is it just a mass of contradictory desires, pursuits, fulfilments and frustrations, with sorrow outweighing joy?

"It may be what you suggest, but it's better than not knowing anything at all."

Better the known than the unknown, is that it? But the known is so small, so petty, so confining. The known is sorrow, and yet you crave for its continuance.

"Think of me, be compassionate, don't be so unyielding. If only I knew, I could die happily."

Sir, don't struggle so hard to know. When all effort to know ceases, then there is something which the mind has not put together. The unknown is greater than the known; the known is but as a barque on the ocean of the unknown. Let all things go and be.

His wife came in just then to give him something to drink, and the child got up and ran out of the room without looking at us. He told his wife to close the door as she went out, and not to let the boy come in again.

"I am not worried about my family; their future is cared for. It's with my own future that I am concerned. I know in my heart that what you say is true, but my mind is like a galloping horse without a rider. Will you help me, or am I beyond all help?"

Truth is a strange thing; the more you pursue it, the more it will elude you. You cannot capture it by any means, however subtle and cunning; you cannot hold it in the net of your thought. Do realize this, and let everything go. On the journey of life and death, you must walk alone; on this journey there can be no taking of comfort in knowledge, in experience, in memories. The mind must be purged of all the things it has gathered in its urge to be secure; its gods and virtues must be given back to the society that bred them. There must be complete, uncontaminated aloneness.

"My days are numbered, my breath is short, and you are asking a very hard thing: that I die without knowing what death is. But I am well instructed. Let be my life, and may there be a blessing upon it."

DETERIORATION OF THE MIND

ALONG THE top of the long, wide bend in the river was the town, very holy and very dirty. The river made a big sweep here, and its main force struck the edge of the town, often washing away the steps leading down to the water, and some of the old houses. But whatever damage it did in its fury, the river still remained holy and beautiful. It was particularly beautiful that evening, with the sun setting below the dark town, and behind the single minaret, which seemed to be the reaching up of the whole town towards the heavens. The clouds were golden-red, aflame with the brilliance of a sun that had travelled over a land of intense beauty and sadness. And as the brilliance faded, there, over the dark town, was the new moon, tender and delicate. From the opposite shore, some distance down the river, the whole enchanting sight seemed magical, yet perfectly natural, without a touch of artificiality. Slowly the young moon went down behind the dark mass of the town, and lights began to appear; but the river still held the light of the evening sky, a golden splendour of incredible softness. On this light, which was the river, there were hundreds of small fishing boats. All afternoon thin, dark men with long poles had been laboriously poling their way upstream against the current, in single file close to the bank; starting at the fishing village below the town, each man in his boat, sometimes with a child or two, had pushed slowly up the river past the long, heavy bridge, and now they were coming down by the hundreds, carried by the strong current. They would be fishing all night, catching big, heavy fish, ten to fifteen inches long, which would afterwards be dumped, some of them still writhing, into larger boats tied up along the bank, to be sold the next day.

The streets of the town were crowded with bullock-carts, buses, cycles, and pedestrians, with here and there a cow or two. Narrow lanes, lined with dimly-lit shops and winding endlessly in and out, were muddy with the recent rains, and filthy with the dirt of man and beast. One of the lanes led to the wide steps which descended to the very edge of the river, and on these steps everything was going on. Some people were sitting close to the water, with eyes shut, in silent meditation; next to them a man was chanting in front of an enthusiastic crowd, which extended far up the steps; further on, a leprous beggar held out his withered hand, while a man with ashes on his forehead and matted hair was instructing the people. Nearby a *sannyasi*, clean of face and skin, with newly-washed robes, sat motionless, his eyes closed, his mind intent with long and easy practice. A man with cupped hand was silently begging the heavens to fill it; and a mother, her left breast bare, was suckling her baby, oblivious of everything. Further down the river, dead bodies, brought from the neighbouring villages and from the sprawling, dirty town, were being burnt in great, roaring fires. Here everything was going on, for this was the most holy and sacred of towns. But the beauty of the still-flowing river seemed to wipe away all the chaos of man, while the heavens above him looked down with love and wonder.

There were several of us, two women and four men. One of the women, with a good head and sharp eyes, had been very well educated at home and abroad; the other was more modest, with a sorrowful, begging look. One of the men, an ex-Communist who had left the party several years ago, was forceful and demanding; another was an artist, shy and retiring, but bold enough to assert himself when the occasion demanded; the third was an official in the governmental bureaucracy; and the fourth was a teacher, very gentle, with a swift smile, and eager to learn.

Everyone was silent for a while, and presently the former Communist spoke.

"Why is there so much deterioration in every department of life? I can understand how power, even in the name of the people, is essentially evil and corrupting, as you have pointed out. One sees this fact demonstrated in history. The seed of evil and corruption is inher-

65

ent in all political and religious organizations, as has been shown in the church through the centuries, and in modern Communism, which promised so much, but which has itself become corrupt and tyrannical. Why does everything have to deteriorate in this way?"

"We know so much about so many things," added the well-educated lady, "but knowledge does not seem to arrest the dry-rot that is in man. I write a little, and have had a book or two published, but I see how easily the mind can go to pieces when once it has caught the knack of a thing. Learn the technique of good expression, dig up a few interesting or exciting themes, get into the habit of writing, and you are set for life; you become popular, and you are done for. I am not saying this out of any malice or bitterness because I am a failure, or only an indifferent success, but because I see this process operating in others and in myself. We don't seem to get away from the corrosion of routine and capacity. To get something started demands energy and initiative, but once started, the seed of corruption is inherent in it. Can one ever escape from this corruptive process?"

"I too," said the bureaucrat, "am caught in the routine of decay. We plan for the future of five or ten years from now, we build dams and encourage new industries, all of which is good and necessary; but even though the dams may be beautifully built and perfectly maintained, and the machines made to function with a minimum of inefficiency, our thinking, on the other hand, becomes more and more inefficient, stupid and lazy. The computers and other complex electronic gadgets outdo man at every turn, yet without man they could not exist. The plain fact is, a few brains are active, creative, and the rest of us live on them, rotting and often rejoicing in our rot."

"I am only a teacher, but I am interested in a different kind of education—an education which will prevent the setting-in of this dry-rot of the mind. At present we 'educate' a living human being to become some stupid bureaucrat—forgive me—with a big job and a handsome salary, or with a clerk's pay and a still more miserable existence. I know what I am talking about, because I am caught in it. But apparently this is the kind of education the governments want, for they are pouring money into it, and every so-called educator, including myself, is aiding and abetting this rapid deterioration of man. Will a better method or technique put an end to this deterioration? Please believe me, sir, I am very serious in asking this question, I am not asking it just for the sake of talking. I have read recent books on education, and invariably they deal with some method or other; and since hearing you, I have begun to question the whole thing."

"I am an artist of sorts, and one or two museums have bought my things. Unfortunately, I shall have to be personal, which I hope the others won't mind, for their problem is also mine. I may paint for a time, then turn to pottery, and then do some sculpturing. It is the same urge expressing itself in different ways. Genius is this force, this extraordinary feeling that must be given form, not the man or the medium through which it expresses itself. I may not be putting it properly, but you know what I mean. It is this creative power that has to be kept alive, potent, under tremendous pressure, like steam in a boiler. There are periods when one feels this power; and having once tasted it, nothing on earth can prevent one from wanting to recapture it. From then on, one is in torture, ever dissatisfied, because that flame is never constant, never there completely. Therefore it has to be fed, nourished; and every feeding makes it more feeble, less and less complete. So the flame gradually dies, though the flair and technique carry on, and one may become famous. The gesture remains, but love has gone, the heart is dead; and so deterioration sets in."

Deterioration is the central factor—is it not?—whatever may be the way of our life. The artist may feel it in one way, and the teacher in another; but if we are at all aware of others, and of our own mental processes, it is fairly obvious, with the old and with the young, that deterioration of the mind does take place. Deterioration seems to be inherent in the very activities of the mind itself. As a machine wears itself out through use, so the mind seems to worsen through its own action.

"We all know this," said the educated lady. "The fire, the creative force fades away after one or two spurts, but the capacity remains, and this *ersatz* creativity becomes in time a substitute for the real thing. We know this only too well. My question is, how can that creative something remain without losing its beauty and force?"

What are the factors of deterioration? If one knew them, perhaps it might be possible to put an end to them.

"Are there any specific factors clearly to be pointed out?" asked the former party member. "Deterioration may be inherent in the very nature of the mind."

The mind is a product of the society, of the culture in which it has been brought up; and as society is always in a state of corruption, always destroying itself from within, a mind that continues to be influenced by society must also be in a state of corruption or deterioration. Isn't that so?

"Of course; and it is because we perceived this fact," explained the ex-Communist, "that some of us worked hard and rather brutally, I'm afraid, to create a new and rigid pattern according to which we felt society should function. Unfortunately, a few corrupt individuals seized power, and we all know the result."

May it not be, sir, that deterioration is inevitable when a pattern is created for the individual and collective life of man? By what authority, other than the cunning authority of power, has any individual or group the right to create the all-knowing pattern for man? The church has done it, by the power of fear, flattery and promise, and has made a prisoner of man.

"I thought I knew, as the priest thinks he knows, what is the right manner of life for man; but now, along with many others, I see what stupid arrogance that is. The fact remains, however, that deterioration is our lot; and can anyone escape from it?"

"Can we not educate the young," asked the teacher, "to be so aware of the factors of corruption and deterioration, that they will instinctively avoid them, as they would avoid the plague?"

Aren't we going round and round the subject without getting at it? Let us consider it together. We know that our minds deteriorate in different ways, according to our individual temperaments. Now, can one put an end to this process? And what do we mean by the word 'deterioration'? Let us go slowly into it. Is deterioration a state of mind that's known through comparison with an incorruptible state which the mind has momentarily experienced and is now living in the memory of, hoping by some means to revive it? Is it the state of a mind that is frustrated in its desire for success, self-fulfilment, and so on? Has the mind tried and failed to become something, and does it therefore feel itself to be deteriorating?

"It's all of that," said the educated lady. "At least, I seem to be in one, if not all, of the states you have just described."

When did that flame of which you were speaking earlier come into being?

"It came unexpectedly, without my seeking it, and when it went away, I was unable to get it back. Why do you ask?"

It came when you were not seeking it; it came neither through your desire for success, nor through the longing for that intoxicating sense of elation. Now that it has gone, you are pursuing it, because it gave momentary meaning to a life that otherwise had no meaning; and as you cannot recapture it, you feel that deterioration has set in. Isn't that so?

"I think it is—not only with me, but with most of us. The clever ones build a philosophy round the memory of that experience, and thereby catch innocent people in their net."

Doesn't all this point to something which may be the central and dominant factor of deterioration?

"Do you mean ambition?"

That's only one facet of the accumulating core: this purposive, self-centred focus of energy which is the 'me', the ego, the censor, the experiencer who judges the experience. May it not be that this is the central, the only factor of deterioration?

"Is it a self-centred, egotistic activity," asked the artist, "to realize what one's life is without that creative intoxication? I can hardly believe it."

It's not a matter of credulity or belief. Let's consider it further. That creative state came into being without your invitation, it was there without your seeking it. Now that it has faded away and become a thing remembered, you want to revive it, which you have tried to do through various forms of stimulation. You may occasionally have touched the hem of it, the outer edges of it, but that's not enough, and you are ever hungering after it. Now, is not all craving, even for the highest, an activity of the self? Is it not self-concern?

"It seems so, when you put it that way," conceded the artist. "But it is craving in one form or another that motivates us all, from the austere saint to the lowly peasant."

"Do you mean," asked the teacher, "that all self-improvement is egotistic? Is every effort to improve society a self-centred activity? Is not education a matter of self-expansive improvement, of making progress in the right direction? Is it selfish to conform to a better pattern of society?"

Society is always in a state of degeneration. There is no perfect society. The perfect society may exist in theory, but not in actuality. Society is based on human relationship motivated by greed, envy, acquisitiveness, fleeting joy, the pursuit of power, and so on. You can't improve envy; envy has to cease. To put a civilized coating on violence through the double-talk of ideals, is not to bring violence to an end. To educate a student to conform to society is only to encourage in him the deteriorating urge to be secure. Climbing the ladder of success, becoming somebody, gaining recognition—-this is the very substance of our degenerating social structure, and to be part of it is to deteriorate.

'Are you suggesting," inquired the teacher rather anxiously, "that one must renounce the world and become a hermit, a *sannyasi?*"

It's comparatively easy, and in its way profitable, to renounce the outward world of home, family, name, property; but it's quite another matter to put an end—without any motive, without the promise of a happy future—to the inner world of ambition, power, achievement, and really to be as nothing. Man begins at the wrong end, with things, and so ever remains in confusion. Begin at the right end; start near to go far.

"Must not a definite practice be adopted to put an end to this deterioration, this inefficiency and laziness of the mind?" asked the government official.

Practice or discipline implies an incentive, the gaining of an end; and isn't this a self-centred activity? Becoming virtuous is a process of self-interest, leading to respectability. When you cultivate in yourself a state of non-violence, you are still violent under a different name. Besides all this, there is another degenerating factor: effort, in all its subtle forms. This doesn't mean that one is advocating laziness.

"Good heavens, sir, you are certainly taking everything away from us!" exclaimed the official. "And when you take everything away, what's left of us? Nothing!"

Creativeness is not a process of becoming or achieving, but a state of being in which self-seeking effort is totally absent. When the self makes an effort to be absent, the self is present. All effort on the part of this complex thing called the mind must cease, without any motive or inducement.

"That means death, doesn't it?"

Death to all that's known, which is the 'me'. It is only when the totality of the mind is still, that the creative, the nameless, comes into being.

"What do you mean by the mind?" asked the artist.

The conscious as well as the unconscious; the hidden recesses of the heart as well as the educated bits of the mind.

"I have listened," said the silent lady, "and my heart understands."

In the early morning sunlight, the leaves of the tree just outside the window were making dancing shadows on the white wall of the room. There was a gentle breeze, and those shadows were never still; they were as alive as the leaves themselves. One or two moved gently, with grace and ease, but the motion of the others was violent, jerky and restless. The sun had just come up from behind a deep-wooded hill. The day was not going to be hot, for the breeze was blowing from the snowy mountains to the north. At that early hour, there was a strange quietness—the quietness of the slumbering earth before man begins his toil. Within this quietness were the screeches of the parrots, flying crazily to the fields and woods; within it were the raucous calls of the crows, and the chatter of many birds; within it were the distant hoots of a train, and the blast of a factory whistle announcing the hour. It was the hour when the mind is as open as the heavens and as vulnerable as love.

The road was very crowded, and the people walking on it were paying scant attention to the vehicular traffic; they would smilingly step aside, but first they had to look around to see who was making so much noise behind them. There were cycles, buses and bullock-carts, and men drawing lighter carts loaded with sacks of grain. The shops, selling everything that man could want, from needles to motor-cars, were spilling over with people.

This same road led through the wealthy part of the city, with its usual aloofness and tidiness, into the open country; and not far out was the famous tomb. You left the car at the outer entrance, and went up a few steps, through an open archway, into a well-kept and watered garden. Walking along a sandy path, and up more steps, you passed through another archway, blue with tiles, and entered an inner garden with a wall completely around it. It was enormous; there were acres of luscious, green lawns, lovely trees and fountains. It was cool in the shade, and the sound of falling water was pleasant. The circular path that went along the wall on the edge of the lawn had a border of brilliant flowers, and it would have taken quite a while to walk around it. Following the path that cut across the lawn, you wondered how so much space and beauty and work could be given to a tomb. Presently you climbed a long flight of steps, which opened on a vast platform covered with slabs of reddish-brown sandstone. On this platform rose the stately tomb. It was built of smooth, polished marble, and the single marble coffin within it shone with the soft light of the sun that filtered through the intricately-latticed marble window. It seemed lonely in its peace, though surrounded with grandeur and beauty.

From the platform you could see where the ancient town, with its domes and gateways, met the new, with its steel pylons for the radio broadcasting station. It was strange to see the coming together of the old and the new, and the impact of it stirred your whole being. It was as though the past and the present of all life lay before you as a simple fact, without the interference of the censor and his choice. The blue horizon stretched far away beyond the city and the woods; it would always remain, while the new became the old.

There were three of them, all quite young, a brother, a sister and a friend. Well-dressed and very well-educated, they spoke several languages easily, and could talk of the latest books. It was strange to see them in that bare room; there were only two chairs, and one of the young men had to sit uncomfortably on the floor, spoiling the crease in his well-pressed trousers. A sparrow that had its nest just outside suddenly appeared on the sill of the open window, but seeing the new faces, it fluttered and flew away again.

"We have come to talk over a rather personal problem," explained the brother, "and we hope you don't mind. May I plunge into it? You see, my sister is going through a beastly time. She feels shy about explaining it, so I am doing the talking for the moment. We like each other very much, and have been almost inseparable ever since we were youngsters. There is nothing unhealthy about our being together, but she has been twice married and twice divorced. We have been through it all together. The husbands were all right in their way, but I am concerned about my sister. We consulted a well-known psychiatrist, but somehow it didn't work out. We needn't go into all that now. Though I had never met you personally, I had known about you for several years, and had read some of your published talks; so I persuaded my sister and our mutual friend to come along with me, and here we are." He hesitated for a few moments, and then went on.

"Our difficulty is that my sister doesn't seem to be satisfied with anything. Literally nothing gives her any sort of satisfaction or contentment. Discontent has become almost a mania with her, and if something isn't done, she's going to crack up completely."

Isn't it a good thing to be discontented?

"To some extent, yes," he replied; "but there are limits to everything, and this is going too far."

What's wrong with being totally discontented? What we generally call discontent is the dissatisfaction which arises when a particular desire is not fulfilled. Isn't that so?

"Perhaps; but my sister has tried so many things, including these two marriages, and she hasn't been happy in either of them. Fortunately, there have been no children, which would have further complicated matters. But I think she can speak for herself now; I only wanted to set the ball rolling."

What is contentment, and what is discontent? Will discontent lead to contentment? Being discontented, can you ever find the other?

"Nothing really satisfies me," said the sister. "We are well off, but the things that money can buy have lost their meaning. I have read a great deal, but as I'm sure you know, it doesn't lead anywhere. I have dabbled in various religious doctrines, but they all seem so utterly phoney; and what have you left after that? I have thought about it a great deal, and I know it isn't for want of children that I am like this. If I had children, I would give them my love, and all that kind of thing, but this torment of discontent would certainly go on. I can't find a way of directing or canalising it, as most people seem to do, into some absorbing activity or interest. Then it would be easy sailing; there would be an occasional squall, which is inevitable in life, but one would always be within reach of calm waters. I feel as though I were in a perpetual storm, without any safe port. I want to find some comfort, somewhere; but, as I said, what the religions have to offer seems to me so utterly stupid, nothing but a lot of superstitions. Everything else, including worship of the State, is only a rational substitute for the real thing—and I don't know what the real thing is. I have tried various entertaining side issues, including the current philosophy of hopelessness in France, but I am left empty-handed. I have even experimented with taking one or two of the latest drugs; but that, of course, is the ultimate act of despair. One might just as well commit suicide. Now you know all about it."

"If I may put in a word," said the friend, "it seems to me that the whole thing would be resolved if she could only find something that really interested her. If she had a vital interest that occupied her mind and her life, then this discontent that is eating her up would disappear. I have known this lady and her brother for many years, and I keep telling her that her misery arises from not having something that will take her mind off herself. But nobody pays much attention to what is said by an old friend."

May I ask, why shouldn't you be discontented? Why shouldn't you be consumed by discontent? And what do you mean by that word?

"It is a pain, an agonizing anxiety, and naturally one wants to get out of it. It would be a form of sadism to want to remain in it. After all, one should be able to live happily, and not be ceaselessly driven by the pain of dissatisfaction."

I am not saying that you should enjoy the pain of it, or merely put up with it; but why should you try to escape from it through an interesting occupation, or through some other form of abiding satisfaction?

"Isn't that a most natural thing to do?" asked the friend. "If you are in pain, you want to get rid of it."

We are not understanding each other. What do we mean by being discontented? We are not inquiring into the mere verbal or explanatory meaning of that word, nor are we seeking the causes of discontent. We shall come to the causes presently. What we are trying to do, is to examine the state of the mind that is caught in the pain of discontent.

"In other words, what is my mind doing when it is discontented? I don't know, I have never before asked myself that question. Let me see. But first of all, have I understood the question?"

"I think I see what you are asking, sir," put in the brother. "What is the *feeling* of the mind that is in the throes of discontent? Isn't that it?"

Something like that. A feeling is extraordinary in itself—is it not? —apart from its pleasure or pain.

"But can there be any feeling at all," asked the sister, "if it is not identified with pleasure or pain?"

Does identification bring about feeling? Can there be no feeling without identification, without naming? We may come to that question presently; but again, what do we mean by discontent? Does discontent exist by itself, as an isolated feeling, or is it related to something?

74

"It is always related to some other factor, to some urge, desire or want, isn't it?" said the friend. "There must always be a cause; discontent is only a symptom. We want to be or to acquire something, and if for any reason we cannot, we become discontented. I think this is the source of her discontent."

Is it?

"I don't know, I haven't thought that far," replied the sister.

Don't you know why you are discontented? Is it because you haven't found anything in which you can lose yourself? And if you did find some interest or activity with which you could completely occupy your mind, would the pain of discontent go? Is it that you want to be contented?

"God, no!" she exploded. "That would be terrible, that would be stagnation."

But isn't that what you are seeking? You may have a horror of being contented, yet in wanting to be free of discontent, you are pursuing a very superior kind of contentment, aren't you?

"I don't think I want contentment; but I do want to be free from this endless misery of discontent."

Are the two desires different? Most people are discontented, but they generally tame it by finding something which gives them satisfaction, and then they function mechanically and go to seed, or they become bitter, cynical, and so on. Is that what you are after?

"I don't want to become cynical, or just go to seed, that would be too stupid; I only want to find a way to soften the ache of this uncertainty."

The ache exists only when you resist uncertainty, when you want to be free of it.

"Do you mean I must remain in this state?"

Please listen. You condemn the state you are in; your mind is opposing it. Discontent is a flame that must be kept burning brightly, and not be smothered by some interest or activity that is pursued as a reaction from the pain of it. Discontent is painful only when it is resisted. A man who is merely satisfied, without understanding the full significance of discontent, is asleep; he is not sensitive to the whole movement of life. Satisfaction is a drug, and it is comparatively easy to find. But to understand the full significance of discontent, the search for certainty must cease.

"It is difficult not to want to be certain about something."

Apart from mechanical certainties, is there any certainty at all, any psychological permanency? Or is there only impermanency? All relationship is impermanent; all thought, with its symbols, ideals, projections, is impermanent. Property is lost, and even life itself ends in death, in the unknown, though man builds a thousand cunning structures of belief to overcome it. We separate life from death, and so both remain unknown. Contentment and discontent are like the two sides of one coin. To be free from the ache of discontent, the mind must cease to seek contentment.

"Then is there no fulfilment?"

Self-fulfilment is a vain pursuit, isn't it? In the very fulfilment of the self, there is fear and disappointment. That which is gained becomes ashes; but we again struggle to gain, and again we are caught in sorrow. If once we are aware of this total process, then self-fulfilment in any direction, at any level, has no significance at all.

"Then to struggle against discontent is to smother the flame of life," she concluded. "I think I understand the meaning of what you have been saying."

Outward Modification and Inward Disintegration

THE TRAIN south was very crowded, but more people were squeezing in, with their bundles and their trunks. They were dressed in every kind of way. Some wore heavy overcoats, while others had hardly anything on, even though it was quite cold. There were long coats and tight *chudidars*, sloppily-tied turbans, and turbans that were neatly tied and of different colours. When everybody had more or less settled down, the shouts could be heard of the vendors on the station platform. They were selling almost everything: soda water, cigarettes, magazines, peanuts, tea and coffee, sweets and cooked things, toys, rugs—and, strangely enough, a flute, made of polished bamboo. Its vendor was playing upon a similar one, and it had a sweet tone. It was an excited and noisy crowd. Many people had come to see off a man who must have been a fairly important person, for he was weighed down with garlands, which had a goodly smell amidst the acrid smoke of the engine and the other unpleasant odours associated with railroad stations. Two or three people were helping an old woman get into a compartment, for she was rather stout and insisted on carrying her own heavy bundle. An infant was screaming at the top of its voice, while the mother was trying to hold it to her breast. A bell rang, the engine whistle screeched, and the train began to move, not to stop again for several hours.

It was beautiful country, and the dew was still on the fields and on the leaves of the spreading trees. We ran for some distance beside a full-flowing river, and the countryside seemed to open out into endless beauty and life. Here and there were small, smoky villages, with cattle roaming about the fields, or pulling water from a well. A boy clad in dirty rags was driving two or three cows before him along a path; he waved, smiling, as the train roared by. On that morning the sky was intensely blue, the trees were washed and the fields well-watered by the recent rains, and the people were going about their work; but it wasn't for this reason that heaven was very close to the earth. There was in the air a feeling of something sacred, to which one's whole being responded. The quality of the blessing was strange and healing; the solitary man walking along that road, and the hovel by the wayside, were bathed in it. You would never find it in churches, temples or mosques, for these are hand-made and their gods hand-wrought. But there in the open country, and in that rattling train, was the inexhaustible life, a blessing that can neither be sought nor given. It was there for the taking, like that small yellow flower springing up so close to the rails. The people in the train were chatting and laughing, or reading their morning paper, but it was there among them, and among the tender, growing things of the early spring. It was there, immense and simple, the love which no book can reveal, and which the mind cannot touch. It was there on that wondrous morning, the very life of life.

There were eight of us in the room, which was pleasantly dark, but only two or three took part in the conversation. Just outside they were cutting the grass; someone was sharpening a scythe, and the children's voices came into the room. Those who had come were very much in earnest. They all worked hard in various ways for the betterment of society, and not for outward, personal gain; but vanity is a strange thing, it hides under the cloak of virtue and respectability.

"The institution we represent is disintegrating," began the oldest one; "it has been sinking for the past several years, and we must do something to stop this disintegration. It is so easy to destroy an organization, but so very difficult to build it up and maintain it. We have faced many crises, and somehow we have always managed to survive them, bruised, but still able to function. Now, however, we have reached a point where we have to do something drastic; but what? That is our problem."

What needs to be done depends on the symptoms of the patient, and upon those who are responsible for the patient.

"We know very well the symptoms of disintegration, they are all too obvious. Though outwardly the institution is recognized and flourishing, inwardly it is rotting. Our workers are what they are; we have had our differences, but have managed to pull along together for more years than I care to remember. If we were satisfied with mere outward appearances, we would consider all to be well; but those of us who are on the inside, know there is a decline."

You and others who have built up and are responsible for this institution, have made it what it is; you *are* the institution. And disintegration is inherent in every institution, in every society or culture, is it not?

"That is so," agreed another. "As you say, the world is of our own making; the world is us, and we are the world. To change the world, we must change ourselves. This institution is part of the world; as we rot, so do the world and the institution. Regeneration must therefore begin with ourselves. The trouble is, sir, that life to us is not a total process; we act at different levels, each in contradiction with the others. This institution is one thing, and we are another. We are managers, presidents, secretaries, the top officials by whom the institution is run. We don't regard it as our own life; it is something apart from us, something to be managed and reformed. When you say that the organization is what we are, we admit it verbally, but not inwardly; we are concerned with operating upon the institution, and not upon ourselves."

Do you see that you are in need of an operation?

"I see that we are in need of a drastic operation," said the oldest one; "but who is to be the surgeon?"

Each one of us is the surgeon and the patient; there is no outside authority who is going to wield the knife. The very perception of the fact that an operation is necessary sets in motion an action which will in itself be the operation. But if there's to be an operation, it means considerable disturbance, disharmony, for the patient has to stop living in a routine manner. Disturbance is inevitable. To avoid all disturbance of things as they are is to have the harmony of the graveyard, which is well-kept and orderly, but full of buried putrefaction.

"But is it possible, being constituted as we are, to operate upon ourselves?"

Sir, by asking that question, are you not building a wall of resistance which prevents the operation from taking place? Thus you are unconsciously allowing deterioration to continue.

"I want to operate upon myself, but I don't seem able to do it."

When you try to operate upon yourself, there is no operation at all. Making an effort to stop deterioration is another way of avoiding the fact; it is to allow deterioration to go on. Sir, you don't really want an operation; you want to tinker, to improve outward appearances with little changes here and there. You want to reform, to cover the rot with gold, in order that you may have the world and the institution you desire. But we are all getting old, and we are going to die. I am not foisting this on you; but why don't you remove your hand and let there be an operation? Clean, healthy blood will flow if you don't hinder it.

To Change Society, You Must Break Away from It

THE SEA was very calm that morning, more so than usual, for the wind from the south had ceased blowing, and before the north-easterly winds began, the sea was taking a rest. The sands were bleached by the sun and salt water, and there was a strong smell of ozone, mixed with that of seaweed. There wasn't anyone yet on the beach, and one had the sea to oneself. Large crabs, with one claw much bigger than the other, moved slowly about, watching, with the large claw waving in the air. There were also smaller crabs, the usual kind, that raced to the lapping water, or darted into round holes in the wet sand. Hundreds of sea-gulls stood about, resting and preening themselves. The rim of the sun was just coming out of the sea, and it made a golden path on the still waters. Everything seemed to be waiting for this moment—and how quickly it would pass! The sun continued to climb out of the sea, which was as quiet as a sheltered lake in some deep woods. No woods could contain these waters, they were too restless, too strong and vast; but that morning they were mild, friendly and inviting.

Under a tree above the sands and the blue water, there was going on a life independent of the crabs, the salt water and the sea-gulls. Large, black ants darted about, not making up their minds where to go. They would go up the tree, then suddenly scurry down for no apparent reason. Two or three would impatiently stop, move their heads about, and then, with a fierce burst of energy, go all over a piece of wood which they must have examined hundreds of times before; they would investigate it again with eager curiosity, and lose interest in it a second later. It was very quiet under the tree, though everything about one was very much alive. There was not a breath of air stirring among the leaves, but every leaf was abundant with the beauty and light of the morning. There was an intensity about the tree—not the terrible intensity of reaching, of succeeding, but the intensity of being complete, simple, alone and yet part of the earth. The colours of the leaves, of the few flowers, of the dark trunk, were intensified a thousandfold, and the branches seemed to sustain the heavens. It was incredibly clear, bright and alive in the shade of that single tree.

Meditation is an intensification of the mind which is in the fullness of silence. The mind is not still like some tamed, frightened or disciplined animal; it is still as the waters are still many fathoms down. The stillness there is not like that on the surface when the winds die. This stillness has a life and a movement of its own which is related to the outer flow of life, but is untouched by it. Its intensity is not that of some powerful machine which has been put together by cunning, capable hands; it is as simple and natural as love, as lightning, as a full-flowing river.

He said he had been in politics up to his ears. He had done the usual things to climb the ladder of success—cultivated the right people, got on familiar terms with the leaders who had themselves climbed the very same ladder—and his climb had been rapid. He had been sent abroad on many of the important committees, and was regarded with respect by those who count; for he was sincere and incorruptible, albeit as ambitious as the rest of them. Added to all this, he was well-read, and words came easily to him. But now, by some fortunate chance, he was tired of this game of helping the country by boosting himself and becoming a very important person. He was tired of it, not because he couldn't climb any higher, but because, through a natural process of intelligence, he had come to see that man's deep betterment does not lie entirely in planning, in efficiency, in the scramble for power. So he had thrown it all overboard, and was beginning to consider anew the whole of life.

What do you mean by the whole of life?

"I have spent many years on a branch of the river, as it were, and I want to spend the remaining years of my life on the river itself. Although I enjoyed every minute of the political struggle, I am not leaving politics regretfully; and now I wish to contribute to the betterment of society from my heart and not from the ever-calculating mind. What I take from society must be returned to it at least tenfold."

If one may ask, why are you thinking in terms of giving and taking?

"I have taken so much from society; and all that it has given me I must give back to it many times."

What do you owe to society?

"Everything I have: my bank account, my education, my name— Oh, so many things!"

In actuality, you have not taken anything from society, because you are part of it. If you were a separate entity, unconnected with society, then you could give back what you have taken. But you are part of society, part of the culture which has put you together. You can return borrowed money; but what can you give back to society as long as you are part of society?

"Because of society I have money, food, clothing, shelter, and I must do something in return. I have profited by my gathering within the framework of society, and it would be ungrateful of me to turn my back on it. I must do some good work for society—good work in the large sense, and not as a 'do-gooder'."

I understand what you mean; but even if you returned all you have gathered, would that absolve you from your debt? What society has yielded through your efforts is comparatively easy to return; you can give it to the poor, or to the State. And then what? You still have your 'duty' to society, for you are still part of it; you are one of its citizens. As long as you belong to society, identify yourself with it, you are both the giver and the taker. You maintain it; you support its structure, do you not?

"I do. I am, as you say, an integral part of society; without it, I am not. Since I am both the good and the bad of society, I must remove the bad and uphold the good."

In any given culture or society, the 'good' is the accepted, the respectable. You want to maintain that which is noble within the structure of society; is that it?

"What I want to do is to change the social pattern in which man is caught. I mean this most earnestly."

The social pattern is set up by man; it is not independent of man, though it has a life of its own, and man is not independent of it; they are interrelated. Change within the pattern is no change at all; it is mere modification, reformation. Only by breaking away from the social pattern without building another can you 'help' society. As long as you belong to society, you are only helping it to deteriorate. All societies, including the most marvellously utopian, have within them the seeds of their own corruption. To change society, you must break away from it. You must cease to be what society is: acquisitive, ambitious, envious, power-seeking, and so on.

"Do you mean I must become a monk, a *sannyasi?*"

Certainly not. The *sannyasi* has merely renounced the outer show of the world, of society, but inwardly he is still a part of it; he is still burning with the desire to achieve, to gain, to become.

"Yes, I see that."

Surely, since you have burnt yourself in politics, your problem is not only to break away from society, but to come totally to life again, to love and be simple. Without love, do what you may, you will not know the total action which alone can save man.

"That is true, sir: we don't love, we aren't really simple."

Why? Because you are so concerned with reforms, with duties, with respectability, with becoming something, with breaking through to the other side. In the name of another, you are concerned with yourself; you are caught in your own cockle-shell. You think you are the centre of this beautiful earth. You never pause to look at a tree, at a flower, at the flowing river; and if by some chance you do look, your eyes are filled with the things of the mind, and not with beauty and love.

"Again, that is true; but what is one to do?"

Look and be simple.

WHERE THE SELF IS, LOVE IS NOT

THE ROSE-BUSHES just inside the gate were covered with bright red roses, heavy with perfume, and butterflies were hovering about them. There were also marigolds and sweet peas in bloom. The garden overlooked the river, and that evening it was full of the golden light of the setting sun. Fishing boats, shaped somewhat like gondolas, were dark on the still surface of the river. The village among the trees on the opposite side was over a mile away, and yet voices came clearly across the water. From the gate there was a path leading down .to the river. It joined a rough road which was used by the villagers on their way to and from the town. This road ended abruptly at the bank of a stream that flowed into the big river. It was not a sandy bank, but heavy with damp clay, and the feet sank into it. Across the stream at this point they would presently build a bamboo bridge; but now there was a clumsy barge laden with the quiet villagers, who were returning from their day of trading in the town. Two men punted us across, while the villagers sat huddled in the evening cold. There was a small brazier to be lit when it got a little darker, but the moon would give them light. A little girl was carrying a basket of firewood; she had put it down while crossing the stream, and was now having difficulty in lifting it again. It was quite heavy for a little girl, but with some help she got it carefully placed on her small head, and her smile seemed to fill the universe. We all climbed the steep bank with careful steps, and soon the villagers went chattering off down the road.

Here it was open country, and the soil was very rich with the silt of many centuries. The flat, well-cultivated land, dotted with marvellous old trees, stretched out to the horizon. There were fields of sweet-smelling peas, white with blossom, as well as winter wheat and other grain. On one side flowed the river, wide and curving, and overlooking the river there was a village, noisy with activity. The path here was very ancient; the Enlightened One was said to have walked on it, and the pilgrims had been using it for many centuries. It was a holy path, and there were small temples here and there along that sacred way. The mango and tamarind trees were also very old, and some were dying, having seen so much. Against the golden evening sky they were stately, their limbs dark and open. A little further along there was a grove of bamboos, yellowing with age, and in a small orchard a goat tied to a fruit tree was bleating for its kid, which was jumping and skipping all over the place. The path led on through another grove of mangoes, and beside a tranquil pond. There was a breathless stillness, and everything knew the blessed hour. The earth and everything upon it became holy. It was not that the mind was aware of this peace as something outside of itself, something to be remembered and communicated, but there was a total absence of any movement of the mind. There was only the immeasurable.

He was a youngish man, in his early forties he said; and though he had faced audiences and spoken with great confidence, he was still rather shy. Like so many others of his generation, he had played with politics, with religion, and with social reform. He was given to writing poetry, and could put colour on canvas. Several of the prominent leaders were his friends, and he could have gone far in politics; but he had chosen otherwise, and was content to keep his light covered in a distant mountain town.

"I have been wanting to see you for many years. You may not remember it, but I was once on the same boat with you going to Europe before the second world war. My father was very interested in your teachings, but I drifted away into politics and other things. My desire to talk to you again finally became so persistent that it could not be put off any longer. I want to expose my heart—something I have never done to anyone else, for it isn't easy to discuss oneself with others. For some time I have been attending your talks and discussions in different places, but recently I have had a strong urge to see you privately, because I have come to an impasse."

Of what kind?

"I don't seem to be able to 'break through'. I have done some meditation, not the kind that mesmerizes you, but trying to be aware of my own thinking, and so on. In this process I invariably fall asleep. I suppose it is because I am lazy, easy-going. I have fasted, and I have tried various diets, but this lethargy persists."

Is it due to laziness, or to something else? Is there a deep, inward frustration? Has your mind been made dull, insensitive, by the events of your life? If one may ask, is it that love is not there?

"I don't know, sir; I have vaguely thought about these matters, but have never been able to pin anything down. Perhaps I have been

84

smothered by too many good and evil things. In a way, life has been too easy for me, with family, money, certain capacities, and so on. Nothing has been very difficult, and that may be the trouble. This general feeling of being at ease and having the capacity to find my way out of almost any situation may have made me soft."

Is that it? Is that not just a description of superficial happenings? If those things had affected you deeply, you would have led a different kind of life, you would have followed the easy course. But you have not, so there must be a different process at work that is making your mind sluggish and inept.

"Then what is it? I am not bothered by sex; I have indulged in it, but it has never been a passion with me to the extent that I became a slave to it. It began with love and ended in disappointment, but not in frustration. Of that I am pretty sure. I neither condemn nor pursue sex. It's not a problem to me, anyway."

Has this indifference destroyed sensitivity? After all, love is vulnerable, and a mind that has built defences against life ceases to love.

"I don't think I have built a defence against sex; but love is not necessarily sex, and I really do not know if I love at all."

You see, our minds are so carefully cultivated that we fill the heart with the things of the mind. We give most of our time and energy to the earning of a livelihood, to the gathering of knowledge, to the fire of belief, to patriotism and the worship of the State, to the activities of social reform, to the pursuit of ideals and virtues, and to the many other things with which the mind keeps itself occupied; so the heart is made empty, and the mind becomes rich in its cunningness. This does make for insensitivity, doesn't it?

"It is true that we over-cultivate the mind. We worship knowledge, and the man of intellect is honoured, but few of us love in the sense you are talking about. Speaking for myself, I honestly do not know if I have any love at all. I don't kill to eat. I like nature. I like to go into the woods and feel their silence and beauty; I like to sleep under the open skies. But does all this indicate that I love?"

Sensitivity to nature is part of love; but it isn't love, is it? To be gentle and kind, to do good works, asking nothing in return, is part of love; but it isn't love, is it?

"Then what *is* love?"

Love is all these parts, but much more. The totality of love is not within the measure of the mind; and to know that totality, the mind must be empty of its occupations, however noble or self-centred. To ask how to empty the mind, or how not to be self-centred, is to pursue a method; and the pursuit of a method is another occupation of the mind.

"But is it possible to empty the mind without some kind of effort?"

All effort, the 'right' as well as the 'wrong', sustains the centre, the core of achievement, the self. Where the self is, love is not. But we were talking of the lethargy of the mind, of its insensitivity. Have you not read a great deal? And may not knowledge be part of this process of insensitivity?

"I am not a scholar, but I read a lot, and I like to browse in libraries. I respect knowledge, and I don't quite see why you think that knowledge necessarily makes for insensitivity."

What do we mean by knowledge? Our life is largely a repetition of what we have been taught, is it not? We may add to our learning, but the repetitive process continues and strengthens the habit of accumulating. What do you know except what you have read or been told, or what you have experienced? That which you experience now is shaped by what you have experienced before. Further experience is what has been experienced already, only enlarged or modified, and so the repetitive process is maintained. Repetition of the good or the bad, of the noble or the trivial, obviously makes for insensitivity, because the mind is moving only within the field of the known. May not this be why your mind is dull?

"But I can't put away all that I know, all that I have accumulated as knowledge."

You are this knowledge, you are the things that you have accumulated; you are the gramophone record that is ever repeating what is impressed on it. You are the song, the noise, the chatter of society, of your culture. Is there an uncorrupted 'you', apart from all this chatter? This self-centre is now anxious to free itself from the things it has gathered; but the effort it makes to be free is still part of the accumulative process. You have a new record to play, with new words, but your mind is still dull, insensitive.

"I see that perfectly; you have described very well my state of mind. I have learnt, in my time, the jargons of various ideologies, both religious and political; but, as you point out, my mind has in essence remained the same. I am now very clearly aware of this; and I am also aware that this whole process makes the mind superficially alert, clever

86

and outwardly pliable, while below the surface it is still that same old self-centre which is the 'me'."

Are you aware of all this as a fact, or do you know it only through another's description? If it is not your own discovery, something that you have found out for yourself, then it is still only the word and not the fact that is important.

"I don't quite follow this. Please go slowly, sir, and explain it again."

Do you know anything, or do you only recognize? Recognition is a process of association, memory, which is knowledge. That is true, isn't it?

"I think I see what you mean. I know that bird is a parrot only because I have been told so. Through association, memory, which is knowledge, there is recognition, and then I say: 'It is a parrot'."

The word 'parrot' has blocked you from looking at the bird, the thing that flies. We almost never look at the fact, but at the word or the symbol that stands for the fact. The fact recedes, and the word, the symbol, becomes all-important. Now; can you look at the fact, whatever it may be, dissociated from the word, the symbol?

"It seems to me that perception of the fact, and awareness of the word representing the fact, occur in the mind at the same time."

Can the mind separate the fact from the word?

"I don't think it can."

Perhaps we are making this more difficult than it is. That object is called a tree; the word and the object are two separate things, are they not?

"Actually it is so; but, as you say, we always look at the object through the word."

Can you separate the object from the word? The word 'love' is not the feeling, the fact of love.

"But, in a way, the word is a fact too, isn't it?"

In a way, yes. Words exist to communicate, and also to remember, to fix in the mind a fleeting experience, a thought, a feeling; so the mind itself is the word, the experience, it is the memory of the fact in terms of pleasure and pain, good and bad. This whole process takes place within the field of time, the field of the known; and any revolution within that field is no revolution at all, but only a modification of what has been.

"If I understand you correctly, you are saying that I have made my mind dull, lethargic, insensitive, through traditional or repetitive thinking, of which self-discipline is a part. To bring the repetitive process to an end, the gramophone record, which is the self, must be broken; and it can be broken only by seeing the fact, and not through effort. Effort, you say, only keeps the recording machine wound up, so in that there is no hope. Then what?"

See the fact, the what *is,* and let that fact operate; don't you operate on the fact—the 'you' being the repetitive mechanism, with its opinions, judgments, knowledge.

"I will try," he said earnestly.

To try is to oil the repetitive mechanism, not to put an end to it.

"Sir, you are taking everything away from one, and nothing is left. But that may be the new thing."

It is.

The Fragmentation of Man Is Making Him Sick

It was still very early, and there was a slight ground mist hiding the bushes and the flowers. A heavy dew had made a circle of dampness around each tree. The sun was just coming up behind a mass of trees, which were quiet now, for the chattering birds had all scattered for the day. The engines of the airplanes were being warmed up, and their roar filled the early morning air; but very soon they would be leaving for different parts of the big continent, and except for the usual daily noises of a town, everything would be quiet again.

A beggar with a nice voice was singing in the street, and the song had that nostalgic quality which is so familiar. His voice had not become raucous, and amidst the rattling of buses and the shouts of people calling across the street, it had a pleasant and welcoming sound. You would hear him every morning if you lived around there. Many beggars do tricks, or have monkeys that do the tricks; they are knowing and sophisticated, with a cunning look and an easy smile. But this beggar was altogether of a different kind. He was a simple beggar, with a long staff and torn, dirty clothes. He had no pretensions, no wheedling ways. The others received more alms than he did, for people like to be flattered, to be called pleasant names, or to be blessed and wished prosperity. But this beggar did none of those things. He begged, and if you gave, he bowed his head and went on; there was no pose, no gesticulation. He would walk the whole length of the long, shady street, always giving way to people; at the end of the street he would turn right into a narrower and quieter street, and begin his singing again, finally wandering off into one of the little lanes. He was quite young, and there was a pleasant feeling about him.

The plane took off at the appointed time and climbed smoothly over the city, with its domes, its ancient tombs, and its long blocks of ugly buildings, pretentious and recently constructed. Beyond the city was the river, winding and open, its waters a pale blue-green; and the plane followed it, going mostly south-east. We had levelled off at about six thousand feet, and the country lay below us, all neatly broken up into irregular grey-green patches, each man owning a little piece. The river went meandering past many villages, and from it there were straight, narrow, man-made canals extending into the fields. Hundreds of miles away to the east, the snow-covered mountains began to appear, ethereal and unreal in their rosy glow. They seemed at first to be floating above the horizon, and it was difficult to believe that they were mountains, with sharp peaks and massive formations. From the surface of the earth, at that distance, they couldn't be seen, but from this altitude they were visible and spectacularly beautiful. One could hardly take one's eyes off them, for fear of missing the slightest nuance in their beauty and grandeur. One range slowly gave place to another, one massive peak to another. They covered the north-eastern horizon, and even after we had been flying for two hours, they were still there. It was really incredible: the colour, the immensity and the solitude. One forgot everything else—the passengers, the captain asking questions, and the hostess requesting the tickets. It was not the absorption of a child in a toy, nor of the monk in his cell, nor of the *sannyasi* on the bank of a river. It was a state of total attention in which there was no distraction. There was only the beauty and the glory of the earth. There was no watcher.

A psychologist, an analyst, and an M.D., he was plump, with a large head and serious eyes. He had come, he said, to talk over several points; however, he would not use the jargon of psychology and analysis, but would keep to words with which we were both familiar. Having studied the famous psychologists, and himself been analysed by one of them, he knew the limitations of modern psychology, as well as its therapeutic value. It was not always successful, he explained, but it had great possibilities in the hands of the right people. Of course, there were many quacks, but that was to be expected. He had also studied, although not extensively, oriental thought and the oriental idea of consciousness.

"When the subconscious was first discovered and described here in the West, no university had a place for it, and no publisher would undertake to bring out the book; but now, of course, after only two decades, the word is on everybody's lips. We like to think that we are the discoverers of everything, and that the Orient is a jungle of mysticism and disappearing-rope tricks; but the fact is that the Orient undertook the exploration of consciousness many centuries ago, only they used different symbols, with more extensive meanings. I am saying this only to indicate that I am eager to learn, and have not the usual bias in this matter. We specialists in the field of psychology do help the maladjusted to return to society, and that seems to be our main concern. But somehow I personally am not satisfied with this—which brings me to one of the points I want to discuss. Is that all we psychologists can do? Can we not do more than just help the maladjusted individual to return to society?"

Is society healthy, that an individual should return to it? Has not society itself helped to make the individual unhealthy? Of course, the unhealthy must be made healthy, that goes without saying; but why should the individual adjust himself to an unhealthy society? If he is healthy, he will not be a part of it. Without first questioning the health of society, what is the good of helping misfits to conform to society?

"I don't think society is healthy; it is run by and for frustrated, power-seeking, superstitious people. It is always in a state of convulsion. During the last war I helped in the work of trying to straighten out the misfits in the army who couldn't adjust themselves to the horrors of the battlefield. They were probably right, but there was a war on, and it had to be won. Some of those who fought and survived still need psychiatric help, and to bring them back into society is going to be quite a job."

To help the individual to fit into a society which is ever at war with itself—is this what psychologists and analysts are supposed to do? Is the individual to be healed only in order to kill or be killed? If one is not killed, or driven insane, then must one only fit into the structure of hate, envy, ambition and superstition, which can be very scientific?

90

"I admit society is not what it should be, but what can you do? You can't get out of society; you have to work in it, make a living in it, suffer and die in it. You can't become a recluse, or one of those people who withdraw and think only of their own salvation. We must save society in spite of itself."

Society is man's relationship with man; its structure is based on his compulsions, ambitions, hates, vanities, envies, on the whole complexity of his urge to dominate and to follow. Unless the individual breaks away from this corruptive structure, what fundamental value can there be in the physician's help? He will only be made corrupt again.

"It is the duty of a physician to heal. We are not reformers of society; that department belongs to the sociologists."

Life is one, it's not to be departmentalized. We have to be concerned with the whole of man: with his work, with his love, with his conduct, with his health, his death and his God—as well as with the atomic bomb. It's this fragmentation of man that's making him sick.

"Some of us realize this, sir, but what can we do? We ourselves are not whole men with an over-all outlook, an integrated drive and purpose. We heal one part while the rest disintegrates, only to see that the deep rot is destroying the whole. What is one to do? As a physician, what is my duty?"

To heal, obviously; but isn't it also the responsibility of the physician to heal society as a whole? There can be no reformation of society; there can only be a revolution outside the pattern of society.

"But I come back to my point: as an individual, what can one do?"

Break away from society, of course; be free, not from mere outward things, but from envy, ambition, the worship of success, and so on.

"Such freedom would give one more time for study, and there certainly would be greater tranquillity; but would it not lead to a rather superficial, useless existence?"

On the contrary, freedom from envy and fear would bring to the individual a state of integration, would it not? It would put a stop to the various forms of escape which inevitably cause confusion and self-contradiction, and life would have a deeper, wider significance.

"Aren't some escapes beneficial to a limited intelligence? Religion is a splendid escape for many people; it gives significance, however illusory, to their otherwise drab existence."

So do cinemas, romantic novels and some drugs; and would you encourage such forms of escape? The intellectuals also have their escapes, crude or subtle, and almost every person has his blind spots; and when such people are in positions of power, they breed more mischief and misery. Religion is not a matter of dogmas and beliefs, of rituals and superstitions; nor is it the cultivation of personal salvation, which is a self-centred activity. Religion is the total way of life; it is the understanding of truth, which is not a projection of the mind.

"You are asking too much of the average person, who wants his amusements, his escapes, his self-satisfying religion, and someone to follow or to hate. What you are hinting at demands a different education, a different world-society, and neither our politicians nor our average educators are capable of this wider vision. I suppose man has got to go through the long, dark night of misery and pain before he will emerge as an integrated, intelligent human being. For the moment, that is not my concern. My concern is with individual human wrecks, for whom I can and *do* do a great deal; but it seems so little in this vast sea of misery. As you say, I shall have to bring about a state of integration in myself, and that's quite an arduous undertaking.

"There is another thing, personal in nature, which I would like to talk over with you, if I may. You said earlier something about envy. I realize that I am envious; and although I allow myself to be analysed from time to time, as most of us analysts do, I haven't been able to go beyond this thing. I am almost ashamed to admit it, but envy is there, ranging from petty jealousy up to its more complex forms, and I don't seem able to shake it off."

Is the mind capable of being free from envy, not in little bits, but completely? Unless there is total freedom from it, right through one's whole being, envy keeps repeating itself in different forms, at different times.

"Yes, I realize that. Envy must be wholly eliminated from the mind, just as a malignant growth must be totally removed from the body, otherwise it will recur; but how?"

The 'how' is another form of envy, isn't it? When one asks for a method, one wants to get rid of envy in order to be something else; so envy is still operating.

"It was a natural question, but I see what you mean. This aspect of the matter had never struck me before."

We always seem to fall into this trap, and for ever after we are caught in it; we are always trying to be free from envy. Trying to be free gives rise to the method, and so the mind is never free either from envy or from the method. Inquiring into the possibility of total freedom from envy is one thing, and seeking a method to help one to be free is another. In seeking a method, one invariably finds it, however simple or complex it may be. Then all inquiry into the possibility of total freedom ceases, and one is stuck with a method, a practice, a discipline. Thus envy goes on and is subtly sustained.

"Yes, as you point it out, I see that's perfectly true. In effect you are asking me if I am really concerned with total freedom from envy. You know, sir, I have found envy to be stimulating at times; there has been pleasure in it. Do I want to be free from the totality of envy, from both the pleasure and the painful anxiety of it? I confess I have never before asked myself that question, nor have I been asked it by others. My first reaction is, I don't know if I want to or not. I suppose what I would really like, is to keep the stimulating side of envy and get rid of the rest. But it is obviously impossible to retain only the desirable parts of it, and one must accept the whole content of envy, or be free of it completely. I am beginning to see the meaning of your question. The urge is there to be free from envy, and yet I want to hold on to certain parts of it. We human beings are certainly irrational and contradictory! This requires further analysis, sir, and I hope you will have the patience to go through to the end of it. I can see there is fear involved in this. If I were not driven by envy, which is covered over by professional words and requirements, there might be a slipping back; I might not be so successful, so prominent, so financially well-off. There is a subtle fear of losing all this, a fear of insecurity, and other fears which it's not worth going into now. This underlying fear is certainly stronger than the urge to be free from even the unpleasant aspects of envy, to say nothing of being totally free from it. I now see the intricate patterns of this problem, and I am not at all sure I want to be free from envy."

As long as the mind thinks in terms of the 'more,' there must be envy; as long as there's comparison, though through comparison we think we understand, there must be envy; as long as there's an end, a goal to be achieved, there must be envy; as long as the additive process exists, which is self-improvement, the gaining of virtue, and so on, there must be envy. The 'more' implies time, does it not? It implies time in order to change from what one *is* to what one *should* be, the ideal; time as a means of gaining, arriving, achieving.

"Of course. To cover distance, to move from one point to another, whether physically or psychologically, time is necessary."

Time as a movement from here to there is a physical, chronological fact. But is time needed to be free from envy? We say, "I am *this*, and to become *that*, or to change this quality into that, needs time." But is time the factor of change? Or is any change within the field of time no change at all?

"I am getting rather confused here. You are suggesting that change in terms of time is no change at all. How is that?"

Such change is a modified continuity of what has been, is it not?

"Let me see if I understand this. To change from the fact, which is envy, to the ideal, which is non-envy, needs time—at least, that's what we think. This gradual change through time, you say, is no change at all, but merely a further wallowing in envy. Yes, I can see that."

As long as the mind thinks in terms of changing through time, of bringing about a revolution in the future, there is no transformation in the present. This is a fact, isn't it?

"All right, sir, we both see this to be a fact. Then what?"

How does the mind react when it is confronted with this fact?

"Either it runs away from the fact, or it stops and looks at it."

Which is your reaction?

"Both, I am afraid. There is an urge to escape from the fact, and at the same time I want to examine it."

Can you examine something when there's fear concerning it? Can you observe a fact about which you have an opinion, a judgment?

"I see what you mean. I am not observing the fact, but evaluating it. My mind is projecting its ideas and fears upon it. Yes, that's right."

In other words, your mind is occupied with itself, and is therefore incapable of being simply aware of the fact. You are operating upon the fact, and not allowing the fact to operate upon your mind. The fact that change within the field of time is no change at all, that there can only be total and not partial, gradual freedom from envy—the very truth of this fact will operate on the mind, setting it free.

"I really think the truth of it is making its way through my blockages."

The Vanity of Knowledge

THERE WERE four who were chanting, and it was pure sound. They were quiet, elderly men, uninterested in worldly things, but not by way of renunciation; they were simply not drawn to the world. Wearing old but clean clothes, and with solemn faces, they would hardly have been noticed if they had passed you on the street. But the moment they began to chant, their faces were transformed and became radiant, ageless, and they created, with the sound of the words and the powerful intonation, that extraordinary atmosphere of a very ancient language. They *were* the words, the sound and the meaning. The sound of the words had great depth. It was not the depth of a stringed instrument, or of a drum, but the depth of a human voice alive to the significance of words made holy by time and usage. The chant was in the language that has been polished and made perfect, and its sound filled the big room, and penetrated the walls, the garden, the mind and the heart. It wasn't the sound of a singer on the stage, but there was the silence that exists between two movements of sound. You felt your body being uncontrollably shaken by the sound of the words, which was in the marrow of your bones; you sat completely still, and it held you in its movement; it was living, dancing, vibrant, and your mind was of it. It wasn't a sound that lulled you to sleep, but one that shook and almost hurt you. It was the depth and the beauty of pure tone, untouched by applause, by fame, and by the world; it was the tone from which all sound, all music comes.

A boy of three or so was sitting up in front without moving, his back straight, his eyes closed; he wasn't asleep. After an hour he quickly got up and went away, without any awkward shyness. He was equal to all, for the sound of the words was in his heart.

You never got tired during those two hours; you didn't want to move, and the world, with all its noise, didn't exist. Presently the chanting stopped, and the sound came to an end; but it went on inside you, and it would go on for many a day. The four bowed and saluted, and became once more the men of every day. They said they had practised that form of chanting for over ten years, and it had called for great patience and a dedicated life. It was a dying art, for there was hardly anyone nowadays willing to devote his life to that kind of chanting; there was no money in it, no fame, and who wanted to enter that kind of world? They were delighted, they said, to chant before people who really appreciated their effort. Then they went their way, poor and lost in a world of noise, cruelty and greed. But the river had listened, and was silent.

He was a well-known scholar, and had come with some of his friends and a disciple or two. He had a large head, and his small eyes peered through thick glasses. He knew Sanskrit as others know their own languages, and spoke it as easily; and he also knew Greek and English. He was as familiar with the major oriental philosophies, including their various branches, as you are with addition and subtraction, and he had studied western philosophers as well, both the ancient and the modern. Rigorous in his self-discipline, he had days of silence and fasting, and had practised, he said, various forms of meditation. For all this, he was quite a youngish man, probably in his late forties, simply attired and eager. His friends and disciples sat around him and waited with that devout expectancy which precludes any questioning. They were all of that world of scholars who possess encyclopaedic knowledge, have visions and psychic experiences, and are certain of their own understanding. They took no part in the conversation, but listened, or rather heard what was going on. Later they would ardently discuss it among themselves, but now they must maintain a reverential silence in the presence of higher authority. There was a period of silence, and presently he began. There was no arrogance or pride of knowledge about him.

"I have come as an inquirer, not to flaunt what I know. What do I know beyond what I have read and experienced? To learn is a great virtue, but to be content with what one knows is stupid. I have not come in the spirit of argumentation, though argument is necessary when doubt arises. I have come to seek, and not to refute. As I said, I have for many years practised meditation, not only the Hindu and Buddhist forms of it, but western types as well. I am saying this so that you may know to what extent I have sought to find that which transcends the mind."

Can a mind which practises a system ever discover that which is beyond the mind? Is a mind which is held within the framework of its own discipline capable of search? Must there not be freedom to discover?

"Surely, to seek and to observe there must be a certain discipline; there must be the regular practice of some method if one is to find, and to understand that which one finds."

Sir, we all seek a way out of our misery and trials; but search comes to an end when a method is adopted by means of which we hope to put an end to sorrow. Only in the understanding of sorrow is there an ending of it, and not in the practice of a method.

"But how can there be an ending of sorrow if the mind is not well-controlled, one-pointed and purposive? Do you mean to say that discipline is unnecessary for understanding?"

Does one understand when, through discipline, through various practices, one's mind is shaped by desire? Must not the mind be free for understanding to take place?

"Freedom, surely, comes at the end of the journey; at the beginning, one is a slave to desire and the things of desire. To free oneself from attachment to the pleasures of the senses, there must be discipline, the practice of various *sadhanas;* otherwise the mind yields to desire and is caught in its net. Unless the groundwork of righteousness is well laid, the house will tumble."

Freedom is at the beginning, and not at the end. The understanding of greed, of the whole content of it—its nature, its implications, and its effects, both pleasurable and painful—must be at the beginning. Then there is no need for the mind to build a wall of resistance, to discipline itself against greed. When the totality of that which inevitably leads to misery and confusion is perceived, discipline against it has no meaning. If he who now spends much time and energy in the practice of a discipline, with all its conflicts, were to give the same thought and attention to the understanding of the total significance of sorrow, there would be a complete ending of sorrow. But we are caught in the tradition of resistance, discipline, and so there is no understanding of the ways of sorrow.

"I am listening, but I do not understand."

Can there be listening as long as the mind clings to conclusions based on its assumptions and experiences? Surely, one listens only when the mind is not translating what it hears in terms of what it knows. Knowledge prevents listening. One may know a great deal; but to listen to something which may be totally different from what one knows, one must put aside one's knowledge. Isn't that so, sir?

"Then how can one tell whether what's being said is true or false?"

97

The true and the false are not based on opinion or judgment, however wise and old. To perceive the true in the false, and the false in what is said to be true, and to see the truth as truth, demands a mind that is not held in its own conditioning. How can one see whether a statement is true or false, if one's mind is prejudiced, caught in the framework of its own or another's conclusions and experiences? For such a mind, what is important is to be aware of its own limitations.

"How is a mind that's enmeshed in the net of its own making to disentangle itself?"

Does this question reflect the search for a new method, or is it put to discover for oneself the whole significance of seeking and practising a method? After all, when one practises a method, a discipline, the intention is to achieve a result, to gain certain qualities, and so on. Instead of worldly things, one hopes to gain so-called spiritual things; but gain is the purpose in both cases. There is no difference, except in words, between the man who meditates and practises a discipline in order to attain the other shore, and the man who works hard to fulfil his worldly ambition. Both are ambitious, both are greedy, both are concerned with themselves.

"That being the fact, sir, how are envy, ambition, greed, and so on, to be put aside?"

Again, if it may be pointed out, the 'how', the method that will seemingly bring about freedom, only puts an end to one's inquiry into the problem, and arrests the understanding of it. To grasp fully the significance of the problem, one has to consider the whole question of effort. A petty mind making an effort not to be petty remains petty; a greedy mind disciplining itself to be generous is still greedy. Effort to be or not to be something is the continuance of the self. This effort may identify itself with the *Atman,* the soul, the indwelling God, and so on, but the core of it is still greed, ambition, which is the self, with all its conscious and unconscious attributes.

"You are maintaining, then, that all effort to achieve an end, worldly or spiritual, is essentially the same, in that selfishness is the basis of it. Such effort only sustains the ego."

That is so, isn't it? The mind that practises virtue ceases to be virtuous. Humility cannot be cultivated; when it is, it is no longer humility.

"That is clear and to the point. Now, since you cannot be advocating indolence, what is the nature of true effort?"

When we are aware of the full significance of effort, with all its implications, is there then any effort at all of which we are conscious?

"You have pointed out that any becoming, positive or negative, is the perpetuation of this 'me', which is the result of identification with desire and the objects of desire. When once this fact is understood, you are asking, is there then any effort as we know it now? I can perceive the possibility of a state of being in which all such effort has ceased."

Merely to perceive the possibility of that state is not to understand the total meaning of effort in everyday existence. As long as there's an observer who is trying to change, or to gain, or to put aside that which he observes, there must be effort; for after all, effort is the conflict between what *is* and what *should* be, the ideal. When this fact is understood, not merely verbally or intellectually, but deeply, then the mind has entered that state of being in which all effort, as we know it, is not.

"To experience that state is the ardent desire of every seeker, including myself."

It cannot be sought; it comes uninvited. The desire for it drives the mind to gather knowledge and practise discipline as a means of gaining it—which is again to conform to a pattern in order to be successful. Knowledge is an impediment to the experiencing of that state.

"How can knowledge be an impediment?" he asked in rather a shocked voice.

The problem of knowledge is complex, is it not? Knowledge is a movement of the past. To know is to assert that which has been. He who asserts that he knows ceases to understand reality. After all, sir, what is it that we know?

"I know certain scientific and ethical facts. Without such knowledge, the civilized world would revert to savagery—and you are obviously not advocating *that*. Apart from these facts, what do I know? I know there is the infinitely compassionate, the Supreme."

That's not a fact, it is a psychological assumption on the part of a mind that has been conditioned to believe in the existence of the Supreme. One who has been conditioned differently will maintain that the Supreme is not. Both are bound by tradition, by knowledge, and so neither will discover the reality of it. Again, what is it that we know? We know only what we have read or experienced, what we have been taught by the ancient teachers and the modern *gurus* and interpreters.

"Again I am forced to agree with you. We are the product of the past in conjunction with the present. The present is shaped by the past."

And the future is a modified continuity of the present. But this is not a matter of agreement, sir. Either one sees the fact, or one does not. When the fact is seen by both of us, agreement is unnecessary. Agreement exists only where there are opinions.

"You are saying, sir, that we know only what we have been taught; that we are merely the repetition of what has been; that our experiences, visions and aspirations are the responses of our conditioning, and nothing more. But is this entirely so? Is the *Atman* of our own making? Can it be a mere projection of our own desires and hopes? It is not an invention, but a necessity."

That which is necessary is soon fashioned by the mind, and the mind is then taught to accept what it has fashioned. The minds of a whole people can be trained to accept a given belief, or its contrary, and both are the outcome of necessity, of hope, of fear, of the desire for comfort or power.

"By your very reasoning, you are forcing me to see certain facts, not the least of which is my own state of confusion. But there still remains the question, what is a mind to do that is caught in its own entangling net?"

Let it just be choicelessly aware of the fact that it is confused; for any action born of that confusion can only lead to further confusion. Sir, must not the mind die to all knowledge if it is to discover the reality of the Supreme?

"That is a very hard thing you are asking. Can I die to everything I have learnt, read, experienced? I really don't know."

But is it not necessary for the mind—spontaneously, without any motive or compulsion—to die to the past? A mind that is the result of time, a mind that has read, studied, that has meditated upon what it has been taught, and is in itself a continuance of the past—how can such a mind experience reality, the timeless, the ever-new? How can it ever fathom the unknown? Surely, to know, to be certain, is the way of vanity, arrogance. As long as one knows, there is no dying, there is only continuity; and what has continuity can never be in that state of creation which is the timeless. When the past ceases to contaminate, reality *is*. There is then no need to seek it out.

With one part of itself the mind knows that there is no permanency, no corner in which it can rest; but with another part, it is ever disciplining itself, seeking openly or surreptitiously to establish an abode of certainty, of permanence, a relationship beyond dispute. So there is an endless contradiction, a struggle to be and yet not to be, and we spend our days in conflict and sorrow, prisoners within the walls of our own minds. The walls can be broken down, but knowledge and technique are not the instruments of that freedom.

"What Is Life All About?"

THE SUN was beating down on the rough, pebbly road, and it was pleasant in the shade of the big mango tree. People from the villages came along that road carrying on their heads large baskets laden with vegetables, fruit, and other things for the town. They were mostly women, walking with barefooted ease, chatting and laughing, their dark faces bare to the sun. They would put their burdens down along the edge of the road and rest in the cool shade of the mango tree, sitting on the ground and not talking so much. The baskets were rather heavy, and presently each woman would help another to place her basket on her head, the last one somehow managing by almost kneeling on the ground. Then they would be off, with steady pace and an extraordinary grace of movement that had come with years of toil. It wasn't a thing that had been learnt through choice; it had come about through sheer necessity. There was a little girl among them, not more than ten or so, and she too had a basket on her head, though much smaller than the others. She was full of smiles and play, and wouldn't look straight ahead, as the older women did, but would turn round to see if I were following, and we would smile at each other. She too was barefooted, and she too was on the long journey of life.

It was a lovely country, rich and enchanting. There were mango groves and rolling hills, and the water that was still running in the narrow, sandy beds made a pleasant noise as it wandered through the land. The palm trees seemed to tower over the mangoes, which were in bloom and haunted by the murmuring of wild bees. Old banyan trees also grew on either side of the road, which was now busy with the movement of lazy bullock-carts, and with chattering people who were walking from one village to another on some trifling business. They were not in a hurry, and would gather to talk of their doings wherever there was deep shade. Few had anything on their thin, worn feet, and fewer still had bicycles. Now and then they would eat a few nuts, or some fried grain. They had an air of gentle kindliness about them, and they had obviously not caught the contagion of the town. On that road there was peace, though an occasional lorry would pass, carrying, perhaps, sacks of charcoal so badly loaded that some seemed ready to fall off at any moment; but they never did. A bus full of people would come along, making threatening noises with its horn. But it too would soon pass by, leaving the road to the villagers—and to the brown monkeys, of which there were dozens, old and young. When a lorry or a bus came rattling along, the babies would cling to their mothers; they would hold on until everything was quiet again, and then scatter on the road, but never going very far away from their mothers. With their large heads, and their eyes bright with curiosity, they would sit scratching themselves and watching the others. The half-grown monkeys would be all over the place, chasing each other across the road and up the trees, always avoiding the older ones, but not wandering too far away from them either. There was a very large male, old but active, who would sit quietly by the road, keeping watch on things. The others kept their distance, but when he moved away, they all would leisurely follow, running and scattering, but always moving in the same general direction. It was a road of a thousand happenings.

He was a young man, and had come accompanied by two others of about the same age. Rather nervous, with a large forehead and long, restless hands, he explained that he was only a clerk, with little pay and very little future. Even though he had passed his college examinations fairly well, he had found this job only with great difficulty, and was glad to have it. He wasn't yet married, and didn't know if he would ever be, for life was difficult, and you needed money to educate children. However, he was content with the little he earned, for he and his mother could live on it and buy the necessary things of life. In any case, he hadn't come about that, he added, but for an entirely different reason. Both of his companions, one of whom was married, had a problem similar to his, and he had persuaded them to come along with him. They too had been to college, and like him, had minor office jobs. They were all clean, serious and somewhat cheerful, with bright eyes and expressive smiles.

"We have come to ask you a very simple question, hoping for a simple answer. Although we are college-educated, we are not yet very well prepared for deep reasoning and extensive analysis; but we shall listen to what you tell us. You see, sir, we don't know what life is all about. We have messed around here and there, belonging to political parties, joining the social 'do-gooders', attending labour meetings, and all the rest of it; and as it happens, we are all passionately fond of music. We have been to temples, and have dipped into the sacred books, but not too deeply. I am venturing to tell you all this simply to give you some information about ourselves. We three get together practically every evening to talk things over, and the question we would like to ask you is this: what is the purpose of life, and how can we find it?"

Why are you asking this question? And if someone were to tell you what the purpose of life is, would you accept it and guide your lives by it?

"We are asking this question," explained the married one, "because we are confused; we don't know what all this mess and misery is about. We would like to talk it over with someone who is not as confused as we are, and who is not arrogant and authoritarian; someone who will talk to us normally, and not condescendingly, as though they knew everything and we were ignorant school boys who knew nothing. We have heard that you aren't like that, and so we have come to ask you what life is all about."

"It's not only that, sir," added the first one. "We also want to lead a fruitful life, a life with some meaning to it; but at the same time, we don't want to become 'ists', or belong to any particular 'ism'. Some of our friends belong to various groups of religious and political double-talkers, but we have no desire to join them. The political ones are generally pursuing power for themselves in the name of the State; and as for the religious ones, they are for the most part gullible and superstitious. So here we are, and I don't know if you can help us."

Again, if anyone were foolish enough to tell you what is the purpose of life, would you accept it—provided, of course, it were reasonable, comforting and more or less satisfactory?

"I suppose we would," said the first one.

"But he would want to make quite sure that it was true, and not just some clever invention," put in one of his companions.

"I doubt that we are capable of such discernment," added the other.

That's the whole point, isn't it? You have all admitted that you are rather confused. Now, do you think a confused mind can find out what the purpose of life is?

"Why not, sir?" asked the first one. "We are confused, there's no denying that; but if through our confusion we cannot perceive the purpose of life, then there's no hope."

However much it may grope and search, a confused mind can only find that which is further confusing; isn't that so?

"I don't see what you are getting at," said the married one.

We are not trying to get at anything. We are proceeding step by step; and the first thing to find out, surely, is whether or not the mind can ever think clearly as long as it is confused.

"Obviously it cannot," replied the first one quickly. "If I am confused, as in fact I am, I cannot think clearly. Clear thinking implies the absence of confusion. As I am confused, my thinking is not clear. Then what?"

The fact is that whatever a confused mind seeks and finds must also be confused; its leaders, its *gurus*, its ends, will reflect its own confusion. Isn't that so?

"That's hard to realize," said the married one.

It's hard to realize because of our conceit. We think we are so clever, so capable of solving human problems. Most of us are afraid to acknowledge to ourselves the fact that we are confused, for then we would have to admit our own utter insolvency, our defeat—which would mean either despair, or humility. Despair leads to bitterness, to cynicism, and to grotesque philosophies; but when there is true humility, then we can really begin to seek and to understand.

"I quite see the truth of what you are saying," replied the married one.

Isn't it also a fact that choice indicates confusion?

"I don't understand how that can be," said the second one. "We must choose; without choice, there is no freedom."

When do you choose? Only out of confusion, when you are not quite 'certain'. When there's clarity, there's no choice.

"Quite right, sir," put in the married one. "When you love and want to marry a person, there's no choice involved. It is only when there's no love that you shop around. In a way, love is clarity, isn't it?"

That depends on what we mean by love. If 'love' is hedged about by fear, jealousy, attachment, then it is not love, and there is no clarity. But for the present we are not talking about love. When the mind is in a state of confusion, its search for the purpose of life, and its choice of purposes, has no significance, has it?

"What do you mean by 'choice of purposes'?"

When you all came here, asking what is the purpose of life, you were shopping for a purpose, a goal, were you not? Obviously you had asked others the same question, but their replies must have been unsatisfactory, and so you came here. You were choosing; and as we said, choice is born of confusion. Being confused, you wanted to be certain; and a mind that seeks to be certain when it's confused only maintains confusion, doesn't it? Certainty added to inward confusion only strengthens the confusion.

"That is clear," replied the first one. "I am beginning to see that a confused mind can only find confused answers to confused problems. Then what?"

Let's go into it slowly. Our minds are confused, and that is a fact. Then our minds are also shallow, petty, limited; that's another fact, isn't it?

"But we are not entirely petty, there is a part of us which is not," asserted the married one. "If we can find a way to go beyond this shallowness, we can break it up."

That is a comforting hope, but is it actually so? You have the traditional notion that there is an entity—the *Atman,* the soul, the spiritual essence—beyond all this pettiness, an entity that can and does pierce through it. But when a petty mind thinks there is a part of itself which is not petty, it is only sustaining its pettiness. In asserting that there's the *Atman,* the higher self, and so on, a confused, ignorant mind is still held in the bonds of its own confused thought, which is based mostly on tradition, on what it has been taught by others.

"Then what are we to do?"

Isn't this question rather premature? There may be no need to take any particular action. In the very process of understanding the whole issue, there may be a different kind of action altogether.

"You mean that the action to be taken will reveal itself as we go along in our understanding of life," explained the married one. "Now, what do you mean by life?"

Life is beauty, sorrow, joy and confusion; it is the tree, the bird, and the light of the moon on the water; it is work, pain and hope; it is death, the search for immortality, the belief in and the denial of the Supreme; it is goodness, hate and envy; it is greed and ambition; it is love and the lack of it; it is inventiveness, and the power to exploit the machine; it is unfathomable ecstasy; it is the mind, the meditator, and the meditation. It is all things. But how do our petty, confused minds approach life? *That* is important, not the description of what life is. On our approach to life all questions and answers depend.

"I see that this mess which I call life is the outcome of my own mind," said the first one. "I am of it, and it is of me. Can I separate myself from life, and ask myself how I approach it?"

You actually *have* separated yourself from life, have you not? You do not say, "I am the whole of life", and remain still; you want to change this and improve that, you want to reject and to hold. You, the watcher, continue as an immovable, permanent centre in this vast movement, and so you are caught in conflict, in sorrow. Now, you who are separate, how do you approach the whole? How do you come to this vastness, to the beauty of the earth and the heavens?

"I come to it as I am," replied the married man, "with my pettiness, asking for futile answers."

What we ask for, we receive. Our lives are petty, mean, quite shallow and bound to routine; and the gods of the trivial mind are as silly and stupid as their maker. Whether we live in a palace or a village, whether we are clerks in an office or sit in the seats of the mighty, the fact is that our minds are petty, narrow, ambitious, envious; and it is with such minds that we want to find out if there is God, what truth is, what the perfect government is, and seek answers to the innumerable other questions that pop up.

"Yes, sir, that is our life," acknowledged the first one sadly. "What can we do?"

Die to the whole of our existence, not little by little, but totally! It's the petty mind that tries, that struggles, that has ideals and systems, that's everlastingly improving itself by cultivating virtues. Virtue ceases to be virtuous when it's cultivated.

"I can see that we should die to the past," said the first one, "but if I die to the past, what is there then?"

You are saying—aren't you?—that you will die to the past only when you are guaranteed a satisfactory substitute for what you have renounced. That's not renunciation, that's only another gain. A petty mind wanting to know what there is after dying will find its own petty answer. You must die to all of the known for the unknown to be.

"I put that question out of thoughtlessness. I do understand, sir, what you have been saying, and this is not just a polite or merely verbal statement. I think each one of us has felt deeply the truth of it all, and this feeling is the important thing. From this feeling, action can and will take place. May we come again?"

WITHOUT GOODNESS AND LOVE, ONE IS NOT EDUCATED

SEATED ON A raised platform, he was playing a seven-stringed instrument to a small audience of people who were familiar with this type of classical music. They were sitting on the floor in front of him; while from a position behind him another instrument, with only four strings, was being played. He was a young man, but completely the master of the seven strings and of the complex music. He would improvise before each song; then would come the song, in which there would be more improvisation. You would never hear any song played twice in the same way. The words were retained, but within a certain frame there was great latitude, and the musician could improvise to his heart's content; and the more the variations and combinations, the greater the musician. On the strings, words were not possible; but all who sat there knew the words, and they went into ecstasies over them. With nodding heads and gracefully gesturing hands, they kept perfect time, and there would be a gentle slap on the thigh at the end of the rhythm. The musician had closed his eyes and was completely absorbed in his creative freedom, and in the beauty of the sound; his mind and his fingers were in perfect co-ordination. And what fingers! Delicate and rapid, they seemed to have a life of their own. They would be still only at the end of the song in that particular frame, and then they would be quiet and reposed; but with incredible rapidity they would begin another song within a different frame. They almost mesmerized you with their grace and swiftness of movement. And those strings, what melodious sounds they gave! They were pressed by the fingers of the left hand to the proper tension, while the fingers of the right hand plucked them with masterly ease and control.

The moon was bright outside, and the dark shadows were motionless; through the window, the river was just visible, a flow of silver against the dark, silent trees on the other bank. A strange thing was going on in the space which is the mind. It had been watching the graceful movements of the fingers, listening to the sweet sounds, observing the nodding heads and the rhythmical hands of the silent people. Suddenly the watcher, the listener, disappeared; he had not been lulled into abeyance by the melodious strings, but was totally absent. There was only the vast space which is the mind. All the things of the earth and of man were in it, but they were at the extreme outer edges, dim and far off. Within the space where nothing was, there was a movement, and the movement was stillness. It was a deep, vast movement, without direction, without motive, which began from the outer edges, and with incredible strength was coming towards the centre—a centre that is everywhere within the stillness, within the motion which is space. This centre is total aloneness, uncontaminated, unknowable, a solitude which is not isolation, which has no end and no beginning. It is complete in itself, and not made; the outer edges are in it but not of it. It is there, but not within the scope of man's mind. It is the whole, the totality, but not approachable.

There were four of them, all boys of about the same age, sixteen to eighteen. Rather shy, they needed coaxing, but once started, they could hardly stop, and their eager questions came tumbling out. You could see that they had talked it all over among themselves beforehand, and had prepared written questions; but after the first one or two, they forgot what they had written, and their words flowed freely from their own spontaneous thoughts. Though not of well-to-do parents, they were clean and neat in their dress.

"Sir, when you talked to us students two or three days ago," began the nearest one, "you said something about how necessary right education is if we are to be able to face life. I wish you would again explain to us what you mean by right education. We have talked it over amongst ourselves, but we don't quite understand it."

What kind of education do you all have now?

"Oh, we are in college, and we are being taught the usual things which are necessary for a given profession," he replied. "I am going to be an engineer; my friends here are variously studying physics, literature and economics. We are taking the prescribed courses and reading the prescribed books, and when we have time we read a novel or two; but except for games, we are at our studies most of the time."

Do you think this is enough to be rightly educated for life?

"From what you have said, sir, it is not enough," replied the second one. "But that's all we get, and ordinarily we think we are being educated."

Just to learn to read and to write, to cultivate memory and pass some examinations, to acquire certain capacities or skills in order to get a job—is that education?

"Is not all this necessary?"

Yes, to prepare for a right means of livelihood is essential; but that's not all of life. There is also sex, ambition, envy, patriotism, violence, war, love, death, God, man's relationship to man, which is society—and so many other things. Are you being educated to meet this vast affair called life?

"Who is to so educate us?" asked the third one. "Our teachers and professors seem so indifferent. Some of them are clever and well-read, but none of them give any thought to this kind of thing. We are pushed through, and we shall consider ourselves lucky if we take our degrees; everything is getting to be so difficult."

"Except for our sexual passions, which are fairly definite," said the first one, "we know nothing about life; all the rest seems so vague and far off. We hear our parents grumbling about not having enough money, and we realize they are stuck in certain grooves for the rest of their days. So who can teach us about life?"

No one can teach you, but you can learn. There's a vast difference between learning and being taught. Learning goes on throughout life, whereas being taught is over in a few hours or years—and then, for the rest of your life, you repeat what you have been taught. What you have been taught soon turns to dead ashes; and then life, which is a living thing, becomes a battleground of vain efforts. You are thrown into life without the ease or the leisure to understand it; before you know anything about life, you are already right in the middle of it, married, tied to a job, with society pitilessly clamouring around you.

One has to learn about life from early childhood on, not at the last moment; when one is all but grown up, it is almost too late.

Do you know what life is? It extends from the moment you are born to the moment you die, and perhaps beyond. Life is a vast, complex whole; it's like a house in which everything is happening at once. You love and you hate; you are greedy, envious, and at the same time you feel you shouldn't be. You are ambitious, and there is either frustration or success, following in the wake of anxiety, fear and ruthlessness; and sooner or later there comes a feeling of the futility of it all. Then there are the horrors and brutality of war, and peace through terror; there is nationalism, sovereignty, which supports war; there is death at the end of life's road, or anywhere along it. There is the search for God, with its conflicting beliefs and the quarrels between organized religions. There is the struggle to get and keep a job; there are marriage, children, illness, and the dominance of society and the State. Life is all this, and much more; and you are thrown into this mess. Generally you sink into it, miserable and lost; and if you survive by climbing to the top of the heap, you are still part of the mess. This is what we call life: everlasting struggle and sorrow, with a little joy occasionally thrown in. Who is going to teach you about all this? Or rather, how are you going to learn about it? Even if you have capacity and talent, you are hounded by ambition, by the desire for fame, with its frustrations and sorrows. All this is life, isn't it? And to go beyond all this is also life.

"Fortunately, we still know only very little of that whole struggle," went on the first one, "but what you tell us of it is already in us potentially. I want to be a famous engineer, I want to beat them all; so I must work hard and get to know the right people; I must plan, calculate for the future. I must make my way through life."

That is just it. Everyone says that he must make his way through life; each one is out for himself, whether in the name of business, religion or the country. You want to become famous, and so does your neighbour, and so does *his* neighbour; and so it is with everyone, from the highest to the lowest in the land. Thus we build a society based on ambition, envy and acquisitiveness, in which each man is the enemy of another; and you are 'educated' to conform to this disintegrating society, to fit into its vicious frame.

"But what are we to do?" asked the second one. "It seems to me that we must conform to society, or be destroyed. Is there any way out of it, sir?"

At present you are so-called educated to fit into this society; your capacities are developed to enable you to make a living within the pattern. 'Your parents, your educators, your government, are all concerned with your efficiency and financial security, are they not?

"I don't know about the government, sir," put in the fourth one, "but our parents spend their hard-earned money to enable us to have a college degree, so that we can earn a livelihood. They love us."

Do they? Let's see. The government wants you to be efficient bureaucrats to run the State, good industrial workers to maintain the economy, and capable soldiers to kill 'the enemy'; isn't that so?

"I suppose the government does. But our parents are more kind; they think of our welfare and want us to be good citizens."

Yes, they want you to be 'good citizens', which means being respectably ambitious, everlastingly acquisitive, and indulging in that socially accepted ruthlessness which is called competition, so that you and they may be secure. This is what constitutes being a so-called good citizen; but is it good, or something very evil? You say that your parents love you; but is it so? I am not being cynical. Love is an extraordinary thing; without it, life is barren. You may have many possessions and sit in the seat of power, but without the beauty and greatness of love, life soon becomes misery and confusion. Love implies —doesn't it?—that those who are loved be left wholly free to grow in their fullness, to be something greater than mere social machines. Love does not compel, either openly or through the subtle threat of duties and responsibilities. Where there's any form of compulsion or exertion of authority, there's no love.

"I don't think this is quite the kind of love my friend was talking about," said the third one. "Our parents love us, but not in that way. I know a boy who wants to be an artist, but his father wants him to be a business man, and he threatens to cut him off if he doesn't do his duty."

What parents call duty is not love, it's a form of compulsion; and society will support the parents, for what they are doing is very respectable. The parents are anxious for the boy to find a secure job and earn some money; but with such an enormous population, there are a thousand candidates for every job, and the parents think the boy can never earn a livelihood through painting; so they try to force him to get over what they regard as his foolish whim. They consider it a necessity for him to conform to society, to be respectable and secure. This is called love. But is it love? Or is it fear, covered over by the word 'love'?

"When you put it that way, I don't know what to say," replied the third one.

Is there any other way of putting it? What has just been said may be unpleasant, but it is a fact. The so-called education that you have now obviously does not help you to meet this vast complex of life; you come to it unprepared, and are swallowed up in it.

"But who is there to educate us to understand life? We have no such teachers, sir."

The educator has to be educated also. The older people say that you, the coming generation, must create a different world, but they don't mean it at all. On the contrary, with great thought and care they set about 'educating' you to conform to the old pattern, with some modification. Though they may talk very differently, teachers and parents, supported by the government and society in general, see to it that you are trained to conform to tradition, to accept ambition and envy as the natural way of life. They are not at all concerned with a new way of life, and that is why the educator himself is not being rightly educated. The older generation has brought about this world of war, this world of antagonism and division between man and man; and the newer generation is following sedulously in its footsteps.

"But we want to be rightly educated, sir. What shall we do?"

First of all, see very clearly one simple fact: that neither the government, nor your present teachers, nor your parents, care to educate you rightly; if they did, the world would be entirely different, and there would be no wars. So if you want to be rightly educated, you have to set about it yourself; and when you are grown up, you will then see to it that your own children are rightly educated.

"But how can we rightly educate ourselves? We need someone to teach us."

You have teachers to instruct you in mathematics, in literature, and so on; but education is something deeper and wider than the mere gathering of information. Education is the cultivation of the mind so that action is not self-centred; it is learning throughout life to break down the walls which the mind builds in order to be secure, and from which arises fear with all its complexities. To be rightly educated, you have to study hard and not be lazy. Be good at games, not to beat another, but to amuse yourself. Eat the right food, and keep physically fit. Let the mind be alert and capable of dealing with the problems of life, not as a Hindu, a Communist, or a Christian, but as a human being. To be rightly educated, you have to understand yourself; you have to keep on learning about yourself. When you stop learning, life becomes ugly and sorrowful. Without goodness and love, you are not rightly educated.

Hate and Violence

It was quite early; the sun wouldn't be up for an hour or so. The Southern Cross was very clear and strangely beautiful over the palm trees. Everything was very still; the trees were motionless and dark, and even the little creatures of the earth were silent. There was a purity and a blessing over the sleeping world.

The road led through a cluster of palms, past a large pond, and beyond, to where the houses began. Each house had a garden, some well-kept, and others neglected. There was a scent of jasmin in the air, and the dew made the perfume richer. There weren't any lights in the houses yet, and the stars were still clear, but there was an awakening in the eastern sky. A cyclist came along yawning, and went by without turning his head. Someone had started a car and was gently warming it up, and there was an impatient honk. Beyond these houses, the road went past a rice-field and turned left, towards the sprawling town.

A path branched off the road and followed a water-way. The palm trees along its banks were reflected on the still, clear water, and a large white bird was already at work, trying to catch fish. There was still no one else on that path, but soon there would be many, for it was used by the local people as a short cut to the main road. Beyond the water-way there was a secluded house, with a large tree in a rather nice garden. The dawn had now fully come, and the morning star was barely visible over the tree; but the night still held back the day. A woman was sitting on a mat under the tree, tuning a stringed instrument which rested on her lap. Presently she sang something in Sanskrit; it was deeply religious, and as the words filled the morning air, the whole atmosphere of the place seemed to change, becoming charged with a strange fullness and meaning. Then she began to sing a song that is sung only at that hour of the morning. It was enchanting. She was utterly unaware that anyone was listening to her, nor did she care if anyone did, for she was wholly absorbed in that song. She had a good, clear voice, and was thoroughly enjoying herself in a grave and serious manner. One could hardly hear the stringed instrument, but her voice came across the water clear and strong. The words and the sound filled one's whole being, and there was the joy of great purity.

He had come with several of his friends, but some were evidently his followers. A large man, very dark and powerfully built, he seemed vigorous, and he must have been physically very active. He was freshly bathed, and his clothes were spotlessly clean. When he talked, his lips seemed to cover his whole face; some inward fury appeared to be eating him up, and his large head, with heavy hair, was held high with disdain and authority. His smile was forced, and you could see that he laughed with very few. His eyes, direct and without reserve, indicated a complete belief in all that he said. There was something strangely potent about him.

"I hope you will excuse me if I plunge into the subject at once; I do not like to beat about the bush, but prefer to come straight to the point. I am with a large group of people who want to destroy the brahminical tradition and put the Brahmin in his place. He has exploited us ruthlessly, and now it's our turn. He has ruled us, made us feel stupidly inferior and subservient to his gods. We are going to burn his gods. We don't want his words to corrupt our language, which is much older than his. We are planning to drive him out of every prominent position, and we shall make ourselves more clever and cunning than he is. He has deprived us of education, but we shall get even."

Sir, why this hate for other human beings? Do you not exploit? Do you not keep other people down? Do you not prevent others from being rightly educated? Are you not scheming to make others accept your gods and your values? Hate is the same, whether it is in you or in the so-called Brahmin.

"I don't think you understand. People can be kept under only for a certain length of time. This is the day of the down-trodden. We are going to rise up and overthrow the Brahmin rule; we are organized, and we shall work hard to bring this about. We want neither their gods nor their priests; we want to be their equals, or go beyond them."

Wouldn't it be better to talk over more thoughtfully the problem of human relationship? It's so easy to orate about nothing, to fall into slogans, to mesmerize oneself and others with double-talk. We are human beings, sir, though we may call ourselves by different names. This earth is ours, it is not the earth of the Brahmin, the Russian or the American. We torture ourselves with these inane divisions. The Brahmin is no more corrupt than any other man who is seeking power and position; his gods are no more false than the ones you and others have. To throw out one image and put another in its place seems so utterly pointless, whether the image be made by the hand or by the mind.

"All this may be so in theory, but in everyday living we have got to face facts. The Brahmins have exploited other people for centuries; they have grown clever and cunning, and now hold all the choice positions. We are out to take their positions away from them, and we are doing it quite successfully."

You can't take away their acumen, and they will continue to use it for their own purposes.

"But we shall educate ourselves, make ourselves cleverer than they are; we shall beat them at their own game, and then we shall create a better world."

The world isn't made better through hate and envy. Aren't you seeking power and position, rather than to bring about a world in which all hate, greed and violence have come to an end? It is this desire for power and position that corrupts man, whether he be a Brahmin, a non-Brahmin or an ardent reformer. If one group which is ambitious, envious, cunningly brutal, is replaced by another with the same trend of thought—surely this leads nowhere.

"You are dealing in ideologies, and we in facts."

Is that so, sir? What do you mean by a fact?

"In everyday living, our conflicts and our hungers are a fact. To us, what is important is to get our rights, to safeguard our interests, and to see that the future is made safe for our children. To this end, we want to get power into our own hands. These are facts."

Do you mean to say that hate and envy are *not* facts?

"They may be, but we are not concerned with that." He looked around to see what the others were thinking, but they were all respectfully silent. They also were safeguarding their interests.

Does not hate direct the course of outward action? Hate can only breed further hate; and a society based on hate, on envy, a society in which there are competing groups, each safeguarding its own interests —such a society will always be at war within itself, and so with other societies. From what you say, all that you have gained is the prospect that your group may come out on top, thereby being in a position to exploit, to oppress, to cause mischief, as the other group has done in the past. This seems so silly, doesn't it?

"I admit it does; but we have got to take things as they are."

In a way, yes; but we need not continue with them as they are. There must obviously be a change, but not within the same pattern of hate and violence. Don't you feel that this is true?

"Is it possible to bring about a change without hate and violence?"

Again, is there a change at all if the means employed is similar to that used in building up the present society?

"In other words, you are saying that violence can only create an essentially violent society, however new we may think it is. Yes, I can see that." Again he looked around at his friends.

Wouldn't you say that, to build a good social order, the right means is essential? And is the means different from the end? Is not the end contained in the means?

"This is getting a little complicated. I see that hate and violence can only produce a society that is fundamentally violent and oppressive. That much is clear. Now, you say that the right means must be employed to bring about a right society. What is the right means?"

The right means is action which is not the outcome of hate, envy, authority, ambition, fear. The end is not distant from the means. The end *is* the means.

"But how are we to overcome hate and envy? These feelings unite us against a common enemy. There is a certain pleasure in violence, it brings results, and it can't be got rid of so easily."

Why not? When you perceive for yourself that violence only leads to greater harm, is it difficult to drop violence? When, however superficially pleasurable, something gives you deep pain, don't you put it aside?

"On the physical level that is comparatively easy, but it's more difficult with things that are inward."

It is difficult only when the pleasure outweighs the pain. If hate and violence are pleasurable to you, even though they breed untold harm and misery, you will keep on with them; but be clear about it, and don't say that you are creating a new social order, a better way of life, for that is all nonsense.

He who hates, who is acquisitive, who is seeking power or a position of authority, is not a Brahmin, for a true Brahmin is outside the social order that is based upon these things; and if you, on your part, are not free from envy, from antagonism, and from the desire for power, you are no different from the present Brahmin, though you may call yourself by a different name.

"Sir, I am astonished at myself that I am even listening to you. An hour ago, I would have been horrified to think that I might listen to such talk; but I have been listening, and I am not ashamed of it. I see now how easily we are carried away by our own words, and by our more sordid urges. Let's hope things will be different."

The Cultivation of Sensitivity

It was very early in the morning when the plane took off. The passengers were all heavily cloaked, for it was quite cold, and it would be colder still as we gained altitude. The man in the next seat was saying, through the roar of the engines, that these easterners were brilliant, logical, and had behind them the culture of many centuries; but what was their future? On the other hand, the western peoples, while not at all brilliant, except for the few, were very active and produced so much; they were as industrious as ants. Why were they all making so much fuss and killing each other over religious and political differences, and the division of the land? What fools they were! They hadn't learned anything from history. He thanked God that he was a scholar, and not caught up in it all. The man who was now in power had turned out to be a mere politician, not the great statesman one had hoped he would be; but such was the way of the world. It was strange how, centuries ago, one small group had civilized the West, and another had exploded creatively all over the Orient, giving new and deeper significance to life. But where was it all now? Man had become small-minded, miserable, lost.

"After all, when the mind is bound by authority, it shrinks—which is what has happened to the minds of the scholars," he added with a smile. "When bound by tradition, philosophy ceases to be creative, meaningful. Most scholars live in a world of their own, a world into which they escape, and their minds are as shrivelled as last year's fruit dried in the summer sun. But life is like that, isn't it?—full of infinite promise, and ending in misery, frustration. All the same, the life of the mind has its own rewards."

The sky had been a clear, soft blue, but now clouds were piling up, dark and heavy with rain. We were flying between an upper and a lower layer of clouds; it was clear where we were, but there was no sun, only space in which there were no clouds. Heavy drops of rain were falling on the silver wings from the upper layer; it was cold and bumpy, but we would be landing soon. The man in the next seat had fallen asleep; his mouth was twitching, and his hands jerked nervously. In a few minutes there would be the long drive from the airport, through woods and green fields.

Like the two who had come with her, she was a teacher, quite young and enthusiastic.

"We have all taken college degrees," she began, "and have been trained as teachers—which may be partly what's wrong with us," she added with a smile. "We teach in a school for young children, up to the age of adolescence, and we would like to talk over with you some of the problems of the adolescent period, when the sexual urges begin. Of course, we have read about it all, but reading is not quite the same as talking things over. We are all married, and looking back, we realize how much better it would have been if someone had talked to us about sexual matters and helped us to understand that difficult adolescent period. But we haven't come to talk about ourselves, though we too have our problems; and who hasn't?"

"For the most part," added the second one, "children come to that difficult period completely unprepared, with very little help or understanding; though they may know something about it, they are caught up and swept along by the sexual urge. We want to help our students to face it, to understand it, and not become virtual slaves to it; but what with all these cinemas, advertising pictures and sexually provocative magazine covers, it is difficult even for adults to think straightly about it. I am not being respectable or prudish, but the problem is

118

there, and one must be able to understand and deal with it in a practical manner."

"That's it," said the third; "we want to be practical, whatever that may mean, but we still don't know too much about it. Films are now available, telling about sex, and showing from beginning to end how children are born, and all the rest of it; but it's such a colossal subject that one hesitates to tackle it. We want to teach the children what they should know about sex, without arousing any morbid curiosity, and without strengthening their already strong feelings to the point of encouraging them to make experiments. It's a kind of tight rope that one has to walk on; and the parents, with some exceptions, of course, are not much help; they are fearful and anxious to be respectable. So it's not just a problem of adolescence; it includes the parents and the whole social environment, and we can't neglect that aspect of it either. Also, there's the problem of delinquency."

Aren't all these problems interrelated? There's no isolated problem, and no problem can be resolved by itself; isn't that so? Then what's the issue that you want to talk over?

"Our immediate problem is how to help the child to understand this period of adolescence, and yet not do anything that might encourage him to go overboard in his relation with the opposite sex."

How do you now meet the problem?

"We hem and haw, we talk vaguely about controlling one's emotions, disciplining one's desires—and of course there are always the examples, the heroes of virtue," ejaculated the first teacher. "We urge on them the importance of following ideals, leading a clean life of moderation, obeying the social order, and all that kind of thing. On some of the children it has a stabilizing effect, on others no effect at all, and a few are frightened; but I suppose the fear soon wears off."

"We talk about the process of reproduction, pointing it out in nature," added the second one, "but on the whole we are conservative and cautious."

Then what's the problem?

"As my friend said, the problem is how to help the student to cope with the sexual urge when he reaches adolescence, and not be bowled over by it."

Does the sexual urge arise only when the boy or girl reaches adolescence, or does it exist in a simpler, freer way throughout the years which precede adolescence? Must not the child be helped to understand it from the earliest possible age, not just at a certain later period of his development?

"I think you are right," said the third one. "The sexual urge does undoubtedly manifest itself in different ways at a much earlier age, but most of us haven't the time or the interest to consider it much before the child reaches adolescence, when the problem tends to become acute."

If one comes to adolescence without having been rightly educated, then obviously the sexual urge takes on an overwhelming importance, and becomes almost uncontrollable.

"What does it mean to be 'rightly educated'?"

Right education is through the cultivation of sensitivity; and sensitivity must be cultivated, not just at the particular period of growth called adolescence, but throughout one's life; isn't that so?

"Why this emphasis on sensitivity?" asked the first one.

To be sensitive is to feel affection, it is to be aware of beauty, of ugliness; and is not the cultivation of this sensitivity part of the problem you are speaking of?

"I hadn't thought about it before, but now that you point it out, I see they are related."

To be rightly educated is not just to have studied history or physics; it is also to be sensitive to the things of the earth—to the animals, to the trees, to the streams, to the sky, and to other people. But we neglect all that, or we study it as part of a project, something to be learned and stored up for use when occasion demands. Even if one has this sensitivity in childhood, it is generally destroyed by the noise of so-called civilization. The child's environment soon forces him into a mould of the respectable, the conventional. Gentleness, affection, the feeling for beauty, the sensitivity to ugliness—all this is lost; but of course the biological urge is still there.

"That's true," agreed the third one. "We do seem to neglect all that side of life, don't we? And we excuse ourselves by saying we have no time for it, we have the curriculum to think of, and all that!"

Isn't the cultivation of sensitivity at least as important as books and degrees? But we worship success, and we neglect this sensitivity, which destroys the pursuit of success.

"Isn't success necessary in life?"

Insistence upon success breeds insensitivity, it encourages ruthlessness and self-centred activity. How can an ambitious man be sensitive to other people, or to the things of the earth? They are there for his fulfilment, to be used by him in his climb to the top. And this sensitivity is essential, otherwise you have sexual problems.

"How would you cultivate sensitivity in the young?"

'Cultivation' is an unfortunate word, but since we have used it, we will go on with it. Sensitivity is not something to be practised; it is no good merely telling the young to observe nature, or to read the poets, and all the rest of it. But if you yourself are sensitive to the beautiful and to the ugly, if in you there is a sense of gentleness, of love, don't you think you will be able to help your students to have affection, to be considerate, and so on? You see, we stifle or neglect all this, while every form of stimulating diversion is indulged in, so the problem becomes increasingly complex.

"I see what you say to be true, but I don't think you fully appreciate our difficulty. We have classes of thirty or forty boys and girls, and we can't talk to all of them individually, however much we would like to. Moreover, teaching so many at one time is a most exhausting task, and we ourselves get tired out and tend to lose whatever sensitivity we have."

So what are you to do? Care, tenderness, affection—these are essential if the sexual urges are to be understood. Surely, by feeling out the problem, by talking about it, by pointing it out in different ways, sensitivity is gathered by the teacher and its significance communicated to the young child; and when that child becomes adolescent, he will then be able to meet the sexual urges with wider and deeper understanding. But to bring about the right kind of education for the child, you have also to educate the parents, who after all form society.

"The problem is complex and really mountainous, and what can we three do in this mess? What can the individual do?"

It is only as individuals that we can do anything at all. It has always been an individual, here and there, who has really affected society and brought about great changes in thought and action. To be really revolutionary, one must step out of the pattern of society, the pattern of acquisitiveness, envy, and so on. Any reform within the pattern will, in the end, only cause more confusion and misery. Delinquency is but a revolt within the pattern; and the function of the educator, surely, is to help the young to break out of the pattern, which is to be free of acquisitiveness and of the search for power.

"I can see that we shall be of little value unless we also feel these things intensely. And that's one of our major difficulties: we are all so intellectual that our feelings have become paralysed. It is only when we feel strongly that we can really do something."

"Why Have I No Insight?"

IT HAD BEEN raining continuously for a week; the earth was soggy, and there were large puddles all along the path. The water level had risen in the wells, and the frogs were having a splendid time, croaking tirelessly all night long. The swollen river was endangering the bridge; but the rains were welcome, even though great damage was being done. Now, however, it was slowly clearing up; there were patches of blue sky just overhead, and the morning sun was scattering the clouds. It would be months before the leaves of the newly-washed trees would again be covered with fine, red dust. The blue of the sky was so intense that it made you stop and wonder. The air had been purified, and in one short week the earth had suddenly become green. In that morning light, peace lay upon the land.

A single parrot was perched on a dead branch of a nearby tree; it wasn't preening itself, and it sat very still, but its eyes were moving and alert. It was of a delicate green, with a brilliant red beak and a long tail of paler green. You wanted to touch it, to feel the colour of it; but if you moved, it would fly away. Though it was completely still, a frozen green light, you could feel it was intensely alive, and it seemed to give life to the dead branch on which it sat. It was so astonishingly beautiful, it took your breath away; you hardly dared take your eyes off it, lest in a flash it be gone. You had seen parrots by the dozen, moving in their crazy flight, sitting along the wires, or scattered over the red fields of young, green corn. But this single bird seemed to be the focus of all life, of all beauty and perfection. There was nothing but this vivid spot of green on a dark branch against the blue sky. There were no words, no thoughts in your mind; you weren't even conscious that you weren't thinking. The intensity of it brought tears to your eyes and made you blink—and the very blinking might frighten the bird away! But it remained there, unmoving, so sleek, so slender, with every feather in its place. Only a few minutes must have passed, but those few minutes covered the day, the year and all time;

in those few minutes all life was, without an end or a beginning. It is not an experience to be stored up in memory, a dead thing to be kept alive by thought, which is also dying; it is totally alive, and so cannot be found among the dead.

Someone called from the house beyond the garden, and the dead branch was suddenly bare.

There were three of them, a woman and two men, and they were all quite young, probably in their middle thirties. They had come early, freshly bathed and clothed, and were obviously not of those who have money. Their faces shone with thought; their eyes were clear and simple, without that veiled look that comes with much learning. The woman was a sister of the oldest of them, and the other man was her husband. We all sat on a mat with a red border at each end. The traffic made an awful noise, and one window had to be closed, but the other opened upon a secluded garden in which there was a wide-spreading tree. They were a bit shy, but soon would be talking freely.

"Although our families are well-to-do, all three of us have chosen to lead a very simple life, without pretensions," began the brother. "We live near a small village, read a little, and are given to meditation. We have no desire to be rich, and have just enough to get by. I know a certain amount of Sanskrit, but hesitate to quote the Scriptures authoritatively. My brother-in-law is more studious than I, but we are both too young to be learned. By itself, knowledge has very little meaning; it is helpful only in that it can guide us, keep us on the straight road."

I wonder if knowledge is helpful; may it not be a hindrance?

"How can knowledge ever be a hindrance?" he asked rather anxiously. "Surely, knowledge is always helpful."

Helpful in what way?

"Helpful in finding God, in leading a righteous life."

Is it? An engineer must have knowledge to build a bridge, to design machines, and so on. Knowledge is essential to those who are concerned with the order of things. The physicist must have knowledge, it's part of his education, part of his very existence, and without it he cannot go forward. But does knowledge set the mind free to discover? Though knowledge is necessary to put to use what has already been discovered, surely the actual state of discovery is free from knowledge.

"Without knowledge, I might wander off the path that leads to God."

Why shouldn't you wander off the path? Is the path so clearly marked, and the end so definite? And what do you mean by knowledge?

"By knowledge I mean all that one has experienced, read, or been taught of God, and of the things one must do, the virtues one must practise, and so on, in order to find Him. I am not, of course, referring to engineering knowledge."

Is there so much difference between the two? The engineer has been taught how to achieve certain physical results by the application of knowledge which man has gathered through the centuries; whereas, you have been taught how to achieve certain inner results by controlling your thoughts, cultivating virtue, doing good works, and so on, all of which is equally a matter of knowledge gathered through the centuries. The engineer has his books and teachers, as you have yours. Both of you have been taught a technique, and both of you desire to achieve an end, you in your way, and he in his. You are both after results. And is God, or truth, a result? If it is, then it's put together by the mind; and what is put together can be rent asunder. So, is knowledge helpful in discovering reality?

"I'm not at all sure that it's not, sir, in spite of what you say," replied the husband. "Without knowledge, how can the path be trodden?"

If the end is static, if it is a dead thing, without movement, then one or many paths can lead to it; but is reality, God, or whatever name you may give it, a fixed abode with a permanent address?

"Of course not," said the brother eagerly.

Then how can there be a path to it? Surely, truth has no path.

"In that case, what's the function of knowledge?" asked the husband.

You are the result of what you have been taught, and on that conditioning your experiences are based; and your experiences, in turn, strengthen or modify your conditioning. You are like a gramophone, playing different records, perhaps, but still a gramophone; and the records you play are made up of what you have been taught, whether by others or by your own experiences. That is so, isn't it?

"Yes, sir," replied the brother, "but is there not a part of me which has *not* been taught?"

124

Is there? Surely, that which you call the *Atman*, the soul, the higher self, and so on, is still within the realm of what you have read or been taught.

"Your statements are so clear and meaningful, one is convinced in spite of oneself," said the brother.

If you are merely convinced, then you do not see the truth of it. Truth is not a matter of conviction or agreement. You can agree or disagree about opinions or conclusions, but a fact needs no agreement; it's so. If once you see for yourself that what has been said is a fact, then you are not merely convinced: your mind has undergone a fundamental transformation. It no longer looks at the fact through a screen of conviction or belief; it approaches truth, or God, without knowledge, without any record. The record is the 'me', the ego, the conceited one, the one who knows, the one who has been taught, who has practised virtue—and who is in conflict with the fact.

"Then why do we struggle to acquire knowledge?" asked the husband. "Isn't knowledge an essential part of our existence?"

When there's an understanding of the self, then knowledge has its rightful place; but without this understanding, the pursuit of self-knowledge gives a feeling of achievement, of getting somewhere; it is as exciting and pleasurable as success in the world. One may renounce the outward things of existence, but in the struggle to acquire self-knowledge there is the sensation of accomplishment, of the hunter catching the hunted, which is similar to the satisfaction of worldly gain. There is no understanding of the self, of the 'me', the ego, through accumulating knowledge of what *has* been or what *is*. Accumulation distorts perception, and it is not possible to understand the self in its daily activities, its swift and cunning reactions, when the mind is weighed down by knowledge. As long as the mind is burdened with knowledge, and is itself the result of knowledge, it can never be new, uncorrupted.

"May I be permitted to ask a question?" inquired the lady, rather nervously. She had been quietly listening, hesitant to ask questions out of respect for her husband; but now that the other two were reluctantly silent, she spoke up. "I would like to ask, if I may, why it is that one person has insight, total perception, while others see only the various details and are incapable of grasping the whole. Why can't we all have this insight, this capacity to see the whole, which you seem to have? Why is it that one has it, and another has not?"

Do you think it's a gift?

"It would seem so," she replied. "Yet that would mean that divinity is partial, and then there would be very little chance for the rest of us. I hope it's not like that."

Let us inquire into it. Now, why are you asking this question?

"For the simple and obvious reason that I want that deep insight." She had lost her shyness now, and was as eager to talk as the other two.

So your inquiry is motivated by a desire to gain something. Gaining, achieving, or becoming something, implies a process of accumulation, and identification with what has been accumulated. Isn't this true?

"Yes, sir."

Gaining also implies comparison, does it not? You, who have not that insight, are comparing yourself with someone who has.

"That is so."

But all such comparison is obviously the outcome of envy; and is insight to be awakened through envy?

"No, I suppose not."

The world is full of envy, ambition, which can be seen in the everlasting pursuit of success, in the relation of the disciple to the Master, of the Master to the higher Master, and so on endlessly; and it does develop certain capacities. But is total perception, total awareness, such a capacity? Is it based on envy, ambition? Or does it come into being only when all desire to gain has ceased? Do you understand?

"I don't think I do."

The desire to gain is based on conceit, is it not?

She hesitated, and then said slowly, "Now that you point it out, I see that fundamentally it is."

So it is your conceit, in the large as well as in the petty sense, that is making you ask this question.

"I'm afraid that's also true."

In other words, you are asking this question out of the desire to be successful. Now, can this same question—Why is it that I have no deep insight?—be asked without envy, without giving any emphasis to the 'I'?

"I don't know."

Can there be any inquiry at all as long as the mind is tethered to a motive? As long as thought is centred in envy, in conceit, in the

126

desire to be successful, can it wander far and freely? Really to inquire, must not the centre cease?

"Do you mean that envy, or ambition, which is the desire to be or to become something, must wholly disappear, if one is to have deep insight?"

Again, if it may be pointed out, you want to *possess* that capacity, so you will set about disciplining yourself in order to acquire it. You, the would-be possessor, are still important, not the capacity itself. This capacity arises only when the mind has no motive of any kind.

"But you said earlier, sir, that the mind is the result of time, of knowledge, of motive; and how can such a mind be without any motive whatsoever?"

Put that question to yourself, not just verbally, superficially, but as seriously as a hungry man wants food. When you are asking, inquiring, it is important to find out for yourself the cause of your inquiry. You can ask out of envy, or you can ask without any motive. The state of the mind which is really inquiring into the capacity of total perception is one of complete humility, complete stillness; and this very humility, this stillness, is that capacity itself. It is not something to be gained.

REFORM, REVOLUTION AND THE SEARCH FOR GOD

THE RIVER that morning was grey, like molten lead. The sun rose out of the sleeping woods, big, with burning radiance, but the clouds just over the horizon soon hid it; and all day long the sun and the clouds were at war with each other for final victory. Generally there were fishermen on the river, in their gondola-shaped boats; but that morning they were absent, and the river was alone. The bloated carcass of some large animal came floating by, and several vultures were on it, screeching and tearing at the flesh. Others wanted their share, but they were driven off with huge, flapping wings, till those already on the body had had their fill. The crows, furiously cawing, tried to get in between the larger, clumsier birds, but they had no chance. Except for this noise and flutter around the dead body, the wide, curving river was peaceful. The village on the other bank had been awake for an hour or two. The villagers were shouting to each other, and their strong voices came clearly over the water. That shouting had something pleasant about it; it was warm and friendly. A voice would call from across the river, rolling along in the clear air, and another would answer it from somewhere up-stream, or from the opposite bank. None of this seemed to disturb the quietness of the morning, in which there was a sense of great, abiding peace.

The car went along a rough, neglected road, raising a cloud of dust which settled on the trees and on the few villagers who were making their way to and from the filthy, sprawling town. School children also used that road, but they didn't seem to mind the dust; they were too engrossed in their laughter and their play. Entering the main road, the car passed through the town, crossed the railway, and soon was again in the clean, open country. It was beautiful here; there were cows and goats in the green fields and under the huge, old trees, and it was as though you had never seen them before. Passing through the town, with its filth and squalor, seemed to have taken away the beauty of the earth; but now it was given back to you again, and you were surprised to see the goodness of the earth, and of the things of the earth. There were camels, big and well-fed, each carrying a great bundle of jute. They never hurried, but kept a steady gait, with their heads held straight up in the air; and on top of each bundle sat a man, urging the awkward beast forward. With a shock of astonishment you saw on that road two huge, slow-swinging elephants, gayly covered with gold-embroidered red cloth, their tusks decorated with silver bands. They were being taken to some religious affair, and were dressed for the occasion; but they were stopped, and there was a conversation. Their huge bulk towered above you; but they were gentle, all enmity and anger were gone. You stroked their rough skin; the tip of a trunk touched your palm softly, curiously, and moved away. The man shouted to get them going again, and the earth seemed to move with them. A small, two-wheeled carriage came along, drawn by a thin, worn-out horse; it had no top, and was carrying a dead human body, wrapped in white cloth. The body was loosely tied to the floor of the unsprung vehicle, and as the horse trotted along over the uneven road, both driver and corpse were bouncing up and down.

The plane from the north had arrived, and the passengers were alighting to take the half-hour rest before starting again. Three were politicians, and by the look of them, they must have been very important people—cabinet ministers, it was said. They came down the cement walk like a ship passing through a narrow channel, all-powerful and altogether above the common herd. The other passengers kept several paces behind them. Everybody knew who they were; if anybody didn't, he was soon told, and the crowd became silent, watching the big men in their glory. But the earth was still green, a dog was barking, and on the horizon were the snow-covered mountains, an astonishing sight to behold.

A small group had gathered in that large, bare room, but only four of them spoke, and somehow these four seemed to speak for them all. It was not a prearranged thing, but it happened quite naturally, and the others were evidently glad that it was so. One of the four, a large man with an assured air, was given to quick and easy statements. The second was not quite so big physically, but he had sharp eyes and a certain ease of manner. The other two were smaller men; but all of them must have been well-read, and words came easily to them. They appeared to be in their forties, and they had all seen something of life, they said, working at the various things in which they were interested.

"I want to talk about frustration," said the large man. "It's the curse of my generation. We all seem to be frustrated in one way or another, and some of us become bitter and cynical, always criticizing others and eager to tear them down. Thousands have been liquidated in political purges; but we should remember that we can also kill others by word and gesture. Personally, I am not cynical, though I have given a great part of my life to social work and the improvement of society. Like so many other people, I have played with Communism, and have found nothing in it; if anything, it's a retrogressive movement, and is certainly not of the future. I have been in the government, and somehow it hasn't meant much to me. I have read fairly widely, but reading doesn't make one's heart any lighter. Though I am quick at argument, my intellect says one thing, and my heart says another. I have been at war with myself for years, and there seems to be no way out of this inner conflict. I am a mass of contradictions, and inwardly I am slowly dying . . . I didn't mean to talk about all this, but somehow I am talking. Why do we inwardly die and wither away? It's not only happening to me, but also to the great of the land."

What do you mean by dying, withering away?

"One may hold a responsible position, one may work hard and come to the top, but inwardly one is dead. If you told the so-called great among us—those whose names appear every day in the papers over a report of their doings and speeches—that they are essentially dull and stupid, they would be horrified; but like the rest of us, they too are withering away, inwardly deteriorating. Why? We lead moral, respectable lives, yet behind the eyes there's no flame. Some of us are not out for ourselves—at least I don't think so—and yet our inner life is ebbing away; whether we know it or not, and whether we live in ministerial houses or in the bare rooms of devoted workers, spiritually we have one foot in the grave. Why?"

May it not be that we are choked by our conceits, by the pride of success and achievement, by the things that have great value for the mind? When the mind is weighed down by the things it has gathered, the heart withers. Isn't it very strange that everybody wants to climb the ladder of success and recognition?

"We are brought up on it. And I suppose that as long as one is climbing the ladder, or sitting at the top of it, frustration is inevitable. But how is one to get over this sense of frustration?"

Very simply, by not climbing. If you see the ladder and know where it leads, if you understand its deeper implications and do not set foot even on its first rung, you can never be frustrated.

"But I can't just sit still and decay!"

You are decaying now, in the midst of your ceaseless activity; and if, like the self-disciplining hermit, you merely sit still while inwardly burning with desire, with all the fears of ambition and envy, you will continue to wither away. Isn't it true, sir, that decay comes with respectability? This does not mean that one must become disreputable. But you are very virtuous, are you not?

"I try to be."

The virtue of society leads to death. To be conscious of one's virtue is to die respectably. Outwardly and inwardly you are conforming to the rules of social morality, aren't you?

"Unless most of us did, the whole structure of society would crumble. Are you preaching moral anarchy?"

Am I? Social morality is mere respectability. Ambition, greed, the conceit of achievement and its recognition, the brutality of power and position, killing in the name of an ideology or a country—this is the morality of society.

"Nevertheless, our social and religious leaders do preach against at least some of these things."

The fact is one thing, and preaching is another. To kill for an ideology or a country is very respectable, and the killer, the general who organizes mass murder, is highly regarded and decorated. The man of power has the important place in the land. The preacher and the preached-at are in the same boat, are they not?

"All of us are in the same boat," put in the second one, "and we are struggling to do something about it."

If you see that the boat has many holes and is sinking fast, won't you jump out?

"The boat is not as bad as all that. We must patch it up, and everybody should lend a hand. If everybody did, the boat would stay afloat on the river of life."

You are a social worker, are you not?

"Yes, sir, I am, and I have had the privilege of being closely associated with some of our greatest reformers. I believe that reform, not revolution, is the only way out of this chaos. Look what the Russian revolution has come to! No, sir, the really great men have always been reformers."

What do you mean by reform?

"To reform is gradually to improve the social and economic conditions of the people through the various schemes that we have formulated; it is to lessen poverty, to remove superstition, to get rid of class divisions, and so on."

Such reformation is always within the existing social pattern. A different group of people may come out on top, new legislation may be enacted, there may be the nationalization of certain industries, and all the rest of it; but it is always within the present framework of society. That is what's called reform, isn't it?

"If you object to that, then you can only be advocating revolution; and we all know that the great revolution following the first world war has since proved itself to be a retrogressive movement, as my friend pointed out, guilty of every kind of horror and suppression. Industrially the Communists may advance, they may equal or surpass other nations; but man doesn't live by bread alone, and we certainly don't want to follow *that* pattern."

A revolution within the pattern, within the framework of society, is no revolution at all; it may be progressive or retrogressive, but like reform, it is only a modified continuation of what has been. However good and necessary the reform, it can only bring about a superficial change, which will again require further reform. There is no end to this process, because society is ever disintegrating within the pattern of its own existence.

"Do you then maintain, sir, that all reform, however beneficial, is just so much patchwork, and that no amount of reform can bring about a total transformation of society?"

Total transformation can never take place within the pattern of any society, whether that society be tyrannical or so-called democratic.

"Is not a democratic society more significant and worth while than a police or tyrannical State?"

Of course.

"Then what do you mean by the pattern of society?"

The pattern of society is human relationship based on ambition, envy, on the personal or collective desire for power, on the hierarchical attitude, on ideologies, dogmas, beliefs. Such a society may and generally does profess to believe in love, in goodness; but it is always ready to kill, to go to war. Within this pattern, change is no change at all, however revolutionary it may appear. When the patient needs a major operation, it's foolish merely to alleviate the symptoms.

"But who's to be the surgeon?"

You have to operate on yourself, and not rely on another, however good a specialist you may think him to be. You have to step out of the pattern of society, the pattern of greed, of acquisitiveness, of conflict.

"Will my stepping out of the pattern affect society?"

First step out of it, and see what happens. To stay within the pattern and ask what will happen if you step out of it is a form of escape, a perverted and useless inquiry.

"Unlike these two gentlemen," said the third one in a mild and pleasant voice, "I know none of the eminent people; I move in a different circle altogether. I have never thought of becoming famous, but have remained in the background, anonymously doing my part. I gave up my wife, put away the joys of having a home and children, and devoted myself completely to the work of liberating our country. I did all this most earnestly and with great diligence. I sought no power for myself; I only wanted our country to be free, to grow into a holy nation, to have again the glory and the grace that was India. But I have seen all the things that have been going on; I have watched the conceit, the pomp, the corruption, the favouritism, and have heard the double-talk of the various politicians, including the leaders of the party to which I belonged. I didn't sacrifice my life, my pleasures, my wife, my money, in order that corrupt men might rule the land. I eschewed power for the good of the country—only to see these ambitious politicians rise to positions of power. I now realize that I have spent vainly the best years of my life, and I feel like committing suicide."

The others were silent, appalled by what had been said; for they were all politicians, in fact and at heart.

Sir, most people do give a perverted twist to their lives, and perhaps discover it too late, or never at all. If they attain position and power, they do damage in the name of the country; they become mischief-makers in the name of peace, or of God. Conceit and ambition rule the land everywhere, with varying degrees of barbarity and ruthlessness. Political activity is concerned with only a very small part of life; it has its importance, but when it usurps the whole field of existence, as it is doing now, it becomes monstrous, corrupting thought and action. We glorify and respect the man in power, the leader, because in us there is the same craving for power and position, the same desire to control and to dictate. It is every individual who brings into being the leader; it is out of every man's confusion, envy, ambition, that the leader is made, and to follow the leader is to follow one's own demands, urges and frustrations. The leader and the follower are both responsible for the sorrow and the confusion of man.

"I recognize the truth of what you are saying, though it is hard for me to acknowledge it. And now, after all these years, I really do not know what to do. I have wept with the tears of my heart, but what's the good of all that? I cannot undo what is done. I have encouraged thousands, by word and action, to accept and to follow. Many of them are like me, though not in my extreme plight; they have changed their allegiance from one leader to another, from one party to another, from one set of catch-words to another. But I am out of it all, and I don't want to go near any of the leaders again. I have striven in vain all these years; the garden I so carefully cultivated has turned to rubble and stone. My wife is dead, and I have no companion. I see now that I have followed man-made gods: the State, the authority of the

133

leader and the subtle vanities of one's own importance. I have been blind and foolish."

But if you really perceive that all you have worked for is foolish and vain, that it only leads to further misery, then there is already the beginning of clarity. When your intention is to go north, and you discover that you have actually been moving south, that very discovery is a turning to the north. Isn't that so?

"It's not quite as simple as that. I see now that the path I have been following leads only to the misery and destruction of man; but I do not know any other path to take."

There is no path to that which is beyond all the paths that men have made and trodden. To find that pathless reality, you have to see the truth in the false, or the false as the false. If you perceive that the path you have trodden is false—not in comparison with something else, not through the judgment of disappointment, nor through the evaluation of social morality, but false in itself—then that very perception of the false is awareness of the true. You do not have to follow the true: the true sets you free from the false.

"But I still feel impelled to take my own life and end it all."

The desire to end it all is the outcome of bitterness, of deep frustration. If the path you were following, even though utterly false in itself, had led to that which you had thought of as the goal; if, in a word, you had been successful, there would have been no sense of frustration, no bitter disappointment. Until you met with this final frustration, you never questioned what you were doing, you never inquired to find out if it were true or false in itself. If you had, things might have been very different. You were swept along by the current of self-fulfilment; and now it has left you isolated, frustrated, disappointed.

"I think I see what you mean. You are saying that any form of self-fulfilment—in the State, in good works, in some utopian dream—must inevitably lead to frustration, to this barren state of mind. I am now aware of that very clearly."

The rich flowering of goodness in the mind—which is very different from being 'good' in order to achieve an end, or to become something —is in itself right action. Love is its own action, its own eternity.

"Though it is late," said the fourth one, "may I ask a question? Will belief in God help one to find Him?"

To find truth, or God, there must be neither belief nor disbelief. The believer is as the non-believer; neither will find the truth, for their thought is shaped by their education, by their environment, by their culture, and by their own hopes and fears, joys and sorrows. A mind that is not free from all these conditioning influences can never find the truth, do what it will.

"Then to seek God is not important?"

How can a mind that is fearful, envious, acquisitive, discover that which is beyond itself? It will find only its own projections, the images, beliefs and conclusions in which it is caught. To find out what is true, or what is false, the mind must be free. To seek God without understanding oneself has very little meaning. Search with a motive is no search at all.

"Can there ever be search without a motive?"

When there's a motive for search, the end of the search is already known. Being unhappy, you seek happiness; therefore you have ceased to seek, for you think you already know what happiness is.

"Then is search an illusion?"

One among many. When the mind has no motive, when it is free and not urged on by any craving, when it is totally still, then truth *is*. You do not have to seek it; you cannot pursue or invite it. It must come.

THE NOISY CHILD AND THE SILENT MIND

THE CLOUDS had been coming through the wide gap in the mountains all day; piling themselves up against the western hills, they remained dark and threatening over the valley, and it would probably rain towards evening. The red earth was dry, but the trees and the wild bushes were green, for it had rained some weeks before. Many small streams wandered through the valley, but they would never reach the sea, for the people used the water to irrigate their rice-fields. Some of these fields were cultivated and under water, ready to be planted, but most of them were already green with the sprouting rice. That green was incredible; it wasn't the green of well-watered mountain slopes, nor the green of well-kept lawns, nor the green of spring, nor the green of tender shoots among the older leaves of an orange tree. It was an altogether different green; it was the green of the Nile, of the olive, of verdigris, a blending of all these and more. There was in it a touch of the artificial, of the chemical; and in the morning, when the sun was just over the eastern hills, that green had the splendour and richness of the oldest parts of the earth. It was hard to believe that such a green could exist in this valley, known to so few, where only the villagers lived. To them it was a daily sight, a thing they had toiled for, knee-deep in water; and now, after long preparation and care, there were these fields of incredible green. The rain would help, and the dark clouds held a promise.

Everywhere there was the darkness of the coming night, and of the low-hanging clouds; but a single ray of the setting sun touched the smooth side of a great rock on the hills towards the east, and it stood out in the gathering gloom. A group of villagers passed, talking loudly and driving their cattle before them. A goat had wandered off, and a little boy was making noises to call it back; it paid no attention, so he ran after it, angrily throwing stones, till at last it returned to the fold. It was now quite dark, but you could still see the edge of the path, and a white flower on a bush. An owl called from somewhere nearby, and another answered it from across the valley. The deep tone of their call vibrated inside of you, and you stopped to listen. A few drops of rain fell. Presently it began in earnest, and there was the goodly smell of rain on dry earth.

It was a clean, pleasant room, with a red mat on the floor. There were no flowers in the room, but there was no need of them. Outside there was the green earth; in the blue sky a single cloud was wandering by, and a bird was calling.

There were three of them, a woman and two men. One of the men had come from far up in the mountains, where he spent his life in solitude and contemplation. The other two were teachers from a school in one of the nearby towns. They had come by bus, as it was too far to bicycle. The bus was crowded, and the road was bad; but it was worth it, they said, for they had several things to talk over. They were both quite young, and said that they would soon be married. They explained how absurdly little they were paid, and said that it was going to be difficult to make ends meet, as prices were going up; but they seemed pleasant and happy, and enthusiastic about their work. The man from the mountains listened and was silent.

"Among many other problems," began the lady teacher, "is that of noise. There is often so much noise in a school for younger children, that at times it becomes almost unbearable; you can hardly hear yourself speak. Of course, you can punish them, force them to be quiet; but it seems so natural for them to shout and let off steam."

"But you have to forbid noise in certain places, such as the class-room and the dining hall, otherwise life would be impossible," replied the other teacher. "You can't allow shouting and chattering all day long; there must be periods when all noise is stopped. Children have to be taught that there are others in this world besides themselves. Consideration of others is as important as arithmetic. I agree it is no good just forcing them to keep quiet through the threat of punishment; but on the other hand, reasonably talking things over with them doesn't seem to stop their constant yelling."

"Noise-making is part of life at that age," went on his companion, "and it's unnatural for them to be silent in that stupid manner. But to be quiet is also part of existence, and though they don't seem to care for it at all, we have somehow to help them to be quiet when quietness is called for. In silence one hears more and sees more; that's why it's important for them to know silence."

"I agree that they should be silent at certain times," said the other teacher, "but how are we to teach them to be silent? It would be absurd to see rows of children compelled to sit in silence; it would be a most unnatural, inhuman thing."

Perhaps we can approach the problem differently. When are you irritated by a noise? A dog begins barking in the night; it wakes you, and you may or may not be able to do something about it. But it's only when there's a resistance to noise that it becomes a tiresome thing, a pain, an irritant.

"It's more than an irritant when it lasts all day long," remonstrated the male teacher. "It gets on your nerves, until you want to shout too."

If it may be suggested, let us for the present put aside the noise of the children, and consider noise itself and its effect on each one of us. If necessary, we will consider the children and their noise later on.

Now, when are you aware of a noise, in the disturbing sense? Surely, only when you resist it; and you resist it only when it's unpleasant.

"That is so," he admitted. "I welcome the pleasurable sounds of music; but the horrible yelling of the children I resist, and not always very happily."

This resistance to noise increases the disturbance it makes. And that's what we do in our daily life: keeping the beautiful, we reject the ugly; resisting evil, we cultivate the good; eschewing hate, we think of love, and so on. There's always within us this self-contradiction, this conflict of the opposites; and such conflict leads nowhere. Isn't that so?

"Self-contradiction is not a pleasant state," replied the lady teacher. "I know it all too well; and I suppose it's also quite useless."

To be only partly sensitive is to be paralysed. To be open to beauty and resist ugliness is to have no sensitivity; to welcome silence and reject noise is not to be whole. To be sensitive is to be aware of both silence and noise, neither pursuing the one nor resisting the other; it is to be without self-contradiction, to be whole.

"But in what way does this help the children?" asked the male teacher.

When are the children silent?

"When they are interested, absorbed in something. Then there's perfect peace."

"It is not only then that they are silent," added his companion quickly. "When one is really quiet within oneself, the children somehow catch that feeling, and they also become quiet; they look at one rather awed, wondering what has happened. Haven't you noticed it?"

"Of course I have," he replied.

So that may be the answer. But we are so rarely silent; though we may not be talking, the mind goes right on chattering, carrying on a silent conversation, arguing with itself, imagining, recalling the past or speculating about the future. It is restless, noisy, always struggling with something, is it not?

"I had never thought of that," said the male teacher. "In that inward sense, one's mind is of course as noisy as the children themselves."

We are noisy in other ways too, are we not?

"Are we?" asked his companion. "When?"

When we are emotionally stirred up: at a political meeting, at a festive board, when we are angry, when we are thwarted, and so on.

"Yes, yes, that is so," she agreed. "When I am really excited, at games and so on, I do often find myself shouting, inwardly if not outwardly. Good Lord, there isn't much difference between us and the children, is there? And their noise is probably far more innocent than the noise we adults make."

Do we know what silence is?

"I am silent when I am absorbed in my work," the male teacher replied. "I am unaware of everything that's happening about me."

So is the child when he is absorbed in a toy; but is that silence?

"No," put in the solitary man from the hills. "There is silence only when one has complete control of the mind, when thought is dominated and there's no distraction. Noise, which is the chattering of the mind, must be suppressed for the mind to be still and silent."

Is silence the opposite of noise? Suppression of the chattering mind indicates control in the sense of resistance, does it not? And is silence the result of resistance, control? If it is, is it silence?

"I don't quite understand what you mean, sir. How can there be silence unless the mind's chattering is stopped, its wanderings brought under control? The mind is like a wild horse that must be tamed."

As one of these teachers said earlier, it is no good forcing a child to be quiet. If you do, he may be quiet for a few minutes, but he will soon again begin making a noise. And is a child really quiet when you force him to be? Outwardly he may sit still through fear, or through hope of reward, but inwardly he is seething, waiting for a chance to resume his noisy chatter. This is so, isn't it?

"But the mind is different. There is the higher part of the mind which must dominate and guide the lower."

The teacher may also regard himself as a higher entity who must guide or shape the child's mind. The similarity is fairly obvious, isn't it?

"Indeed it is," said the lady teacher. "But we still don't know what to do about the noisy child."

Let's not consider what to do until we have fully understood the problem. This gentleman has said that the mind is different from a child; but if you observe them both, you will see that they are not so very different. There's a great similarity between the child and the mind. Suppression of either only tends to increase the urge to make noise, to chatter; there is an inward building up of tension which must and does find release in various ways. It's like a boiler building up a head of steam; it must have an outlet, or it will burst.

"I don't want to argue," went on the man of the hills, "but how is the mind to stop its noisy chattering if not through control?"

The mind may be stilled, and have transcendental experiences, through years of control, of suppression, of practising a system of yoga; or, by taking a modern drug, the same results may sometimes be achieved overnight. However you may achieve them, the results depend on a method, and a method—perhaps the drug also—is the way of resistance, suppression, is it not? Now, is silence the suppression of noise?

"It is," asserted the solitary man.

Is love, then, the suppression of hate?

"That's what we ordinarily think," put in the lady teacher, "but when one looks at the actual fact, one sees the absurdity of that way of thinking. If silence is merely the suppression of noise, then it's still related to noise, and such 'silence' is noisy, it's not silence at all."

"I don't quite understand this," said the man from the hills. "We all know what noise is, and if we eliminate it, we shall know what silence is."

Sir, instead of talking theoretically, let's make an experiment right now. Let's go slowly and hesitantly, step by step, and see if we can directly experience and understand the actual functioning of the mind.

"That would be greatly beneficial."

If I ask you a simple question, like 'Where do you live?', your reply is immediate, is it not?

"Of course."

Why?

"Because I know the answer, it is quite familiar to me."

So the thinking process takes only a second, it is over in a flash; but a more complex question requires a longer time to answer; there's a certain hesitancy. Is this hesitancy silence?

"I don't know."

A gap of time exists between a complex question and your response to it, because your mind is looking into the records of memory to find an answer. This time-gap is not silence, is it? In this interval there is going on an inquiry, a groping, a seeking out. It's an activity, a movement into the past; but it's not silence.

"I see that. Any movement of the mind, whether into the past or into the future, is obviously not silence."

Now, let's go a little further. To a question whose answer you cannot find in the records of memory, what is your reply?

"I can only say that I don't know."

And what then is the state of your mind?

"It's a state of eager suspense," put in the lady teacher.

In that suspense you are waiting for an answer, aren't you? So there's still a movement, an expectancy in the gap between two chatterings, between the question and the final answer. This expectancy is not silence, is it?

"I am beginning to see what you are getting at," replied the solitary one. "I perceive that neither this waiting for an answer nor the scrutiny of past things is silence. Then what *is* silence?"

If all movement of the mind is noise, then is silence the opposite of that noise? Is love the opposite of hate? Or is silence a state totally unrelated to noise, to chatter, to hate?

"I don't know."

Please consider what you are saying. When you say you don't know, what's the state of your mind?

"I'm afraid I'm again waiting for an answer, expecting you to tell me what silence is."

In other words, you are expecting a verbal description of silence; and any description of silence must be related to noise; so it's part of noise, isn't it?

"I really don't understand this, sir."

A question sets the machine of memory going, which is a thinking process. If the question is very familiar, the machine answers instantaneously. If the question is more complex, the machine takes a longer time to reply; it has to grope among the records of memory to find the answer. And when a question is asked whose answer is not on the record, the machine says, 'I don't know'. Surely, this whole process is the mechanism of noise. However outwardly silent, the mind is in operation all the time, isn't it?

"Yes," he replied eagerly.

Now, is silence merely the stopping of this mechanism? Or is silence totally apart from the mechanism, be it stopped or working?

"Are you saying, sir, that love is wholly apart from hate, whether hate is there or not?" asked the lady teacher.

Isn't it? Into the fabric of hate, love can never be woven. If it is, then it's not love. It may have all the appearance of love, but it's not; it's something entirely different. This is really important to understand.

An ambitious man can never know peace; ambition must cease entirely, and only then will there be peace. When a politician talks of peace, it is merely double-talk, for to be a politician is to be at heart ambitious, violent.

The understanding of what is true and what is false is its own action, and such action will be efficient, effective, 'practical'. But most of us are so caught up in action, in doing or organizing something, or in carrying out some plan, that to be concerned with what is true and what is false seems complex and unnecessary. That is why all our action inevitably leads to mischief and misery.

The mere absence of hate is not love. To tame hate, to force it to be still, is not to love. Silence is not the outcome of noise, it is not a reaction whose cause is noise. The 'silence' that grows from noise has its roots in noise. Silence is a state totally outside the machinery of the mind; the mind cannot conceive of it, and the mind's attempts to reach silence are still part of noise. Silence is in no way related to noise. Noise must totally cease for silence to be.

When there is silence in the teacher, it will help the children to be silent.

Where There Is Attention, Reality *Is*

The clouds were against the hills, hiding them and the mountains beyond. It had been raining all day, a soft drizzle which didn't wash away the earth, and there was in the air the pleasant smell of the jasmine and the rose. The grain was ripening in the fields; among the rocks, where the goats fed, were low bushes, with here and there a gnarled old tree. There was a spring high up on the hillside that was always flowing, summer and winter, and the water made a pleasant sound as it ran down the hill, past a grove of trees, and disappeared among the open fields beyond the village. A small bridge of cut stone was being built over the stream by the villagers, under the supervision of a local engineer. He was a friendly old man, and they worked in a leisurely manner when he was about. But when he was not there, only one or two carried on; the rest of them, putting down their tools and their baskets, sat around and talked.

Along the path by the stream came a villager with a dozen donkeys. They were returning from the nearby town with empty sacks. These donkeys had thin, graceful legs, and they were trotting along quite fast, pausing now and then to nibble the green grass on each side of the path. They were going home, and had not to be driven. All along the path there were little plots of cultivated land, and a gentle breeze was stirring among the young corn. In a small house. a woman with a clear voice was singing; it brought tears to your eyes, not from some nostalgic remembrance, but from the sheer beauty of the sound. You sat under a tree, and the earth and the heavens entered your being. Beyond the song and the red earth was the silence, the total silence in which all life is in movement. There were now fireflies among the trees and bushes, and in the gathering darkness they were bright and clear; the amount of light they gave was surprising. On a dark rock, the soft, flashing light of a single firefly held the light of the world.

He was young and very earnest, with clear, sharp eyes. Although in his thirties, he was not yet married; but sex and marriage were not a serious problem, he added. A well-built man, he had vigour in his gestures and in his walk. He was not given to much reading, but he had read a certain number of serious books, and had thought about things. Employed in some governmental office, he said his pay was good enough. He liked outdoor games, especially tennis, at which he was evidently quite good. He didn't care for cinemas, and had but few friends. It was his practice, he explained, to meditate morning and evening for about an hour; and after hearing the previous evening's talk, he had decided to come along to discuss the meaning and significance of meditation. As a boy, he often used to go with his father into a small room to meditate; he could bring himself to stay there for only ten minutes or so, and his father didn't seem to mind. That room had a single picture on the wall, and no member of the family went into it except for the purpose of meditation. While his father had neither encouraged nor discouraged him in the matter, and had never told him how to meditate, or what it was all about, somehow, ever since he was a boy, he had liked to meditate. While he was in college, it had been difficult for him to keep regular hours; but later, once he got a job, he had meditated for an hour every morning and every evening, and now he wouldn't miss those two hours of meditation for anything in the world.

"I have come, sir, not to argue, or to defend anything, but to learn. Although I have read about the various types of meditation for different temperaments, and have evolved a way of controlling my thoughts, I am not foolish enough to imagine that what I am doing is really meditation. However, if I am not mistaken, most authorities on meditation do advocate control of thought; that seems to be the essence of it. I have also practised a little yoga as a means of quieting the mind: special breathing exercises, repeating certain words and chants, and so on. All this is merely by way of introducing myself, and it may not be important. The point is, I am really interested in practising meditation, it has become vital to me, and I want to know more about it."

Meditation has significance only when there's an understanding of the meditator. In practising what you call meditation, the meditator is apart from the meditation, isn't he? Why is there this difference, this gap between them? Is it inevitable, or must the gap be bridged? Without really understanding the truth or the falseness of this apparent division, the results of so-called meditation are similar to those which can be brought about by any tranquillizer that is taken to quiet the mind. If one's purpose is to bring thought under domination, then any system or drug that produces the desired effect will do.

"But you wipe away at one stroke all the yogic exercises, the traditional systems of meditation that have been practised and advocated through the centuries by the many saints and ascetics. How can they all be wrong?"

Why shouldn't they all be wrong? Why this gullibility? Is not a tempered scepticism helpful in understanding this whole problem of meditation? You accept because you are eager for results, for success; you want to 'arrive'. To understand what meditation is, there must be questioning, inquiry; and mere acceptance destroys inquiry. You have to see for yourself the false as the false, and the truth in the false, and the truth as the truth; for none can instruct you concerning it. Meditation is the way of life, it is part of daily existence, and the fullness and beauty of life can only be understood through meditation. Without understanding the whole complexity of life, and the everyday reactions from moment to moment, meditation becomes a process of self-hypnosis. Meditation of the heart is the understanding of daily problems. You can't go very far if you don't begin very near.

"I can understand that. One cannot climb the mountain without first going through the valley. I have endeavoured in my daily life to remove the obvious barriers, like greed, envy, and so on, and somewhat to my own surprise I have managed to put aside the things of the world. I quite see and appreciate that a right foundation must be laid, otherwise no building can stand. But meditation isn't merely a matter of taming the burning desires and passions. The passions must be subjugated, brought under control; but surely, sir, meditation is something more than this, isn't it? I am not quoting any authority, but I do feel that meditation is something far greater than merely laying the right foundation."

That may be; but at the very beginning is the totality. It is not that one must first lay the right foundation, and then build, or first be free from envy, and then 'arrive'. In the very beginning is the ending. There's no distance to be covered, no climbing, no point of arrival. Meditation itself is timeless, it's not a way of arriving at a timeless state. It is, without a beginning and without an ending. But these are mere words, and they will remain as such as long as you don't inquire into and understand for yourself the truth and the falseness of the meditator.

"Why is that so important?"

The meditator is the censor, the watcher, the maker of 'right' and 'wrong' effort. He's the centre, and from there he weaves the net of thought; but thought itself has made him; thought has brought about this gap between the thinker and the thought. Unless this division ceases, so-called meditation only strengthens the centre, the experiencer who thinks of himself as apart from the experience. The experiencer is always craving more experience; each experience strengthens the accumulation of past experiences, which in turn dictates, shapes the present experience. Thus the mind is ever conditioning itself. So experience and knowledge are not the liberating factors that they are supposed to be.

"I'm afraid I don't understand all this," he said, rather bewildered.

The mind is free only when it is no longer conditioned by its own experiences, by knowledge, by vanity, envy; and meditation is the freeing of the mind from all these things, from all self-centred activities and influences.

"I realize that the mind must be free from all self-centred activities, but I do not quite follow what you mean by influences."

Your mind is the result of influence, isn't it? From childhood your mind is influenced by the food you eat, by the climate you live in, by your parents, by the books you read, by the cultural environment in which you are educated, and so on. You are taught what to believe and what not to believe; your mind is a result of time, which is memory, knowledge. All experiencing is a process of interpreting in terms of the past, of the known, and so there's no freedom from the known; there is only a modified continuity of what has been. The mind is free only when this continuity comes to an end.

"But how does one know that one's mind is free?"

This very desire to be certain, to be secure, is the beginning of bondage. It's only when the mind is not caught in the net of certainty, and is not seeking certainty, that it is in a state of discovery.

"The mind does want to be certain about everything, and I see now how this desire can be a hindrance."

What is important is to die to everything that one has accumulated, for this accumulation is the self, the ego, the 'me'. Without the ending of this accumulation, there is the continuity of the desire to be certain, as there is the continuation of the past.

"Meditation, I am beginning to see, is not simple. Just to control thought is comparatively easy, and to worship an image, or to repeat certain words and chants, is merely to put the mind to sleep; but real meditation seems to be much more complex and arduous than I ever imagined."

It is really not complex, though it may be arduous. You see, we don't start with the actual, with the fact, with what we are thinking, doing, desiring; we start with assumptions, or with ideals, which are not actualities, and so we are led astray. To start with facts, and not with assumptions, we need close attention; and every form of thinking not originating from the actual is a distraction. That's why it is so important to understand what is actually taking place both within and around one.

"Are not visions actualities?"

Are they? Let's find out. If you are a Christian, your visions follow a certain pattern; if you are a Hindu, a Buddhist, or a Moslem, they follow a different pattern. You see Christ or Krishna, according to your conditioning; your education, the culture in which you have been brought up, determines your visions. Which is the actuality: the vision, or the mind which has been shaped in a certain mould? The vision is the projection of the particular tradition which happens to form the background of the mind. This conditioning, not the vision which it projects, is the actuality, the fact. To understand the fact is simple; but it is made difficult by our likes and dislikes, by our condemnation of the fact, by the opinions or judgments we have *about* the fact. To be free of these various forms of evaluation is to understand the actual, the what *is*.

"You are saying that we never look at a fact directly, but always through our prejudices and memories, through our traditions and our experiences based upon those traditions. To use your word, we are never aware of ourselves as we actually are. Again, I see that you are right, sir. The fact is the one thing that matters."

Let us look at the whole problem differently. What is attention? When are you attentive? And do you ever really pay attention to anything?

"I pay attention when I am interested in something."

Is interest attention? When you are interested in something, what's actually happening to the mind? You are evidently interested in watching those cattle go by; what is this interest?

"I am attracted by their movement, their colour, their form, against the green background."

Is there attention in this interest?

"I think there is."

A child is absorbed in a toy. Would you call that attention?

"Isn't it?"

The toy absorbs the interest of the child, it takes over his mind, and he's quiet, no longer restless; but take away the toy, and he again becomes restless, he cries, and so on. Toys become important because they keep him quiet. It is the same with grown-ups. Take away their toys—activity, belief, ambition, the desire for power, the worshipping of gods or of the state, the championing of a cause—and they too become restless, lost, confused; so the toys of the grown-ups also become important. Is there attention when the toy absorbs the mind? The toy is a distraction, is it not? The toy becomes áll-important, and not the mind which is taken over by the toy. To understand what attention is, we must be concerned with the mind, not with the toys of the mind.

"Our toys, as you call them, hold the mind's interest."

The toy which holds the mind's interest may be the Master, a picture, or any other image made by the hand or by the mind; and this holding of the mind's interest by a toy is called concentration. Is such concentration attention? When you are concentrated in this manner and the mind is absorbed in a toy, is there attention? Is not such concentration a narrowing down of the mind? And is this attention?

"As I have practised concentration, it is a struggle to keep the mind fixed upon a particular point to the exclusion of all other thoughts, all distractions."

Is there attention when there is resistance against distractions? Surely, distractions arise only when the mind has lost interest in the toy; and then there's a conflict, isn't there?

"Certainly, there's a conflict to overcome the distractions."

Can you pay attention when there's a conflict going on in the mind?

"I am beginning to see what you are driving at, sir. Please proceed."

When the toy absorbs the mind, there's no attention; neither is there attention when the mind is struggling to concentrate by excluding distractions. As long as there's an object of attention, is there attention?

"Aren't you saying the same thing, only using the word 'object' instead of 'toy'?"

The object, or toy, may be external; but there are also inward toys, are there not?

"Yes, sir, you have enumerated some of them. I am aware of this."

A more complex toy is motive. Is there attention when there's a motive to be attentive?

"What do you mean by a motive?"

A compulsion to action; an urge towards self-improvement, based on fear, greed, ambition; a cause that drives you to seek; suffering that makes you want to escape, and so on. Is there attention when some hidden motive is in operation?

"When I am compelled to be attentive by pain or pleasure, by fear or the hope of reward, then there's no attention. Yes, I see what you mean. This is very clear, sir, and I am following you."

So there's no attention when we approach anything in that manner. And does not the word, the name, interfere with attention? For example, do we ever look at the moon without verbalization, or does the word 'moon' always interfere with our looking? Do we ever listen to anything with attention, or do our thoughts, our interpretations, and so on, interfere with our listening? Do we ever really pay attention to anything? Surely, attention has no motive, no object, no toy, no struggle, no verbalization. This is true attention, is it not? Where there is attention, reality *is*.

"But it's impossible to pay such full attention to anything!" he exclaimed. "If one could, there wouldn't be any problems."

Every other form of 'attention' only increases the problems, doesn't it?

"I see that it does, but what is one to do?"

When you see that any concentration on toys, any action based on motive, whatever it be, only furthers mischief and misery, then in this seeing of the false there's the perception of the true; and truth has its own action. All this is meditation.

"If I may say so, sir, I have rightly listened, and have really understood many of the things you have explained. What is understood will have its own effect, without my interfering with it. I hope I may come again."

SELF-INTEREST DECAYS THE MIND

WINDING FROM one side of the valley to the other, the path crossed over a small bridge where the swiftly-running water was brown from the recent rains. Turning north, it led on over gentle slopes to a secluded village. That village and its people were very poor. The dogs were mangy, and they would bark from a distance, never venturing near, their tails down, their heads held high, ready to run. Many goats were scattered about on the hillside, bleating, and eating the wild bushes. It was beautiful country, green, with blue hills. The bare granite projecting from the tops of the hills had been washed by the rains of countless centuries. These hills were not high, but they were very old, and against the blue sky they had a fantastic beauty, that strange loveliness of measureless time. They were like the temples that man builds to resemble them, in his longing to reach the heavens. But that evening, with the setting sun on them, these hills seemed very close. Far to the south a storm was gathering, and the lightning among the clouds gave a strange feeling to the land. The storm would break during the night; but the hills had stood through the storms of untold ages, and they would always be there, beyond all the toil and sorrow of man.

The villagers were returning to their homes, weary after a day's work in the fields. Soon you would see smoke rising from their huts as they prepared the evening meal. It wouldn't be much; and the children, waiting for their meal, would smile as you went by. They were large-eyed and shy of strangers, but they were friendly. Two little girls held small babies on their hips while their mothers were cooking; the babies would slip down, and get jerked up onto the hips again. Though only ten or twelve years old, these little girls were already used to holding babies; and they both smiled. The evening breeze was among the trees, and the cattle were being brought in for the night.

On that path there was now no other person, not even a lonely villager. The earth seemed suddenly empty, strangely quiet. The new, young moon was just over the dark hills. The breeze had stopped, not a leaf was stirring; everything was still, and the mind was completely alone. It wasn't lonely, isolated, enclosed within its own thought, but alone, untouched, uncontaminated. It wasn't aloof and distant, apart from the things of the earth. It was alone, and yet with everything; because it was alone, everything was of it. That which is separate knows itself as being separated; but this aloneness knew no separation, no division. The trees, the stream, the villager calling in the distance, were all within this aloneness. It was not an identification with man, with the earth, for all identification had utterly vanished. In this aloneness, the sense of the passing of time had ceased.

There were three of them, a father, his son and a friend. The father must have been in his late fifties, the son in his thirties, and the friend was of uncertain age. The two older men were bald, but the son still had plenty of hair. He had a well-shaped head, a rather short nose and wide-set eyes. His lips were restless, though he sat quietly enough. The father had seated himself behind his son and the friend, saying that he would take part in the talk if necessary, but otherwise would just watch and listen. A sparrow came to the open window and flew away again, frightened by so many people in the room. It knew that room, and would often perch on the window-sill, chirping softly, without fear.

"Though my father may not take part in the conversation," the son began, "he wants to be in on it, for the problem is one that concerns us all. My mother would have come had she not been feeling so unwell, and she is looking forward to the report we shall make to her. We have read some of the things you have said, and my father particularly has followed your talks from afar; but it is only within the last year or so that I have myself taken a real interest in what you are saying. Until recently, politics have absorbed the greater part of my interest and enthusiasm; but I have begun to see the immaturity of politics. The religious life is only for the maturing mind, and not for politicians and lawyers. I have been a fairly successful lawyer, but am a lawyer no longer, as I want to spend the remaining years of my life in something vastly more significant and worth while. I am speaking also for my friend, who wanted to accompany us when he heard we were coming here. You see, sir, our problem is the fact that we are all growing old. Even I, though still comparatively young, am coming to that period of life when time seems to fly, when one's days seem so short and death so near. Death, for the moment at least, is not a problem; but old age is."

What do you mean by old age? Are you referring to the aging of the physical organism, or of the mind?

"The aging of the body is of course inevitable, it wears out through use and disease. But need the mind age and deteriorate?"

To think speculatively is futile and a waste of time. Is the deterioration of the mind a supposition, or an actual fact?

"It is a fact, sir. I am aware that my mind is growing old, tired; slow deterioration is taking place."

Is this not also a problem with the young, though they may still be unaware of it? Their minds are even now set in a mould; their thought is already enclosed within a narrow pattern. But what do you mean when you say that your mind is growing old?

"It is not as pliable, as alert, as sensitive as it used to be. Its awareness is shrinking; its responses to the many challenges of life are increasingly from the storage of the past. It's deteriorating, functioning more and more within the limits of its own setting."

Then what makes the mind deteriorate? It is self-protectiveness and resistance to change, is it not? Each one has a vested interest which he is consciously or unconsciously protecting, watching over, and not allowing anything to disturb.

"Do you mean a vested interest in property?"

Not only in property, but in relationships of every kind. Nothing can exist in isolation. Life is relationship; and the mind has a vested interest in its relationship to people, to ideas, and to things. This self-interest, and the refusal to bring about a fundamental revolution within itself, is the beginning of the mind's deterioration. Most minds are conservative, they resist change. Even the so-called revolutionary mind is conservative, for once it has gained its revolutionary success, it also resists change; the revolution itself becomes its vested interest.

Even though the mind, whether it be conservative or so-called revolutionary, may permit certain modifications on the fringes of its activities, it resists all change at the centre. Circumstances may compel it to yield, to adapt itself, with pain or with ease, to a different pattern; but the centre remains hard, and it's this centre that causes the deterioration of the mind.

"What do you mean by the centre?"

Don't you know? Are you seeking a description of it?

"No, sir, but through the description I may touch it, get the feeling of it."

"Sir," put in the father, "we may intellectually be aware of that centre, but actually most of us have never come face to face with it. I have myself seen it cunningly and subtly described in various books, but I have never really confronted it; and when you ask if we know it, I for one can only say that I don't. I only know the descriptions of it."

"It is again our vested interest," added the friend, "our deep-rooted desire for security, that prevents us from knowing that centre. I don't know my own son, though I have lived with him from infancy, and I know even less that which is much closer than my son. To know it one must look at it, observe it, listen to it, but I never do. I am always in a hurry; and when occasionally I do look at it, I am at odds with it."

We are talking of the aging, the deteriorating mind. The mind is ever building the pattern of its own certainty, the security of its own interests; the words, the form, the expression may vary from time to time, from culture to culture, but the centre of self-interest remains. It is this centre that causes the mind to deteriorate, however outwardly alert and active it may be. This centre is not a fixed point, but various points within the mind, and so it's the mind itself. Improvement of the mind, or moving from one centre to another, does not banish these centres; discipline, suppression or sublimation of one centre only establishes another in its place.

Now, what do we mean when we say we are alive?

"Ordinarily," replied the son, "we consider ourselves alive when we talk, when we laugh, when there's sensation, when there's thought, activity, conflict, joy."

So what we call living is acceptance or 'revolt' within the social

152

pattern; it's a movement within the cage of the mind. Our life is an endless series of pains and pleasures, fears and frustrations, wantings and graspings; and when we do consider the mind's deterioration, and ask whether it's possible to put an end to it, our inquiry is also within the cage of the mind. Is this living?

"I'm afraid we know no other life," said the father. "As we grow older, pleasures shrink while sorrows seem to increase; and if one is at all thoughtful, one is aware that one's mind is gradually deteriorating. The body inevitably grows old and knows decay; but how is one to prevent this aging of the mind?"

We lead a thoughtless life, and towards the end of it we begin to wonder why the mind decays, and how to arrest the process. Surely, what matters is how we live our days, not only when we are young, but also in middle life, and during the declining years. The right kind of life demands of us far more intelligence than any vocation for earning a livelihood. Right thinking is essential for right living.

"What do you mean by right thinking?" asked the friend.

There's a vast difference, surely, between right thinking and right thought. Right thinking is constant awareness; right thought, on the other hand, is either conformity to a pattern set by society, or a reaction against society. Right thought is static, it is a process of grouping together certain concepts, called ideals, and following them. Right thought inevitably builds up the authoritarian, hierarchical outlook and engenders respectability; whereas right thinking is awareness of the whole process of conformity, imitation, acceptance, revolt. Right thinking, unlike right thought, is not a thing to be achieved; it arises spontaneously with self-knowledge, which is the perception of the ways of the self. Right thinking cannot be learnt from books, or from another; it comes through the mind's awareness of itself in the action of relationship. But there can be no understanding of this action as long as the mind justifies or condemns it. So, right thinking eliminates conflict and self-contradiction, which are the fundamental causes of the mind's deterioration.

"Is not conflict an essential part of life?" asked the son. "If we did not struggle, we would merely vegetate."

We think we are alive when we are caught up in the conflict of ambition, when we are driven by the compulsion of envy, when desire pushes us into action; but all this only leads to greater misery and

153

confusion. Conflict increases self-centred activity, but the understanding of conflict comes about through right thinking.

"Unfortunately, this process of struggle and misery, with some joy, is the only life we know," said the father. "There are intimations of another kind of life, but they are few and far between. To go beyond this mess and find that other life is ever the object of our search."

To search for what is beyond the actual is to be caught in illusion. Everyday existence, with its ambitions, envies, and so on, must be understood; but to understand it demands awareness, right thinking. There's no right thinking when thought starts with an assumption, a bias. Setting out with a conclusion, or looking for a preconceived answer, puts an end to right thinking; in fact, there is then no thinking at all. So, right thinking is the foundation of righteousness.

"It seems to me," put in the son, "that at least one of the factors in this whole problem of the mind's deterioration is the question of right occupation."

What do you mean by right occupation?

"I have noticed, sir, that those who become wholly absorbed in some activity or profession soon forget themselves; they are too busy to think about themselves, which is a good thing."

But isn't such absorption an escape from oneself? And to escape from oneself is wrong occupation; it is corrupting, it breeds enmity, division, and so on. Right occupation comes through the right kind of education, and with the understanding of oneself. Haven't you noticed that whatever the activity or profession, the self consciously or unconsciously uses it as a means for its own gratification, for the fulfilment of its ambition, or for the achievement of success in terms of power?

"That is so, unfortunately. We seem to use everything we touch for our own advancement."

It is this self-interest, this constant self-advancement, that makes the mind petty; and though its activity be extensive, though it be occupied with politics, science, art, research, or what you will, there is a narrowing down of thinking, a shallowness that brings about deterioration, decay. Only when there's understanding of the totality of the mind, the unconscious as well as the conscious, is there a possibility of the mind's regeneration.

"Worldliness is the curse of the modern generation," said the father.

154

"It is carried away by the things of the world, and does not give thought to serious things."

This generation is like other generations. Worldly things are not merely refrigerators, silk shirts, airplanes, television sets, and so on; they include ideals, the seeking of power, whether personal or collective, and the desire to be secure, either in this world or the next. All this corrupts the mind and brings about its decay. The problem of deterioration is to be understood at the beginning, in one's youth, not at the period of physical decline.

"Does that mean there's no hope for us?"

Not at all. It's more arduous to stop the mind's deterioration at our age, that's all. To bring about a radical change in the ways of our life, there must be expanding awareness, and a great depth of feeling, which is love. With love everything is possible.

THE IMPORTANCE OF CHANGE

THE LARGE black ants had made a path through the grass, across a stretch of sand, over a pile of rubble and through the gap in an ancient wall. A little beyond the wall was a hole which was their home. There was an extraordinary coming and going on that path, an incessant bustle in both directions. Each ant would hesitate a second as it went by another; their heads would touch, and on they would go again. There must have been thousands of them. Only when the sun was directly overhead was that path deserted, and then all activity would be centred around their nest near the wall; they were excavating, each ant bringing out a grain of sand, a pebble or a bit of earth. When you gently knocked on the ground nearby, there was a general scramble. They would pour out of the hole, looking for the aggressor; but soon they would settle down and resume their work. As soon as the sun was on its westerly course and the evening breeze blew pleasantly cool from the mountains, they would march out again on their path, populating the silent world of the grass, the sand and the rubble. They went along that path for quite a distance, hunting, and they would find so many things: the leg of a grasshopper, a dead frog, the remains of a bird, a half-eaten lizard or some grain. Everything was attacked with fury; what couldn't be carried away was eaten on the spot, or taken home in pieces. Only rain stopped their constant activity, and with the last drops they were out again. If you put your finger on their path, they would feel all around the tip, and a few would climb up it, only to come down again.

The ancient wall had a life of its own. Near the top there were holes in which bright green parrots, with curving red beaks, had made their nests. They were a shy lot, and didn't like you to come too near. Screeching and clinging to the crumbling red bricks, they would wait to see what you were going to do. If you didn't come any nearer, they would wriggle into the holes, leaving only their pale green tail feathers sticking out; there would then be another wriggle, the feathers would disappear, and their red beaks and shapely green heads would be showing. They were settling down for the night.

The wall enclosed an ancient tomb whose dome, catching the last rays of the setting sun, glowed as if someone had turned on a light from within. The whole structure was well-built and splendidly proportioned; it had not a line that could jar you, and it stood out against the evening sky, seemingly freed from the earth. All things were intensely alive, and all things—the ancient tomb, the crumbling red bricks, the green parrots, the busy ants, the whistle of a distant train, the silence and the stars—were merged into the totality of life. It was a benediction.

Although it was late, they had wanted to come, so we all went into the room. Lanterns had to be lit, and in the hurry one was broken, but the remaining two gave enough light for us to see each other as we sat in a circle on the floor. One of those who had come was a clerk in some office; he was small and nervous, and his hands were never still. Another must have had a little more money, for he owned a shop and had the air of a man who was making his way in the world. Heavily built and rather fat, he was inclined to easy laughter, but was now serious. The third visitor was an old man, and being retired, he explained, he had more time to study the Scriptures and perform *puja*, a religious ceremony. The fourth was an artist with long hair, who watched with a steady eye every movement, every gesture we made; he wasn't going to miss anything. We were all silent for a while. Through the open window one or two stars could be seen, and the strong perfume of jasmine came into the room.

"I would like to sit quietly like this for a longer period," said the merchant. "It's a blessing to feel this quality of silence, it has a healing effect; but I don't want to waste time explaining my immediate feelings, and I suppose I had better get on with what I came to talk about. I have had a very strenuous life, more so than most people; and while I am not by any means a rich man, I am now comfortably well off. I have always tried to lead a religious life. I haven't been too covetous, I have been charitable, and I haven't deceived others unnecessarily; but when you are in business, you have sometimes to avoid telling the exact truth. I could have made a great deal more money, but I denied myself that pleasure. I amuse myself in simple ways, but on the whole I have led a serious life; it could have been better, but it really hasn't been bad. I am married, and have two children. Briefly, sir, that's my personal history. I have read some of your books and attended your discourses, and I have come here to be instructed in how to lead a more deeply religious life. But I must let the other gentlemen talk."

"My work is a rather tiresome routine, but I am not qualified for any other job," said the clerk. "My own needs are few, and I am not married; but I have to support my parents, and I am also helping my younger brother through college. I am not at all religious in the orthodox sense, but the religious life appeals to me very strongly. I am often tempted to give up everything and become a *sannyasi*, but a sense of responsibility to my parents and my brother makes me hesitate. I have meditated every day for many years, and since hearing your explanation of what real meditation is, I have tried to follow it; but it's very difficult, at least for me, and I can't seem to get into the way of it. Also, my position as a clerk, which requires me to work all day long at something in which I have not the slightest interest, is hardly conducive to higher thought. But I deeply crave to find the truth, if it's ever possible for me to do so, and while I am young I want to set a right course for the rest of my life; so here I am."

"For my part," said the old man, "I am fairly familiar with the Scriptures, and since retiring as a government official several years ago, my time is my own. I have no responsibilities; all my children are grown up and married, so I am free to meditate, to read, and to talk of serious things. I have always been interested in the religious life. From time to time I have listened attentively to one or other of the various teachers, but I have never been satisfied. In some cases their teachings are utterly childish, while others are dogmatic, orthodox and merely explanatory. I have recently been attending some of your talks and discussions. I follow a great deal of what you say, but there are certain points with which I cannot agree—or rather, which I don't understand. Agreement, as you have explained, can exist with regard to opinions, conclusions, ideas, but there can be no 'agreement' with regard to truth; either one sees it, or one does not. Specifically, I would like further clarification on the ending of thought."

"I am an artist, but not yet a very good one," said the man with the long hair. "I hope one day to go to Europe to study art; here we have mediocre teachers. To me, beauty in any form is an expression of reality; it's an aspect of the divine. Before I start to paint, I meditate, like the ancients, on the deeper beauty of life. I try to drink at the spring of all beauty, to catch a glimpse of the sublime, and only then do I begin my day's painting. Sometimes it comes through, but more often it doesn't; however hard I try, nothing seems to happen, and whole days, even weeks, are wasted. I have also tried fasting, along with various exercises, both physical and intellectual, hoping to awaken the creative feeling; but all to no avail. Everything else is secondary to that feeling, without which one cannot be a true artist, and I will go to the ends of the earth to find it. That is why I have come here."

All of us sat quietly for a time, each with his own thoughts.

Are your several problems different, or are they similar, though they may appear to be different? Is it not possible that there is one basic issue underlying them all?

"I am not sure that my problem is in any way related to that of the artist," said the merchant. "He is after inspiration, the creative feeling, but I want to lead a more deeply spiritual life."

"That's precisely what I want to do too," replied the artist, "only I have expressed it differently."

We like to think that our particular problem is exclusive, that our sorrow is entirely different from that of others; we want to remain separate at all costs. But sorrow is sorrow, whether it is yours or mine. If we don't understand this, we cannot proceed; we shall feel cheated, disappointed, frustrated. Surely, all of us here are after the same thing; the problem of each is essentially the problem of all. If we really feel the truth of this, then we have already gone a long way in our understanding, and we can inquire together; we can help each other, listen to and learn from each other. Then the authority of a teacher has no meaning, it becomes silly. Your problem is the problem of another; your sorrow is the sorrow of another. Love is not exclusive. If this is clear, sirs, let us proceed.

"I think we all now see that our problems are not unrelated," replied the old man, and the others nodded in approval.

Then what is our common problem? Please don't answer immediately, but let us consider.

Is it not, sirs, that there must be a fundamental transformation in oneself? Without this transformation, inspiration is always transitory, and there is a constant struggle to recapture it; without this transformation, any effort to lead a spiritual life can only be very superficial, a matter of rituals, of the bell and the book; without this transformation, meditation becomes a means of escape, a form of self-hypnosis.

"That is so," said the old man. "Without a deep inward change, all effort to be religious or spiritual is a mere scratching on the surface."

"I am entirely one with you, sir," added the man from the office. "I do feel that there must be a fundamental change in me, otherwise I shall go on like this for the rest of my life, groping, asking and doubting. But how is one to bring about this change?"

"I also can see that there must be an explosive change within myself if that which I am groping after is to come into being," said the artist. "A radical transformation in oneself is obviously essential. But, as that gentleman has already asked, how is such a change to be brought about?"

Let us give our minds and hearts to the discovery of the manner of its happening. What is important, surely, is to feel the urgent necessity of changing fundamentally, and not merely be persuaded by the words of another that you ought to change. An exciting description may stimulate you to feel that you must change, but such a feeling is very superficial, and it will pass away when the stimulant is gone. But if you yourself see the importance of change, if you feel, without any form of compulsion, without any motivation or influence, that radical transformation is essential, then this very feeling is the action of transformation.

"But how is one to have this feeling?" asked the merchant.

What do you mean by the word 'how'?

"Since I have not got this feeling for change, how can I cultivate it?"

Can you cultivate this feeling? Must it not arise spontaneously from your own direct perception of the utter necessity for a radical transformation? The feeling creates its own means of action. By logical reasoning you may come to the conclusion that a fundamental change is necessary, but such intellectual or verbal comprehension does not bring about the action of change.

"Why not?" asked the old man.

Is not intellectual or verbal comprehension a superficial response? You hear, you reason, but your whole being does not enter into it. Your surface mind may agree that a change is necessary, but the totality of your mind is not giving its complete attention; it's divided in itself.

"Do you mean, sir, that the action of change takes place only when there's total attention?" asked the artist.

Let's consider it. One part of the mind is convinced that this fundamental change is necessary, but the rest of the mind is unconcerned; it may be in abeyance, or asleep, or actively opposed to such a change. When this happens, there's a contradiction within the mind, one part wanting change, and the other being indifferent or opposed to change. The resulting conflict, in which that part of the mind which wants change is trying to overcome the recalcitrant part, is called discipline, sublimation, suppression; it is also called following the ideal. An attempt is being made to build a bridge over the gap of self-contradiction. There is the ideal, the intellectual or verbal comprehension that there must be a fundamental transformation, and the vague but actual feeling of not wanting to be bothered, the desire to let things go on as they are, the fear of change, of insecurity. So there's a division in the mind; and the pursuit of the ideal is an attempt to bring together the two contradictory parts, which is an impossibility. We pursue the ideal because it doesn't demand immediate action; the ideal is an accepted and respected postponement.

"Then is trying to change oneself always a form of postponement?" asked the man from the office.

Isn't it? Haven't you noticed that when you say, "I will try to change," you have no intention of changing at all? You either change, or you don't; *trying* to change has actually very little significance. Pursuing the ideal, attempting to change, compelling the two contradictory parts of the mind to come together by the action of the will,

160

practising a method or a discipline to achieve such a unification, and so on—all this is useless and wasteful effort which actually prevents any fundamental transformation of the centre, the self, the ego.

"I think I understand what you are conveying," said the artist. "We are playing around with the idea of change, but never changing. Change requires drastic, unified action."

Yes; and unified or integrated action cannot take place as long as there's a conflict between opposing parts of the mind.

"I see that, I really do!" exclaimed the man from the office. "No amount of idealism, of logical reasoning, no convictions or conclusions, can bring about the change we are talking about. But then what will?"

Are you not, by that very question, preventing yourself from discovering the action of change? We are so eager for results that we do not pause between what we have just discovered to be true or false, and the uncovering of another fact. We hasten forward without fully understanding what we have already found.

We have seen that reasoning and logical conclusions will not bring about this change, this fundamental transformation of the centre. But before we ask ourselves what factor *will* bring it about, we must be fully aware of the tricks that the mind uses to convince itself that change is gradual and must be effected through the pursuit of ideals, and so on. Having seen the truth or the falseness of that whole process, we can proceed to ask ourselves what is the factor necessary for this radical change.

Now, what is it that makes you move, act?

"Any strong feeling. Intense anger makes me act; I may afterwards regret it, but the feeling explodes into action."

That is, your whole being is in it; you forget or disregard danger, you are lost to your own safety, security. The very feeling is action; there is no gap between the feeling and the act. The gap is created by the so-called reasoning process, a weighing of the pros and the cons according to one's convictions, prejudices, fears, and so on. Action is then political, it is stripped of spontaneity, of all humanity. The men who are seeking power, whether for themselves, their group or their country, act in this manner, and such action only breeds further misery and confusion.

"Actually," went on the man from the office, "even a strong feeling for fundamental change is soon erased by self-protective reasoning, by thinking what would happen if such a change took place in one, and so on."

The feeling is then hedged about by ideas, by words, is it not? There is a contradictory reaction, born of the desire not to be disturbed. If that is the case, then continue in your old way; don't deceive yourself by following the ideal, by saying that you are trying to change, and all the rest of it. Be simple with the fact that you don't want to change. The realization of this truth is in itself sufficient.

"But I *do* want to change."

Then change; but don't talk unfeelingly about the necessity of changing. It has no meaning.

"At my age," said the old man, "I have nothing to lose in the outward sense; but to give up the old ideas and conclusions is quite another matter. I now see at least one thing: that there can be no fundamental change without an awakening of the feeling for it. Reasoning is necessary, but it's not the instrument of action. To know is not necessarily to act."

But the action of feeling is also the action of knowing, the two are not separate; they are separate only when reason, knowledge, conclusion or belief induces action.

"I am beginning to see this very clearly, and my knowledge of the Scriptures, as a basis for action, is already losing its grip on my mind."

Action based on authority is no action at all; it is mere imitation, repetition.

"And most of us are caught in that process. But one can break away from it. I have understood a great deal this evening."

"So have I," said the artist. "To me, this discussion has been highly stimulating, and I don't think the stimulation will admit of any reaction. I have seen something very clearly, and I am going to pursue it, not knowing where it will lead."

"My life has been respectable," said the merchant, "and respectability is not conducive to change, especially of the fundamental kind we have been talking about. I have cultivated very earnestly the idealistic desire to change, and to lead a more genuinely religious life; but I now see that meditation upon life and the ways of change is far more essential."

"May I add yet another word?" asked the old man. "Meditation is not upon life; it is itself the way of life."

162

KILLING

THE SUN wouldn't be up for two or three hours. There was not a cloud in the sky, and the stars were shouting with joy. The heavens were enclosed by the dark outline of the encircling hills, and the night was completely still; not a dog was barking, and the villagers were not yet up. Even the deep-throated owl was silent. The window let into the room the immensity of the night, and there was that strange feeling of being totally alone—an awakened aloneness. The little stream was flowing under the stone bridge, but you had to listen for it; its gentle murmur was all but inaudible in that vast silence, which was so intense, so penetrating, that your whole being was held in it. It was not the opposite of noise; noise could be in it, but was not of it.

It was still quite dark when we set out in the car, but the morning star was over the eastern hills. The trees and bushes were intensely green in the bright glare of the headlights as the car made its way in and out among the hills. The road was empty, but you couldn't go too fast because of the many curves. There was now the beginning of a glow in the east; and although we were chatting in the car, the awakening of meditation was going on. The mind was completely motionless; it wasn't asleep, it wasn't tired, but utterly still. As the sky became brighter and brighter, the mind went further and further, deeper and deeper. Though it was aware of the huge ball of golden light, and of the talk that was going on, it was alone, moving without any resistance, without any directive; it was alone, like a light in darkness. It did not know it was alone—only the word knows. It was a movement that had no end and no direction. It was happening without a cause, and it would go on without time.

The headlights had been switched off, and in that early morning light the rich, green country was enchanting. There was heavy dew, and wherever the sun's rays touched the earth, countless jewels were sparkling with every colour of the rainbow. At that hour the bare granite rocks seemed soft and yielding—an illusion which the rising sun would soon take away. The road wound on between luscious rice-fields and huge ponds, full to the brim with dancing waters, which would keep the country nourished till the next rainy season. But the rains weren't over yet; and how green and alive everything was! The

163

cattle were fat, and the faces of the people on the road shone with the cool freshness of the morning. There were now many monkeys along the road. They were not the kind with long legs and long bodies that swing with ease and grace from branch to branch, or step lightly and haughtily in the fields, watching with grave faces as you go by. These were small monkeys, with long tails and dirty green-brown fur, full of play and mischief. One of them nearly got caught under the front wheel, but it was saved by its own quickness, and by the alertness of the driver.

Now it was broad daylight, and the villagers were on the move in greater numbers. The car had to go to the side of the road to pass the slow-moving bullock-carts, of which there always seemed to be so many; and the lorries would never give way to let you go by until you had blown your horn for a minute or two. Famous temples towered over the trees, and the car sped past the birthplace of a saintly teacher.

A small group had come, one woman and several men, but only three or four took part in the discussion. They were all earnest people, and you could see that they were good friends, though they had differences of thought. The first man who spoke had a well-trimmed beard, an aquiline nose and a high forehead; his dark eyes were sharp and very serious. The second one was painfully thin; he was bald and clear-skinned, and he couldn't keep his hands off his face. The third was plump, cheerful and easy of manner; he would look at you as though taking stock, and being dissatisfied, would look again to see if his count had been right. He had shapely hands, with long fingers. Though he would laugh easily, there was about him a depth of seriousness. The fourth had a pleasant smile, and his eyes were those of a man who had read a great deal. Though he took very little part in the conversation, he was by no means asleep. All the men were probably in their forties, but the woman appeared to be much younger; she never spoke, though she was attentive to what was going on.

"We have been talking things over amongst ourselves for several months, and we want to discuss with you a problem that has been bothering us," said the first speaker. "You see, some of us are meat-eaters, and others are not. Personally, I have never eaten meat in my life; it's repulsive to me in any form, and I can't bear the idea of killing an animal to fill my stomach. Although we have not been able to agree as to what is the right thing to do in this matter, we have all remained good friends, and shall continue as such, I hope."

"I occasionally eat meat," said the second one. "I prefer not to, but when you travel it's often difficult to maintain a balanced diet without meat, and it's much simpler to eat it. I don't like to kill animals, I am sensitive about that kind of thing, but to eat meat now and then is all right. Many strait-laced cranks on the subject of vegetarianism are more sinful than people who kill to eat."

"My son shot a pigeon the other day, and we had it for dinner," said the third speaker. "The boy was quite excited to have brought it down with his new shotgun. You ought to have seen the look in his eyes! He was both appalled and pleased; feeling guilty, he had at the same time the air of a conqueror. I told him not to feel guilty. Killing is cruel, but it is part of life, and it is not too serious as long as it is practised in moderation and kept under proper control. Eating meat is not the dreadful crime that our friend here makes it out to be. I am not too much for bloody sports, but killing to eat is not a sin against God. Why make so much fuss about it?"

"As you can see, sir," went on the first speaker, "I haven't been able to convince them that killing animals for food is barbarous; and besides, eating meat is an unhealthy thing, as anyone knows who has taken the trouble to make an impartial investigation of the facts. With me, not eating meat is a matter of principle; in my family we have been non-meat-eaters for generations. It seems to me that man must eliminate from his nature this cruelty of killing animals for food if he is to become really civilized."

"That's what he's everlastingly telling us," interrupted the second one. "He wants to 'civilize' us meat-eaters, yet other forms of cruelty do not seem to cause him any concern. He is a lawyer, and he does not mind the cruelty involved in the practice of his profession. However, in spite of our disagreement on this point, we are still friends. We have discussed the whole issue dozens of times, and as we never seem to get any further, we all agreed that we should come and talk it over with you."

"There are bigger and wider issues than killing some wretched animal for food," put in the fourth one. "It's all a matter of how you look at life."

What's the problem, sirs?

"To eat meat, or not to eat it," replied the non-meat-eater.

Is that the main issue, or is it part of a larger issue?

"To me, a man's willingness or unwillingness to kill animals for the satisfaction of his appetite indicates his attitude towards the larger issues of life."

If we can see that to concentrate exclusively on any part does not bring about the comprehension of the whole, then perhaps we shall not get confused over the parts. Unless we are able to perceive the whole, the part assumes greater importance than it has. There's a bigger issue involved in all this, isn't there? The problem is that of killing, and not merely killing animals for food. A man is not virtuous because he doesn't eat meat, nor is he any less virtuous because he does. The god of a petty mind is also petty; his pettiness is measured by that of the mind which puts flowers at his feet. The larger issue includes the many and apparently separate problems that man has created within himself and outside of himself. Killing is really a very great and complex problem. Shall we consider it, sirs?

"I think we should," replied the fourth one. "I am keenly interested in this problem, and to approach it along a wide front appeals to me."

There are many forms of killing, are there not? There is killing by a word or a gesture, killing in fear or in anger, killing for a country or an ideology, killing for a set of economic dogmas or religious beliefs.

"How does one kill by a word or a gesture?" asked the third speaker.

Don't you know? With a word or a gesture you may kill a man's reputation; through gossip, defamation, contempt, you may wipe him out. And does not comparison kill? Don't you kill a boy by comparing him with another who is cleverer or more skilful? A man who kills out of hate or anger is regarded as a criminal and put to death. Yet the man who deliberately bombs thousands of people off the face of the earth in the name of his country is honoured, decorated; he is looked upon as a hero. Killing is spreading over the earth. For the safety or expansion of one nation, another is destroyed. Animals are killed for food, for profit, or for so-called sport; they are vivisected for the 'well-being' of man. The soldier exists to kill. Extraordinary progress is being made in the technology of murdering vast numbers of people in a few seconds and at great distances. Many scientists are wholly occupied with it, and priests bless the bomber and the warship. Also, we kill a cabbage or a carrot in order to eat; we destroy a pest. Where are we to draw the line beyond which we will not kill?

"It's up to each individual," replied the second one.

Is it as simple as that? If you refuse to go to war, you are either shot or sent to prison, or perhaps to a psychiatric ward. If you refuse to take part in the nationalistic game of hate, you are despised, and you may lose your job; pressure is brought to bear in various ways to force you to conform. In the paying of taxes, even in the buying of a postage stamp, you are supporting war, the killing of ever-changing enemies.

"Then what is one to do?" asked the non-meat-eater. "I am well aware that I have legally killed, in the law courts, many times; but I am a strict vegetarian, and I never kill any living creature with my own hands."

"Not even a poisonous insect?" asked the second one.

"Not if I can help it."

"Someone else does it for you."

"Sir," went on the vegetarian lawyer, "are you suggesting that we should not pay taxes or write letters?"

Again, in being concerned first with the details of action, in speculating about whether we should do this or that, we get lost in the particular without comprehending the totality of the problem. The problem needs to be considered as a whole, does it not?

"I quite see that there must be a comprehensive view of the problem, but the details are important too. We can't neglect our immediate activity, can we?"

What do you mean by "a comprehensive view of the problem"? Is it a matter of mere intellectual agreement, verbal assent, or do you actually comprehend the total problem of killing?

"To be quite honest, sir, until now I haven't paid much attention to the wider implications of the problem. I have been concerned with one particular aspect of it."

Which is like not throwing the window wide open and looking at the sky, the trees, the people, the whole movement of life, but peering instead through a narrow crack in the casement. And the mind is like that: a small, unimportant part of it is very active, while the rest is dormant. This petty activity of the mind creates its own petty problems of good and bad, its political and moral values, and so on. If we could really see the absurdity of this process, we would naturally, without any compulsion, explore the wider fields of the mind.

So the issue we are discussing is not merely the killing or the non-killing of animals, but the cruelty and hate that are ever increasing in the world and in each one of us. That is our real problem, isn't it?

"Yes," replied the fourth one emphatically. "Brutality is spreading in the world like a plague; a whole nation is destroyed by its bigger and more powerful neighbour. Cruelty, hate, is the issue, not whether or not one happens to like the taste of meat."

The cruelty, the anger, the hate that exists in ourselves is expressed in so many ways: in the exploitation of the weak by the powerful and the cunning; in the cruelty of forcing a whole people, under pain of being liquidated, to accept a certain ideological pattern of life; in the building up of nationalism and sovereign governments through intensive propaganda; in the cultivation of organized dogmas and beliefs, which are called religion, but which actually separate man from man. The ways of cruelty are many and subtle.

"Even if we spent the rest of our lives looking, we couldn't uncover all the subtle ways in which cruelty expresses itself, could we?" inquired the third one. "Then how are we to proceed?"

"It seems to me," said the first speaker, "that we are missing the central issue. Each one of us is protecting himself; we are defending our self-interests, our economic or intellectual assets, or perhaps a tradition which affords us some profit, not necessarily monetary. This self-interest in everything we touch, from politics to God, is the root of the matter."

Again, if one may ask, is that a mere verbal assertion, a logical conclusion which can be torn to shreds or cunningly defended? Or does it reflect the perception of an actual fact that has significance in our daily life of thought and action?

"You are trying to bring us to distinguish between the word and the actual fact," said the third speaker, "and I am beginning to see how important it is that we should make this distinction. Otherwise we shall be lost in words, without any action—as in fact we are."

To act there must be feeling. A feeling for the whole issue makes for total action.

"When one feels deeply about anything," said the fourth man, "one acts, and such action is not impulsive or so-called intuitive; neither is it a premeditated, calculated act. It is born out of the depth of one's being. If that act causes mischief, pain, one cheerfully pays for it; but such an act is rarely mischievous. The question is, how is one to sustain this deep feeling?"

"Before we go any further," put in the third man earnestly, "let's be clear about what you are explaining, sir. One is aware of the fact that to have complete action, there must be deep feeling, in which there is a full psychological comprehension of the problem; otherwise there are merely bits of action, which never stick together. That much is clear. Then, as we were saying, the word is not the feeling; the word may evoke the feeling, but this verbal evocation does not sustain the feeling. Now, can one not enter the world of feeling directly, without the description of it, without the symbol or the word? Isn't that the next question?"

Yes, sir. We are distracted by words, by symbols; we rarely feel except through the stimulation of the term, the description. The word 'God' is not God, but that word leads us to react according to our conditioning. We can find out the truth or the falseness of God only when the word 'God' no longer creates in us certain habitual physiological or psychological responses. As we were saying earlier, a total feeling makes for total action—or rather, a total feeling *is* total action. A sensation passes away, leaving you where you were before. But this total feeling we are talking about is not a sensation, it does not depend on stimulation; it sustains itself, no artifice is needed.

"But how is this total feeling to be aroused?" insisted the first speaker.

If one may say so, you are not seeing the point. Feeling that can be aroused is a matter of stimulation; it's a sensation, to be nourished through various means, by this or that method. Then the means or the method becomes all-important, not the feeling. The symbol as a means to the feeling is enshrined in a temple, in a church, and then the feeling exists only through the symbol or the word. But is total feeling to be 'aroused'? Consider, sir, don't answer.

"I see what you mean," said the third one. "Total feeling is not to be aroused at all; it's there, or it's not. This leaves us in a rather hopeless state, doesn't it?"

Does it? There's a sense of hopelessness because you want to arrive somewhere, you want to get that total feeling; and since you can't, you feel rather lost. It is this desire to arrive, to achieve, to become, that creates the method, the symbol, the stimulant, through which the mind comforts and distracts itself. So let us again consider the problem of killing, cruelty, hate.

To be concerned with 'humanitarian' killing is quite absurd; to abstain from eating meat while destroying your son by comparing him with another is to be cruel; to take part in the respectable killing for your country or for an ideology is to cultivate hate; to be kind to animals and cruel to your fellow man by act, word, or gesture, is to breed enmity and brutality.

"Sir, I think I understand what you have just said; but how is total feeling to come about? I ask this only as a query in the movement of search. I am not asking for a method: I see the absurdity of that. I see, too, that the desire to achieve builds its own hindrances, and that to feel hopeless, or helpless, is silly. All this is now clear."

If it is clear, not just verbally or intellectually, but with the actuality of the pain that a thorn causes in your foot, then there's compassion, love. Then you have already opened the door to this total feeling of compassion. The compassionate man knows right action. Without love, you are trying to find out what is the right thing to do, and your action only leads to greater harm and misery; it is the action of politicians and reformers. Without love, you cannot comprehend cruelty; a peace of sorts may be established through the reign of terror; but war, killing, will continue at another level of our existence.

"We haven't got compassion, sir, and that's the real source of our misery," said the first man feelingly. "We are hard inside, an ugly thing in ourselves, but we bury it under kindly words and superficial acts of generosity. We are cancerous at heart, in spite of our religious beliefs and social reforms. It's in one's own heart that an operation must take place, and then a new seed can be planted. That very operation is the life of the new seed. The operation has begun, and may the seed bear fruit."

To Be Intelligent Is To Be Simple

THE SEA was very blue, and the setting sun was just touching the tops of the low-lying clouds. A boy of thirteen or fourteen, in a wet cloth, was standing by a car, shivering and pretending to be dumb; he was begging, and was putting on a very good act. Having got a few coins, he was off, sprinting across the sands. The waves were coming in very gently, and they didn't completely obliterate the footprints in passing over them. The crabs were racing with the waves, and dodging one's feet; they would let themselves be caught by a wave, and by the shifting sands, but they would come up again, ready for the next wave. Seated on a few logs tied together, a man had been right out to sea, and he was now coming in with two large fish; he was dark, burnt by many suns. Coming ashore with skill and ease, he drew his raft far up onto the dry sands, out of reach of the waves. Further along there was a grove of palm trees, bending towards the sea, and beyond them the town. A steamer on the horizon stood as if motionless, and a gentle breeze was blowing from the north. It was an hour of great beauty and stillness, in which the earth and the heavens met. You could sit on the sand and watch the waves come in and go out, endlessly, and their rhythmic movement seemed to pass over the land. Your mind was alive, but not as the restless sea; it was alive, and it reached from one horizon to the other. It had no height or depth, it was neither far nor near; there was no centre from which to measure or encircle the whole. The sea, the sky and the land were all there, but there was no observer. It was vast space and measureless light. The light of the setting sun was on the trees, it bathed the village and could be seen beyond the river; but *this* was a light that never set, a light that was ever shining. And strangely, there were no shadows in it; you did not cast your shadow across any part of it. You were not asleep, you had not closed your eyes, for now the stars were becoming visible; but whether you closed your eyes or kept them open, the light was always there. It was not to be caught and put in a shrine.

A mother of three children, she seemed simple, quiet and unassuming, but her eyes were alive and observant; they took in many things. As she talked, her rather nervous shyness disappeared, but she remained quietly watchful. Her eldest son had been educated abroad and was now working as an electronic engineer; the second one had a good job in a textile factory, and the youngest was just finishing college. They were all good boys, she said, and you could see she was proud of them. They had lost their father some years ago, but he had seen to it that they would have a good education and be self-supporting. What little else he had, he had left to her, and she was not in need of anything, for her wants were few. At this point she stopped talking, and was evidently finding it difficult to come out with something that was on her mind. Sensing what she wanted to talk about, I hesitantly questioned her.

Do you love your children?

"Of course I do," she answered quickly, glad of the opening. "Who doesn't love their children? I have brought them up with loving care, and have been occupied all these years with their comings and goings, their sorrows and joys, and with all the other things that a mother cares about. They have been very good children, and have been very good to me. They all did well in their studies, and they will make their way in life; they may not leave their mark upon the world, but after all, so few do. We are all now living together, and when they get married I shall stay, if I am wanted, with one or other of them. Of course, I have my own house too, and I am not economically dependent on them. But it is strange that you should ask me that question."

Is it?

"Well, I have never before talked about myself to anyone, not even to my sister, or to my late husband, and suddenly to be asked that question seemed rather strange—though I *do* want to talk it over with you. It took a lot of courage to come to see you, but now I am glad I came, and that you have made it so easy for me to talk. I have always been a listener, but not in your sense of the word. I used to listen to my husband, and to his business associates whenever they dropped in. I have listened to my children and to my friends. But no one ever seemed to care to listen to me, and for the most part I was silent. In listening to others, one learns, but most of what one hears is nothing that one doesn't already know. The men gossiped as much as the women, besides complaining about their jobs and their bad pay; some talked about their hoped-for promotion, others about social reform, village work or what the *guru* had said. I listened to them all, and never opened my heart to anybody. Some were more clever, and others more stupid than I, but in most things they were not very different from me. I enjoy music, but I listen to it with a different ear. I seem to be listening to somebody or other most of the time; but there is also something else to which I listen, something which always eludes me. May I talk about it?"

Isn't that why you are here?

"Yes, I suppose it is. You see, I am approaching forty-five, and most of those years I have been occupied with others; I have been busy with a thousand and one things, all day and every day. My husband died five years ago, and since then I have been more than ever occupied with the children; and now, in a strange way, I am coming upon myself all the time. With my sister-in-law I attended your talk the other day, and something stirred in my heart, something which I always knew was there. I can't express it very well, and I hope you will understand what it is I want to say."

May I help you?

"I wish you would."

It is difficult to be simple right to the end of anything, isn't it? We experience something that is simple in itself, but it soon becomes complicated; it is hard to keep it within the bounds of its original simplicity. Don't you feel this is so?

"In a way, yes. There is a simple thing in my heart, but I don't know what it all means."

You said that you loved your children. What is the meaning of that word 'love'?

"I told you what it means. To love one's children is to look after them, to see that they don't get hurt, that they don't make too many mistakes; it is to help them prepare for a good job, to see them happily married, and so on."

Is that all?

"What more can a mother do?"

If one may ask, does your love for your children fill your whole life, and not just a part of it?

"No," she admitted. "I love them, but it has never filled my whole life. The relationship with my husband was different. He might have filled my life, but not the children; and now that they have grown to be young men, they have their own lives to live. They love me, and I love them; but the relationship between a man and his wife is different, and they will find their fullness of life in marrying the right woman."

Have you never wanted your children to be rightly educated, so that they would help to prevent wars, and not be killed for some idea or to satisfy some politician's craving for power? Doesn't your love make you want to help them to bring about a different kind of society, a society in which hatred, antagonism, envy, will have ceased to exist?

"But what can *I* do about it? I myself haven't been properly educated, so how can I possibly help to create a new social order?"

Don't you feel strongly about it?

"I'm afraid not. Do we feel strongly about anything?"

Then is love not something strong, vital, urgent?

"It should be, but with most of us it is not. I love my sons, and pray that nothing bad will happen to them. If it does, what can I do but shed bitter tears over it?"

If you have love, isn't it strong enough to make you act? Jealousy, like hate, is strong, and it does bring about forceful, vigorous action; but jealousy is not love. Then do we really know what love is?

"I have always thought that I loved my children, even though it hasn't been the greatest thing in my life."

Is there then a greater love in your life than your love for your children?

It had not been easy to come to this point, and she felt awkward and embarrassed as we came to it. For some time she wouldn't talk, and we sat there without saying a word.

"I have never really loved," she began gently. "I have never felt very deeply about anything. I used to be very jealous, and it was a very strong feeling. It bit into my heart and made me violent; I cried, made scenes, and once, God forgive me, I struck. But that's all over and gone. Sexual desire was also very strong, but with each baby it diminished, and now it has completely disappeared. My feeling for my children isn't what it should be. I have never felt anything very strongly except jealousy and sex; and that doesn't go very far, does it?"

Not very far.

"Then what is love? Attachment, jealousy, even hate, is what I used to consider to be love; and of course sexual relationship. But I see now that sexual relationship is only a very small part of a much greater thing. The greater thing I have never known, and that is why sex became so consumingly important, at least for a time. When that faded away, I thought I loved my sons; but the fact is that I have loved them, if I may use that word at all, only in a very small way; and although they are good boys, they are just like thousands of others. I suppose we are all mediocre, satisfied with petty things: with ambition, prosperity, envy. Our lives are small, whether we live in palaces or huts. This is all very clear to me now, which it has never been before; but as you must know, I am not an educated person."

Education has nothing to do with it; mediocrity is not a monopoly of the uneducated. The scholar, the scientist, the very clever, may also be mediocre. Freedom from mediocrity, from pettiness, is not a matter of class or learning.

"But I have not thought much, I have not felt much; my life has been a sorry thing."

Even when we do feel strongly, it's generally about such petty things: about personal and family security, about the flag, about some religious or political leader. Our feeling is always for or against something; it isn't like a fire that burns brightly, without smoke.

"But who is to give us that fire?"

To depend on another, to look to a *guru*, a leader, is to take away the aloneness, the purity of the fire; it makes for smoke.

"Then, if we are not to ask for help, we must have the fire to begin with."

Not at all. At the beginning, the fire is not there. It has to be nurtured; there must be care, a wise putting away, with understanding, of those things that dampen the fire, that destroy the clarity of the flame. Then only is there the fire that nothing can extinguish.

"But that needs intelligence, which I haven't got."

Yes you have. In seeing for yourself how little your life is, how little you love; in perceiving the nature of jealousy; in beginning to be aware of yourself in everyday relationship, there is already the movement of intelligence. Intelligence is a matter of hard work, quick perception of the subtle tricks of the mind, facing the fact, and clear thinking, without assumptions or conclusions. To kindle the fire of intelligence, and to keep it alive, demands alertness and great simplicity.

"It is kind of you to say that I have intelligence; but *have* I?" she insisted.

It's good to inquire, but not to assert that you have or have not. To inquire rightly is in itself the beginning of intelligence. You hinder intelligence in yourself by your own convictions, opinions, assertions and denials. Simplicity is the way of intelligence—not the mere show of simplicity in outward things and behaviour, but the simplicity of inward non-being. When you say "I know", you are on the path of non-intelligence; but when you say "I don't know", and really mean it, you have already started on the path of intelligence. When a man doesn't know, he looks, listens, inquires. 'To know' is to accumulate, and he who accumulates will never know; he is not intelligent.

"If I am on the path of intelligence because I am simple and don't know much . . ."

To think in terms of 'much' is to be unintelligent. 'Much' is a comparative word, and comparison is based on accumulation.

"Yes, I see that. But, as I was saying, if one is on the path of intelligence because one is simple and really doesn't know anything, then intelligence would seem to be tantamount to ignorance."

Ignorance is one thing, and the state of not knowing is quite another; the two are in no way connected. You may be very learned, clever, efficient, talented, and yet be ignorant. There is ignorance when there is no self-knowledge. The ignorant man is he who is unaware of himself, who does not know his own deceits, vanities, envies, and so on. Self-knowledge is freedom. You may know all about the wonders of the earth and of the heavens, and still not be free from envy, sorrow. But when you say "I don't know", you are learning. To learn is not to accumulate, either knowledge, things or relationships. To be intelligent is to be simple; but to be simple is extraordinarily arduous.

CONFUSION AND CONVICTIONS

THE TOPS of the mountains beyond the lake were in dark, heavy clouds, but the shores of the lake were in the sun. It was early spring, and the sun wasn't warm. The trees were still bare, their branches naked against the blue sky; but they were beautiful in their nakedness. They could wait with patience and certainty, for the sun was upon them, and in a few weeks more they would be covered with tender green leaves. A little path by the lake turned off through the woods, which were mostly evergreens; they extended for miles, and if you went far enough along that path you came to an open meadow, with trees all around it. It was a beautiful spot, secluded and far away. A few cows were sometimes grazing in the meadow, but the tinkling of their bells never seemed to disturb the solitude or take away the feeling of distance, of loneliness and familiar seclusion. A thousand people might come to that enchanted place, and when they had left, with their noise and litter, it would have remained unspoilt, alone and friendly.

That afternoon the sun was on the meadow, and on the tall, dark trees that stood around it, carved in green, stately, without movement. With your preoccupations and inward chatter, with your mind and eyes all over the place, restlessly wondering if the rain would catch you on your way back, you felt as though you were trespassing, not wanted there; but soon you were part of it, part of that enchanted solitude. There were no birds of any kind; the air was completely still, and the tops of the trees were motionless against the blue sky. The lush green meadow was the centre of this world, and as you sat on a rock, you were part of that centre. It wasn't imagination; imagination is silly. It wasn't that you were trying to identify yourself with what was so splendidly open and beautiful; identification is vanity. It wasn't that you were trying to forget or abnegate yourself in this unspoilt solitude of nature; all self-forgetful abnegation is arrogance. It wasn't the shock or the compulsion of so much purity; all compulsion is a denial of the true. You could do nothing to make yourself, or help yourself to be, part of that wholeness. But you were part of it, part of the green meadow, the hard rock, the blue sky and the stately trees. It was so. You might remember it, but then you would not be of it; and if you went back to it, you would never find it.

Suddenly you heard the clear notes of a flute; and along the path you met the player, a mere boy. He was never going to be a professional, but there was joy in his playing. He was looking after the cows. He was too shy to talk, so he played on his flute as you went down the path together. He would have come all the way down, but it was too far, and presently he turned back; but the notes of the flute were still in the air.

They were husband and wife, without children, and comparatively young. Short and well-built, they were a strong, healthy-looking couple. She looked straight at you, but he would look at you only when you weren't looking at him. They had come once or twice before, and there was a change in them. Physically they were about the same, but there was something different in their look, in the way they sat, and in the set of their heads; they had the air of people who were becoming, or had already become, important. Being out of their usual element, they were feeling a little awkward, constrained, and appeared not to be quite sure why they had come, or what to say; so they began by talking about their travels, and about other matters that were not of great interest to them under the present circumstances.

"Of course," said the husband at last, "we do believe in the Masters, but at the moment we are not giving emphasis to all that. People don't understand, and make the Masters into saviours, super-*gurus*— and what you say about *gurus* is perfectly right. To us, the Masters are our own higher selves; they exist, not just as a matter of belief, but as an everyday occurrence in our daily living. They guide our lives; they instruct and point the way."

To what, sir, if one may ask?

"To the evolutionary and nobler processes of life. We have pictures of the Masters, but they are merely symbols, images for the mind to dwell on, in order to bring something greater into our petty lives. Otherwise life becomes tawdry, empty and very superficial. As there are leaders in the political and economic fields, so these symbols act as guides in the realm of higher thought. They are as necessary as light in darkness. We are not intolerant of other guides, other symbols; we welcome them all, for in these troubled times, man needs all the help he can get. So we are not intolerant; but you appear to be both intolerant and rather dogmatic when you deny the Masters as guides, and reject every other form of authority. Why do you insist that man must be free from authority? How could we exist in this world if there were not some kind of law and order, which after all is based on authority? Man is sorely tried, and he needs those who can help and deeply comfort him."

Which man?

"Man in general. There may be exceptions, but the common man needs some kind of authority, a guide who will lead him from a sensate life to the life of the spirit. Why are you against authority?"

There are many kinds of authority, are there not? There is the authority of the State for the so-called common good. There is the authority of the church, of dogma and belief, which is called religion, to save man from evil and help him to be civilized. There is the authority of society, which is the authority of tradition, of greed, envy, ambition; and the authority of personal knowledge or experience, which is the result of our conditioning, of our education. There is also the authority of the specialist, the authority of talent, and the authority of brute force, whether of a government or an individual. Why do we seek authority?

"That's fairly obvious, isn't it? As I said, man needs something to guide himself by; being confused, he naturally seeks an authority to lead him out of his confusion."

Sir, aren't you speaking of man as though he were a being, different from yourself? Don't you also seek authority?

"Yes, I do."

Why?

"The physicist knows more than I about the structure of matter, and if I want to learn the facts in that field, I go to him. If I have a toothache, I go to a dentist. If I am inwardly confused, which often happens, I seek the guidance of the higher self, the Master, and so on. What's wrong with that?"

It is one thing to go to the dentist, or to keep to the right or the left side of the road, or to pay taxes; but is this the same as accepting authority in order to be free from sorrow? The two are entirely different, are they not? Is psychological pain to be understood and eliminated by following the authority of another?

"The psychologist or the analyst can frequently help the disordered mind to resolve its problem. Authority in such cases is obviously beneficial."

But why do you look to the authority of what you call the higher self, or the Master?

"Because I am confused."

Can a confused mind ever seek out what is true?

"Why not?"

Do what it will, a confused mind can only find further confusion; its search for the higher self, and the response it receives, will be according to its confused state. When there's clarity, there's an end to authority.

"There are moments when my mind is clear."

You are saying, in effect, that you are not totally confused, that there is a part of you which is clear; and this supposedly clear part is what you call the higher self, the Master, and so on. I am not saying this in any derogatory manner. But can there be one part of the mind which is confused, and another part which is not? Or is this just wishful thinking?

"I only know there are moments when I am not confused."

Can clarity know itself as being non-confused? Can confusion recognize clarity? If confusion recognizes clarity, then what is recognized is still part of confusion. If clarity knows itself as a state of non-confusion, then it is the result of comparison; it is comparing itself with confusion, and so it's part of confusion.

"You are telling me that I am totally confused, aren't you, sir? But that just isn't so," he insisted.

Are you aware first of confusion or of clarity?

"Isn't that like asking which came first, the chicken or the egg?"

Not quite. When you are happy, you are not aware of it; it is only when happiness is not there that you search for it. When you are aware that you are happy, at that very moment happiness ceases. In looking to the *Atman*—the supra-mind, the Master, or whatever else you may name it—to clear up your confusion, you are acting from confusion; your action is the outcome of a conditioned mind, isn't it?

"Perhaps."

Being confused, you are seeking or establishing an authority so as to clear up that confusion, which only makes matters worse.

"Yes," he agreed reluctantly.

If you see the truth of this, then your only concern is with the clearing up of your confusion, and not with the establishing of authority, which has no meaning.

"But how am I to clear up my confusion?"

By really being honest in your confusion. To admit to oneself that one is totally confused is the beginning of understanding.

"But I have a position to maintain," he said impulsively.

That's just it. You have a position of leadership—and the leader is as confused as those that are led. It is the same all over the world. Out of his confusion, the follower or the disciple chooses the leader, the teacher, the *guru;* so confusion prevails. If you really wish to be free of confusion, then that is your primary concern, and maintaining a position has no longer any importance. But you have been playing this game of hide-and-seek with yourself for some time, haven't you, sir?

"I suppose I have."

Everyone wants to be somebody, and so we bring more confusion and sorrow upon ourselves and upon others; and yet we talk about saving the world! One must first clarify one's own mind, and not be concerned with the confusion of others.

There was a long pause. Then the wife, who had been silently listening, spoke in a rather hurt voice.

"But we want to help others, and we have given our lives to it. You can't take away from us this desire, after all the good work we have done. You are too destructive, too negative. You take away, but what do you give? You may have found the truth, but we haven't; we are seekers, and we have a right to our convictions."

Her husband was looking at her rather anxiously, wondering what was going to come out, but she went right on.

"After working all these years, we have built up for ourselves a position in our organization; for the first time we have an opportunity to be leaders, and it is our duty to take it."

Do you think so?

"I most certainly do."

Then there is no problem. I am not trying to convince you of anything, or to convert you to a particular point of view. To think from a conclusion or a conviction is not to think at all; and living is then a form of death, is it not?

"Without our convictions, life for us would be empty. Our convictions have made us what we are; we believe in certain things, and they have become part of our very make-up."

Whether they have validity or not? Has a belief any validity?

"We have given a great deal of consideration to our beliefs, and have found that they have truth behind them."

How do you find out the truth of a belief?

"We know whether there's an underlying truth in a belief or not," she replied vehemently.

But how do you know?

"Through our intelligence, our experience, and the test of our daily living, of course."

Your beliefs are based on your education, on your culture; they are the outcome of your background, of social, parental, religious or traditional influence, are they not?

"What's wrong with that?"

When the mind is already conditioned by a set of beliefs, how can it ever find out the truth about them? Surely, the mind must first free itself from its beliefs, and only then can the truth concerning them be perceived. It is as absurd for a Christian to scoff at the beliefs and dogmas of Hinduism, as it is for a Hindu to deride the Christian dogma which asserts that only through a certain belief can you be saved, for they are both in the same boat. To understand the truth with regard to belief, conviction, dogma, there must first be freedom from all conditioning as a Christian, a Communist, a Hindu, a Moslem, or what you will. Otherwise you are merely repeating what you have been told.

"But belief based on experience is a different matter," she asserted.

Is it? Belief projects experience, and such experience then strengthens the belief. Our visions are the outcome of our conditioning, the religious as well as the non-religious. This is so, isn't it?

"Sir, what you say is too devastating," she remonstrated. "We are weak, we cannot stand on our own feet, and we need the support of our beliefs."

By insisting that you cannot stand on your own feet, you are obviously making yourself weak; and then you allow yourself to be exploited by the exploiter whom you have created.

"But we need help."

When you do not seek it, help comes. It may come from a leaf, from a smile, from the gesture of a child, or from any book. But if you make the book, the leaf, the image, all-important, then you are lost, for you are caught in the prison of your own making.

She had become quieter now, but was still worried about something. The husband too was on the point of speaking, but restrained himself. We all waited in silence, and presently she spoke.

"From everything you have said, it seems that you regard power as evil. Why? What's wrong with exercising power?"

What do you mean by power? The dominance of a State, of a group, of a *guru*, of a leader, of an ideology; the pressure of propaganda, through which the clever and the cunning exert their influence over the so-called mass—is this what you mean by power?

"Somewhat, yes. But there's the power to do good as well as the power to do evil."

Power in the sense of ascendancy, dominance, forceful influence over another, is evil at all times; there is no 'good' power.

"But there are people who seek power for the good of their country, or in the name of God, peace or brotherhood, aren't there?"

There are, unfortunately. If one may ask, are you seeking power?

"We are," she replied defiantly. "But only in order to do good to others."

That's what they all say, from the most cruel tyrant to the so-called democratic politician, from the *guru* to the irritated parent.

"But we are different. Having suffered so much ourselves, we want to help others to avoid the pitfalls that we have been through. People are children, and they must be helped for their own well-being. We really mean to do good."

Do you know what is the good?

"I think most of us know what is the good: not to do harm, to be kind, to be generous, to abstain from killing, and not to be concerned about oneself."

In other words, you want to tell people to be generous of heart and hand; but does this require a vast, landed organization, with the possibility that one of you may become the head of it?

"Our becoming the head of it is only to keep the organization moving along the right lines, and not for the sake of personal power."

Is having power in an organization so very different from personal power? You both want to enjoy the prestige of it, the opportunities for travel which it affords, the feeling of being important, and so on. Why not be simple about it? Why clothe all this with respectability? Why use a lot of noble words to cover up your desire for success and the recognition of it, which is what most human beings want?

"We only want to help people," she insisted.

Is it not strange that one refuses to see things as they are?

"Sir," chimed in the husband, "I don't think you understand our situation. We are ordinary people, and we don't pretend to be anything else; we have our faults, and we honestly admit our ambition. But those whom we respect, and who have been wise in many ways, have asked us to take this position, and if we didn't take it, it would fall into far worse hands—into the hands of people who are wholly concerned with themselves. So we feel that we must accept our responsibility, though we are not really worthy of it. I sincerely hope you understand."

Is it not rather for you to understand what you are doing? You are concerned with reform, are you not?

"Who isn't? The great leaders and teachers, past and present, have always been concerned with reform. Isolated hermits, *sannyasis*, are of little use to society."

Reform, though necessary, is not of much significance unless the whole of man is considered. Cutting down a few dead branches does not make the tree healthy if the roots are unsound. Mere reforms always need further reform. What is necessary is a total revolution in our thinking.

"But most of us are not capable of such a revolution, and fundamental change must be brought about gradually, through the evolutionary processes. It is our aspiration to aid in this gradual change, and we have dedicated our lives to the service of man. Shouldn't you be more tolerant of human weakness?"

Tolerance is not compassion, it's a thing put together by the cunning mind. Tolerance is the reaction from intolerance; but neither the tolerant nor the intolerant will ever be compassionate. Without love, all so-called good action can only lead to further mischief and misery. A mind that's ambitious, seeking power, does not know love, and it will never be compassionate. Love is not reform, but total action.

ATTENTION WITHOUT MOTIVE

IN THE NARROW, shady lane between two gardens, a young boy was playing a flute; it was a cheap wooden thing, and he was playing a popular cinema tune, but the purity of the notes filled the space in that lane. The white walls of the houses had been washed by the recent rains, and on those walls the shadows were dancing to the music of the flute. It was a sunny morning, there were scattered white clouds in the blue sky, and a pleasant breeze was blowing from the north. Beyond the houses and the gardens was the village, with huge trees towering over the thatched huts. Under those trees, women were selling fish, a few vegetables and some fried things. Little children were playing in the narrow road, and still smaller children were using the ditch as their toilet, unmindful of the grown-ups and the passing cars. There were many goats, and their small black and white kids were cleaner and even more spirited than the children. They were so soft to the touch, and they loved being petted. Passing under the barbed wire of their enclosure, they would run across the road into a small open space, nibble the grass, romp about, butt each other, jump up in the air with abandon, and then race back to their mothers. Cars slowed down to avoid them, and not one was run over. They seemed to have divine protection—only to be killed and eaten.

But the flute player was there among the green foliage, and the clear notes called one out of doors. The boy was dirty, his clothes torn and unwashed, his face aggressively sharp and complaining. No one had taught him to play the flute, and no one ever would; he had picked it up by himself, and as the cinema tune rolled out, the purity of the notes was extraordinary. It was strange for the mind to float on that purity. Moving a few paces away, it continued through the trees, over the houses and towards the sea. Its movement was not in time and space, but in purity. The word 'purity' is not purity; the word is tied to memory, and to the association of many things. This purity was not an invention of the mind; it was not a thing put together, only to be undone, through remembrance and comparison. The flute player was there, but the mind was infinitely far away—not in distance, nor in terms of memory. It was far away within itself, clear, untouched, alone, beyond the measure of time and recognition.

The small room overlooked a tiny garden full of flowers, with a spot of lawn. There was just enough room for the five of us, and for the small boy whom one had brought along. The boy would sit quietly for a while, and then get up and walk out of the door. He wanted to play, and the grown-up conversation was beyond him; but he had a serious air. Each time he came in, he would sit next to one of the men, who turned out to be his father, and their hands would touch; and presently he fell asleep, holding on to a finger.

They were all active men, obviously capable and energetic. Their respective professions as a lawyer, a government official, an engineer and a social worker were, except for that of the last, only a means of livelihood. Their real interest lay elsewhere, and they all seemed to reflect the culture of many generations.

"I am only concerned with myself," said the lawyer, "but not in the narrow, personal sense of self-improvement. The point is, I alone can break through the barrier of centuries and set my mind free. I am willing to listen, reason, discuss, but I abominate all influence. Influence, after all, is propaganda, and propaganda is the most stupid form of compulsion. I read a great deal, but I am constantly watching myself to see that I don't fall under the influence of the author's thought. I have attended many of your talks and discussions, sir, and I agree with you that any form of compulsion prevents understanding. Anyone who is persuaded, consciously or unconsciously, to think along a particular line, however apparently beneficial, is bound to end up in some form of frustration, because his fulfilment is according to the way of another, and so he can never really fulfil himself at all."

Are we not being influenced by something or other, most of the time? One may be unconscious of influence, but isn't it always present in many subtle forms? Is not thought itself the product of influence?

"The four of us have often talked this matter over," responded the official, "and we are still not very clear about it, otherwise we wouldn't be here. Personally, I have visited many teachers at their *ashramas* all over the country; but before meeting the master, I first try to meet the disciples to see how far they have merely been influenced to a better life. Some of the disciples are scandalized by this approach, and they can't understand why I don't want to see the *guru* first. They are almost entirely under the heel of authority; and the *ashramas,* particularly the larger ones, are sometimes very efficiently run, like any office or factory. People turn over all their property and possessions to the central authority, and then remain in the *ashrama,* under guidance, for the rest of their lives. You would be surprised at the kind of people one finds there, a whole cross-section of society: retired government administrators, business men who have made their pile, a professor or two, and so on. And they are all dominated by the so-called spiritual influence of the *guru.* It's pathetic, but there it is!"

Is influence or compulsion restricted to the *ashrama?* The hero, the ideal, the political Utopia, the future as a symbol of achieving or becoming something—do not these things exert their subtle influence on each one of us? And must not the mind also be free of this kind of compulsion?

"We don't go that far," said the social worker. "We stay wisely within certain limits, otherwise there might be utter chaos."

To discard compulsion in one form, only to accept it in a more subtle form, seems a futile endeavor, does it not?

"We want to go step by step, systematically and thoroughly understanding one form of compulsion after another," said the engineer.

Is such a thing ever possible? Mustn't compulsion or influence be tackled as a whole, not bit by bit? In trying to discard one pressure after another, is there not in this very process the maintenance of that which you are trying to discard, perhaps at a different level? Can envy be got rid of little by little? Does not the very effort sustain envy?

"To build anything takes time. One can't put up a bridge all at once. Time is needed for everything—for the seed to bear fruit, and for man to mature."

In certain things, time is obviously necessary. To perform a series of actions, or to move in space from here to there, takes time. But apart from chronology, time is a plaything of the mind, is it not? Time is used as a means to achieve, to become something, positively or negatively; time exists in comparison. The thought "I am *this*, and I shall become *that*" is the way of time. The future is the modified past, and the present becomes merely a movement or passage from the past to the future, and so is of little importance. Time as a means of achievement has tremendous influence, it exerts the pressure of centuries of tradition. Is this process of attraction and compulsion, which is both negative and positive, to be understood bit by bit, or must it be seen as a whole?

"If I may interrupt, I would like to go on with what I was saying at the beginning," protested the lawyer. "To be influenced is not to think at all, and that's why I am only concerned with myself—but not in a self-centred way. If I may be personal, I have read some of the things you have said about authority, and I am working on the same lines. It is for this reason that I no longer go anywhere near the various teachers. Authority—not in the civil or legal sense—is to be avoided by an intelligent man."

Are you merely concerned with freedom from outward authority, from the influence of newspapers, books, teachers, and so on? Must you not also be free from every form of inward compulsion, from the pressures of the mind itself, not merely the surface mind, but the deep unconscious? And is this possible?

"That's one of the things I have been wanting to talk over with you. If one is somewhat aware, it's comparatively easy to observe and be free of the imprint made on the conscious mind by passing influences and pressures from without; but the conditioning and influence of the unconscious is a problem quite difficult to understand."

The unconscious is a result—is it not?—of innumerable influences and compulsions, both self-imposed and imposed by society.

"It is most definitely influenced by the culture or society in which one has been brought up; but whether this conditioning is total, or only segmentary, I am not at all sure."

Do you want to find out?

"Of course I do, that's why I am here."

How is one to find out? The 'how' is the process of inquiry, it is not the search for a method. If one is seeking a method, then inquiry has stopped. It's fairly obvious that the mind is influenced, educated, shaped, not only by the present culture, but by centuries of culture. What we are attempting to find out is whether only part of the mind, or the whole of consciousness, is thus influenced, conditioned.

"Yes, that is the question."

What do we mean by consciousness? Motive and action; desire, fulfilment and frustration; fear and envy; tradition, racial inheritance and the experiences of the individual based upon the collective past; time as past and future—all this is the essence of consciousness, the very centre of it, is it not?

"Yes; and I quite perceive the vast complexity of it."

Does one feel the nature of consciousness for oneself, or is one influenced by another's description of it?

"To be quite honest, both; I feel the nature of my own consciousness, but it helps to have a description of it."

How arduous it is to be free of influence! Putting aside the description, can one feel out the nature of consciousness and not merely theorize about it, or indulge in explanations? It is important to do this, isn't it?

"I suppose it is," put in the official hesitantly. The lawyer was absorbed in his own thoughts.

To feel out for oneself the nature of consciousness is an entirely different experience from recognizing its nature through a description.

"Of course it is," replied the lawyer, back on the scene again. "One is the influence of words, and the other is the direct experiencing of what's taking place."

The state of direct experiencing is attention without motive. When there is the desire to achieve a result, there is experiencing with a motive, which only leads to the further conditioning of the mind. To learn, and to learn with a motive, are contradictory processes, are they not? Is one learning when there's a motive to learn? The accumulation of knowledge, or the acquisition of technique, is not the movement of learning. Learning is a movement which is not away from or towards something; it ceases when there is the accumulation of knowledge in order to gain, to achieve, to arrive. Feeling out the nature of consciousness, learning about it, is without motive; there is no experiencing, or being taught, in order to be or not to be something. To have a motive, a cause, ever brings about pressure, compulsion.

"Are you implying, sir, that true freedom is without a cause?"

Of course. Freedom is not a reaction to bondage; when it is, then that freedom becomes another bondage. That's why it's very important to find out if one has a motive to be free. If one has, then the result is not freedom, but merely the opposite of what *is*.

"Then to feel out the nature of consciousness, which is the direct experiencing of it without any motive, is already a freeing of the mind from influence. Is that it?"

Isn't that so? Haven't you found that a motive invites influence, coercion, conformity? For the mind to be free from pressure, pleasant or unpleasant, all motive, however subtle or noble, must wither away —but not through any form of compulsion, discipline or suppression, which will only bring about another kind of bondage.

"I see," went on the lawyer. "Consciousness is a whole complex of interrelated motives. To understand this complex, one must feel it out, learn about it, without any further motive; for all motives inevitably bring about some kind of influence, pressure. Where there's a motive of any kind, there's no freedom. I am beginning to understand this very clearly."

"But is it possible to act without a motive?" asked the social worker. "It seems to me that motive is inseparable from action."

What do you mean by action?

"The village needs cleaning up, the children must be educated, the law must be enforced, reforms must be carried out, and so on. All this is action, and behind it there's definitely some kind of motive. If action with a motive is wrong, then what's right action?"

The Communist thinks his is the right way of life; so does the capitalist, and the so-called religious man. Governments have five or ten-year plans, and impose certain legislation to carry them out. The social reformer conceives of a way of life, which he insists upon as being right action. Every parent, every school teacher, enforces tradition and attention. There are innumerable political and religious organizations, each with its leader, and each with power, gross or subtle, to enforce what it calls right action.

"Without all this, there would be chaos, anarchy."

We are not condemning or defending any way of life, any leader or teacher; we are trying to understand, through this maze, what right action is. All these individuals and organizations, with their proposals and counter-proposals, are trying to influence thought in this or that direction, and what is called right action by some, is considered by others to be wrong action. This is so, isn't it?

"Yes, to a certain extent," agreed the social worker. "But though it's obviously incomplete, fragmentary, no one thinks of political action, for example, as being either right or wrong in itself; it's just a necessity. Then what is right action?"

Trying to bring together all these conflicting notions does not make for right action, does it?

"Of course not."

Seeing the mess the world is in, the individual reacts to it in different ways; he maintains that he must understand himself first, that he must cleanse his own being, and so on; or else he becomes a reformer, a doctrinaire, a politician, seeking to influence the minds of others to conform to a particular pattern. But the individual who thus reacts to the social confusion and disorder is still part of it; his action, being really a reaction, can only bring about confusion in another form. None of this is right action. Right action, surely, is total action, it is not fragmentary or contradictory; and it is total action alone that can respond adequately to all political and social demands.

"What is this total action?"

Haven't you to find that out for yourself? If you are told what it is, and you agree or disagree, it will only lead to another fragmentary action, won't it? Reformatory activity within society, and activity on the part of the individual as opposed to or apart from society, is incomplete action. Total action lies beyond these two, and that total action is love.

THE VOYAGE ON AN UNCHARTED SEA

THE SUN had just set behind the trees and the clouds, and the golden glow came through a window of the large room, which was filled with people listening to the music of an eight-stringed instrument accompanied by a small drum. Almost everyone in that audience was following the music with complete absorption, especially a girl in a bright dress, who sat like a statue, her hand keeping perfect time as it gently beat out the rhythm on her thigh. That was the only movement she made; with head erect and eyes glued on the man with the instrument, she was oblivious to everything else about her. Several others in the audience were keeping time with their hands or their heads. They were all in raptures, and the world of wars, politicians, worries, had ceased to exist.

Outside the light was fading, and the flowers that shone with bright colours only a few minutes before had disappeared in the gathering darkness. The birds were quiet now, and one of those small owls was beginning to call. Someone was shouting from a house across the way; through the trees one or two stars could be seen, and a lizard on the white garden wall was just visible as it stealthily crawled towards an insect. But the music held the audience. It was pure and subtle music, with great depth of beauty and feeling. Suddenly the stringed instrument stopped, and the little drum took over; it spoke with a clarity and precision that were really quite incredible. The hands were astonishingly gentle and swift as they struck both sides of the little drum, whose sound said more than the wild chattering of men. That drum, if asked, could send out passionate messages with vigour and emphasis; but now it was speaking quietly of many things, and the mind rode upon the waves of its sound.

When the mind is on the flight of discovery, imagination is a dangerous thing. Imagination has no place in understanding; it destroys understanding as surely as does speculation. Speculation and imagination are the enemies of attention. But the mind was aware of this, and so there was no flight from which it had to be recalled. The mind was perfectly still—yet how rapid it was! It had moved to the ends of the earth and was back again even before it had started on its journey. It was faster than the fastest, and yet it could be slow—so slow that no detail escaped it. The music, the audience, the lizard, were only a brief movement within it. It was perfectly still, and because it was still, it was alone. Its stillness was not the stillness of death, nor was it a thing put together by thought, coerced and brought into being by the vanity of man. It was a movement beyond the measure of man, a movement which was not of time, which had no going and coming, but which was still with the unknown depths of creation.

In his late forties, and rather plump, he had been educated abroad; and quietly, in a roundabout way, he conveyed that he knew all the important people. He made his living by writing for the newspapers about serious subjects, and giving talks all over the country; and he also had some other source of income. He appeared to be well-read, and was interested in religion—as most people are, he added.

"I have a *guru* of my own and I go to him as regularly as possible, but I am not one of those blind followers. As I travel a good bit, I have met many teachers, from the far north to the southernmost tip of the country. Some are obviously fakes, with a smattering of book knowledge cleverly disguised as their own experience. There are others who have done years of meditation, who practise various forms of yoga, and so on. A few of these are very advanced, but the majority of them are as superficial as any other set of specialists. They know their limited subject, and are satisfied with it. There are *ashramas* whose spiritual teachers are efficient, capable, assertive and completely autocratic, full of their own sublimated ego. I am telling you all this, not as gossip, but to indicate that I am serious in my search for truth, and that I am capable of discernment. I have attended some of your talks, when time has allowed; and while I have to write for a living and can't give all my time to the religious life, I am entirely serious about it."

If one may ask, what significance do you give to that word 'serious'?

"I do not trifle with religious matters, and I really want to lead a religious life. I set apart a certain hour of the day to meditate, and I give as much time as I can to deepening my inner life. I am very serious about it."

Most people are serious about something, are they not? They are serious about their problems, about the fulfilment of their desires, about their position in society, about their looks, their amusements, their money, and so on.

"Why do you compare me with others?" he asked, rather offended.

I am not belittling your seriousness, but each one of us is serious where his particular interests are concerned. A vain man is serious in his self-esteem; the powerful are serious about their importance and influence.

"But I am sober in my activities, and very earnest in my endeavour to lead a religious life."

Does the desire for something make for seriousness? If it does, then practically everyone is serious, from the cunning politician to the most exalted saint. The object of desire may be worldly or otherwise; but everyone is serious who is after something, isn't he?

"Surely there is a difference," he replied with some irritation, "between the seriousness of the politician or the money-maker, and that of a religious man. The seriousness of a religious man has a quality which is wholly different."

Has it? What do you mean by a religious man?

"The man who is seeking God. The hermit or *sannyasi* who has renounced the world in order to find God, I would call truly serious. The seriousness of the others, including the artist and the reformer, is in a different category altogether."

Is the man who is seeking God really religious? How can he seek God if he does not know Him? And if he knows the God he seeks, what he knows is only what he has been told, or what he has read; or else it is based on his personal experience, which again is shaped by tradition, and by his own desire to find security in another world.

"Aren't you being a little too logical?"

Surely one must understand the myth-making mechanism of the mind before there can be the experiencing of that which is beyond the measure of the mind. There must be freedom from the known for the unknown to be. The unknown is not to be pursued or sought after. Is he serious who pursues a projection of his own mind, even when that projection is called God?

"If you put it that way, none of us are serious."

We are serious in pursuing what is pleasant, satisfying.

"What's wrong with that?"

It's neither right nor wrong, but simply a matter of fact. Is this not what is actually taking place with each one of us?

"I can only speak for myself, and I do not think that I am seeking God for my own gratification. I am denying myself many things, which isn't exactly a pleasure."

You deny yourself certain things for the sake of a greater satisfaction, don't you?

"But to seek God is not a matter of gratification," he insisted.

One may see the foolishness of pursuing worldly things, or be frustrated in the effort to achieve them, or be put off by the pain and strife which such achievement involves; and so one's mind turns to other-worldliness, to the pursuit of a joy or a bliss which is called God. In the very process of self-denial is its gratification. After all, you are seeking some form of permanency, aren't you?

"We all are; that's the nature of man."

So you are not seeking God, or the unknown, that which is above and beyond the transient, beyond strife and sorrow. What you are really seeking is a permanent state of undisturbed satisfaction.

"To put it so baldly sounds terrible."

But that is the actual fact, is it not? It is in the hope of attaining total gratification that we go from one teacher to another, from one religion to another, from one system to another. About that we are very serious.

"Conceded," he said without conviction.

Sir, this is not a matter of concession, or of verbal agreement. It is a fact that we are all serious in our search for contentment, deep satisfaction, however much the manner of achieving it may vary. You may discipline yourself in order to acquire power and position in this world, whereas I may rigorously practise certain methods in the hope of attaining a so-called spiritual state, but the motivation in each case is essentially the same. One pursuit may not be as socially harmful as the other, but both of us are seeking gratification, the continuation of that centre which is ever wanting to succeed, to be or become something.

"Am I really seeking to be something?"

Aren't you?

"I don't care about being known as a writer, but I do want the ideas or principles of which I write to be accepted by the important people."

Aren't you identifying yourself with those ideas?

"I suppose I am. One tends, in spite of oneself, to use ideas as a means to fame."

That's just it, sir. If we can think simply and directly about it, the situation will be clarified. Most of us are concerned, both outwardly and inwardly, with our own advancement. But to perceive the facts about oneself as they are, and not as one would like them to be, is quite arduous; it demands an unbiased perception, without the recognizing memory of right and wrong.

"You are surely not totally condemning ambition, are you?"

To examine what *is*, is neither to condemn nor to justify. Self-fulfilment in any form is obviously the perpetuation of this centre that is striving to be or become something. You may want to become famous through your writing, and I may want to achieve what I call God or reality, which has its own conscious or unconscious benefits. Your pursuit is called worldly, and mine is called religious or spiritual;

but apart from the labels, is there so very much difference between them? The aim of desire may vary, but the underlying motive is the same. Ambition to fulfil, or to become something, has always within it the seed of frustration, fear and sorrow. This self-centred activity is the very nature of egotism, is it not?

"Good heavens, you are stripping me of everything: of my vanities, my desire to be famous, even of my drive to put across some worthwhile ideas. What shall I do when all this is gone?"

Your question indicates that *nothing* is gone, doesn't it? No one can take away from you, inwardly, what you don't want to give up. You will continue on your way to fame, which is the way of sorrow, frustration, fear.

"Sometimes I do want to chuck the whole rotten business, but the pull is strong." His tone had become anxious and earnest. "What will stop me from taking that path?"

Are you asking this question seriously?

"I think I am. Sorrow, I suppose?"

Is sorrow the way of understanding? Or does sorrow exist because there's no understanding? If you examined the whole urge to become something, and the path of fulfilment, not just intellectually, but deeply, then intelligence, understanding, would come into being and destroy the root of sorrow. But sorrow does not bring understanding.

"How is that, sir?"

Sorrow is the result of a shock, it is the temporary shaking up of a mind that has settled down, that has accepted the routine of life. Something happens—a death, the loss of a job, the questioning of a cherished belief—and the mind is disturbed. But what does a disturbed mind do? It finds a way to be undisturbed again; it takes refuge in another belief, in a more secure job, in a new relationship. Again the wave of life comes along and shatters its safeguards, but the mind soon finds still further defences; and so it goes on. This is not the way of intelligence, is it?

"Then what *is* the way of intelligence?"

Why are you asking another? Don't you want to find out for yourself? If I were to give you an answer, you would either refute or accept it, which again would impede intelligence, understanding.

"I see what you have said about sorrow to be perfectly true. That's exactly what we all do. But how is one to get out of this trap?"

No form of external or inward compulsion will help, will it? All compulsion, however subtle, is the outcome of ignorance; it is born of the desire for reward or the fear of punishment. To understand the whole nature of the trap is to be free of it; no person, no system, no belief, can set you free. The truth of this is the only liberating factor —but you have to see it for yourself, and not merely be persuaded. You have to take the voyage on an uncharted sea.

ALONENESS BEYOND LONELINESS

THE MOON was just coming out of the sea into a valley of clouds. The waters were still blue, and Orion was faintly visible in the pale silver sky. The white waves were all along the shore, and the fishermen's huts, square, neat and dark against the white sands, were close to the water. The walls of these huts were made of bamboo, and the roofs were thatched with palm leaves laid one on top of another, sloping downward so that the heavy rains couldn't come inside. Completely round and full, the moon was making a path of light on the moving waters, and it was huge—you couldn't have held it in your arms. Rising above the valley of clouds, it had the heavens to itself. The sound of the sea was unceasing, and yet there was a great silence.

You never remain with any feeling, pure and simple, but always surround it with the paraphernalia of words. The word distorts it; thought, whirling round it, throws it into shadow, overpowers it with mountainous fears and longings. You never remain with a feeling, and with nothing else: with hate, or with that strange feeling of beauty. When the feeling of hate arises, you say how bad it is; there is the compulsion, the struggle to overcome it, the turmoil of thought about it. You want to remain with love; but you break it up, calling it personal or impersonal; you cover it with words, giving it the ordinary meaning, or saying that it is universal; you explain how to feel it, how to maintain it, why it fades away; you think of someone whom you love, or who loves you. There is every kind of verbal movement.

Try remaining with the feeling of hate, with the feeling of envy, jealousy, with the venom of ambition; for after all, that's what you have in daily life, though you may want to live with love, or with the word 'love'. Since you have the feeling of hate, of wanting to hurt somebody with a gesture or a burning word, see if you can stay with that feeling. Can you? Have you ever tried? Try to remain with a feel-

196

ing, and see what happens. You will find it amazingly difficult. Your mind will not leave the feeling alone; it comes rushing in with its remembrances, its associations, its do's and don'ts, its everlasting chatter. Pick up a piece of shell. Can you look at it, wonder at its delicate beauty, without saying how pretty it is, or what animal made it? Can you look without the movement of the mind? Can you live with the feeling behind the word, without the feeling that the word builds up? If you can, then you will discover an extraordinary thing, a movement beyond the measure of time, a spring that knows no summer.

She was a small, elderly lady, with white hair and a face that was heavily lined, for she had borne many children; but there was nothing weak or feeble about her, and her smile conveyed the depth of her feeling. Her hands were wrinkled but strong, and they had evidently prepared many vegetables, for the right thumb and forefinger were covered with tiny cuts, which had become darkened. But they were fine hands—hands that had worked hard and wiped away many tears. She spoke quietly and hesitantly, with the voice of one who had suffered much; and she was very orthodox; for she belonged to an ancient caste that held itself high, and whose tradition it was to have no dealings with other groups, either through marriage or through commerce. They were people who were supposed to cultivate the intellect as a means to something other than the mere acquisition of things.

For a while neither of us spoke; she was gathering herself, and was not sure how to begin. She looked around the room, and seemed to approve of its bareness. There wasn't even a chair, or a flower, except for the one that could be seen just outside the window.

"I am now seventy-five," she began, "and you could be my son. How proud I would be of such a son! It would be a blessing. But most of us have no such happiness. We produce children who grow up and become men of the world, trying to be great in their little work. Though they may occupy high positions, they have no greatness in them. One of my sons is in the capital, and he has a great deal of power, but I know his heart as only a mother can. Speaking for myself, I don't want anything from anybody; I don't want more money, or a bigger house. I mean to live a simple life to the very end. My children laugh at my orthodoxy, but I mean to continue in it. They smoke, drink and often eat meat, thinking nothing of it. Though I love them, I will not eat with them, for they have become unclean; and why should I, in my old age, pander to all their nonsense? They want to marry out of caste, and they don't perform the religious rites, or practise meditation, as their father did. He was a religious man, but . . ." She stopped talking, and considered what she was going to say.

"I didn't come here to talk about my family," she continued, "but I am glad to have said what I did. My sons will go their way, and I cannot hold them, though it saddens me to see what they are coming to. They are losing and not gaining, even though they have money and position. When their names appear in the papers, as often happens, they show me the papers proudly; but they will be like the common run of men, and the quality of our forefathers is fast disappearing. They are all becoming merchants, selling their talents, and I can't do anything to stem the tide. But that's enough about my children."

Again she stopped talking, and this time it was going to be more difficult to speak of what was in her heart. With lowered head she was thinking how to put the words together, but they wouldn't come. She refused to be helped, and was not embarrassed to remain silent for a time. Presently she began.

"It's difficult to speak of things that are very deep, isn't it? One can talk of matters that do not lie too deeply, but it requires a certain confidence in oneself and in the listener to broach a problem, the very existence of which one has hardly admitted even to oneself for fear of awakening the echo of darker things that have been asleep for so long. In this case it isn't that I don't trust the listener," she added quickly. "I have more than confidence in you. But to put certain feelings into words is not easy, especially when one has never before expressed them in words. The feelings are familiar, but the words to describe them are not. Words are terrible things, aren't they? But I know you are not impatient, and I shall go at my own pace.

"You know how young people marry in this country, not by their own choice. My husband and I were married in that way many years ago. He was not a kindly man; he had a quick temper and was given to sharp words. Once he beat me; but I became used to many things in the course of my married life. Though as a child I used to play with my brothers and sisters, I spent a great deal of time by myself, and I always felt apart, alone. In living with my husband, that feeling was pushed into the background; there were so many things to do. I was kept very busy with housekeeping, and with the joy and the pain of bearing and raising children. Nevertheless, the feeling of being alone would still creep over me, and I would want to think about it, but there wasn't time; so it would pass off like a wave, and I would go on with what I had to do.

"When the children had grown up, been educated, and were out on their own—though one of my sons still lives with me—my husband and I lived quietly until he died five years ago. Since his death, this feeling of being alone has come over me more often; it has gradually increased until now, and I am fully immersed in it. I have tried to get away from it by doing *puja*, by talking to some friend, but it's always there; and it's an agony, a fearsome thing. My son has a radio, but I can't escape from this feeling through such means, and I don't like all that noise. I go to the temple; but this sense of being utterly alone is with me on the way, while I am there, and coming back. I am not exaggerating, but only describing the thing as it is." She paused for a moment, and then continued.

"The other day my son brought me along to your talk. I couldn't follow all that you were saying, but you mentioned something about aloneness, and the purity of it; so perhaps you will understand." There were tears in her eyes.

To find out if there is something deeper, something beyond the feeling that comes upon you, and in which you are caught, you must first understand this feeling, must you not?

"Will this agonizing feeling of being alone lead me to God?" she inquired anxiously.

What do you mean by being alone?

"It is difficult to put that feeling into words, but I will try. It is a fear that comes when one feels oneself to be completely alone, entirely by oneself, utterly cut off from everything. Though my husband and children were there, this wave would come upon me, and I would feel myself to be like a dead tree in a wasted land: lonely, unloved and unloving. The agony of it was much more intense than that of bearing a child. It was fearful and breath-taking; I didn't belong to anyone; there was a sense of complete isolation. You understand, don't you?"

Most people have this feeling of loneliness, this sense of isolation, with its fear, only they smother it, run away from it, get themselves lost in some form of activity, religious or otherwise. The activity in which they indulge is their escape, they can get lost in it, and that's why they defend it so aggressively.

"But I have tried my best to run away from this feeling of isolation, with its fear, and I haven't been able to. Going to the temple doesn't help; and even if it did, one can't be there all the time, any more than one can spend one's life performing rituals."

Not to have found an escape may be your salvation. In their fear of being lonely, of feeling cut off, some take to drink, others take drugs, while many turn to politics, or find some other way of escape. So you see, you are fortunate in not having found a means of avoiding this thing. Those who avoid it do a great deal of mischief in the world; they are really harmful people, for they give importance to things that are not of the highest significance. Often, being very clever and capable, such people mislead others by their devotion to the activity which is their escape; if it isn't religion, it's politics, or social reform—anything to get away from themselves. They may seem to be selfless, but they are actually still concerned with themselves, only in a different way. They become leaders, or the followers of some teacher; they always belong to something, or practise some method, or pursue an ideal. They are never just themselves; they are not human beings, but labels. So you see how fortunate you are not to have found an escape.

"You mean it's dangerous to escape?" she asked, somewhat bewildered.

Isn't it? A deep wound must be examined, treated, healed; it's no good covering it up, or refusing to look at it.

"That's true. And this feeling of isolation is such a wound?"

It's something you don't understand, and in that sense it's like a disease that will keep on recurring; so it's meaningless to run away from it. You have tried running away, but it keeps on overtaking you, doesn't it?

"It does. Then you are glad that I haven't found an escape?"

Aren't you?—which is much more important.

"I think I understand what you have explained, and I am relieved that there's some hope."

Now let's both examine the wound. To examine something, you mustn't be afraid of the thing you're going to see, must you? If you are afraid, you won't look; you will turn your head away. When you had babies, you looked at them as soon as possible after they were born. You weren't concerned with whether they were ugly or beautiful; you looked at them with love, didn't you?

"That's exactly what I did. I looked at each new baby with love, with care, and pressed it to my heart."

In the same way, with affection, we must examine this feeling of being cut off, this sense of isolation, of loneliness, mustn't we? If we are fearful, anxious, we shall be incapable of examining it at all.

"Yes, I see the difficulty. I haven't really looked at it before, because I was fearful of what I might see. But now I think I can look."

Surely, this ache of loneliness is only the final exaggeration of what we all feel in a minor way every day, isn't it? Every day you are isolating yourself, cutting yourself off, aren't you?

"How?" she asked, rather horrified.

In so many ways. You belong to a certain family, to a special caste; they are *your* children, *your* grandchildren; it is *your* belief, *your* God, *your* property; you are more virtuous than somebody else; you know, and another does not. All this is a way of cutting yourself off, a way of isolation, isn't it?

"But we are brought up that way, and one has to live. We can't cut ourselves off from society, can we?"

Is this not what you are actually doing? In this relationship called society, every human being is cutting himself off from another by his position, by his ambition, by his desire for fame, power, and so on; but he has to live in this brutal relationship with other men like himself, so the whole thing is glossed over and made respectable by pleasant-sounding words. In everyday life, each one is devoted to his own interests, though it may be in the name of the country, in the name of peace, or God, and so the isolating process goes on. One becomes aware of this whole process in the form of intense loneliness, a feeling of complete isolation. Thought, which has been giving all importance to itself, isolating itself as the 'me', the ego, has finally come to the point of realizing that it's held in the prison of its own making.

"I'm afraid all this is a bit difficult to follow at my age, and I'm not too well-educated either."

This has nothing to do with being educated. It needs thinking through, that's all. You feel lonely, isolated, and if you could, you would run away from that feeling; but fortunately for yourself, you have been unable to find a means of doing so. Since you have found no way out, you are now in a position to look at that from which you have been trying to escape; but you can't look if you are afraid of it, can you?

"I see that."

Doesn't your difficulty lie in the fact that the word itself makes trouble?

"I don't understand what you mean."

You have associated certain words with this feeling that comes over you, words like 'loneliness', 'isolation', 'fear', 'being cut off'. Isn't that so?

"Yes."

Now, just as your son's name doesn't prevent you from perceiving and understanding his real qualities and make-up, so you must not let such words as 'isolation', 'loneliness', 'fear', 'being cut off', interfere with your examination of the feeling they have come to represent.

"I see what you mean. I have always looked at my children in that direct way."

And when you look at this feeling in the same direct way, what happens? Don't you find that the feeling itself isn't frightening, but only what you *think* about the feeling? It is the mind, thought, that brings fear to the feeling, isn't it?

"Yes, that's right; at this moment I understand that very well. But will I be capable of understanding it when I leave here, and you are not there to explain?"

Of course. It is like seeing a cobra. Having once seen it, you can never mistake it; you don't have to depend on anybody to tell you what a cobra is. Similarly, when once you have understood this feeling, that understanding is always with you; when once you have learned to look, you have the capacity to see. But one must go through and beyond this feeling, for there is much more to be discovered. There is an aloneness which is not this loneliness, this sense of isolation. That state of aloneness is not a remembrance or a recognition; it is untouched by the mind, by the word, by society, by tradition. It is a benediction.

"In this one hour I have learned more than in all my seventy-five years. May that benediction be with you and with me."

"Why Did You Dissolve Your Order of the Star?"

Bathed in the light of the evening sun, a fisherman came swinging down the road with a smile on his face. He wore a piece of cloth attached to a string around his waist, but was otherwise completely naked. He had a magnificent body, and you could see that he was very proud of it. A car went by, driven by a chauffeur, and the lady inside was all dressed up. She must have been going to some party. She had jewels round her neck and in her ears, and there were flowers in her dark hair. The chauffeur was doing all the driving, and she was absorbed in herself. She didn't even look at the fisherman, nor was she aware of anything else about her; but the fisherman looked at the car as it went by, to see if he was noticed. He was walking quite fast, with a long, easy stride, never slackening his pace; but as each car passed he turned his head. Just before reaching the village he took a newly-made road of bright red earth, which in the last rays of the setting sun was redder than ever. Passing through a palm grove and along a canal, where there were some light barges loaded with fire-wood, the fisherman crossed a bridge and took a narrow path that led to the river.

It was very quiet by the river, for there were no houses nearby, and the noise of traffic didn't come that far. Land crabs had made large round holes in the damp mud, and a few cattle were about. The breeze was playing with the palms, and they were stately in their movement; they were all dancing, as if to music.

Meditation is not for the meditator. The meditator can think, reason, build up or tear down, but he will never know meditation; and without meditation, his life is as empty as the shell by the sea. Something can be put in that emptiness, but it is not meditation. Meditation is not an act whose worth can be weighed in the market-place; it has its own action, which cannot be measured. The meditator knows only the action of the market-place, with its noise of exchange; and through this noise, the noiseless action of meditation can never be found. The action of cause becoming effect, and effect becoming cause, is an everlasting chain that binds the meditator. Such action, being within the walls of his own prison, is not meditation. The meditator can never know meditation, which is just beyond his walls. It's only the walls that the meditator himself has built, high or low, thick or thin, that divide him from meditation.

He was a young man, just out of college and full of high spirits. Moved by an urge to do good, he had recently joined some movement in order to be more effective, and would like to have devoted his whole life to it; but unfortunately his father was an invalid, and he had to support his parents. He saw the drawbacks of the movement as well as its merits, but the good outweighed the bad. He was not married, he said, and would never be. His smile was friendly, and he was eager to express himself.

"The other day I was present at your talk, in which you were saying that truth cannot be organized, and that no organization can lead one to truth. You were very definite about it, but to me your explanation was not altogether satisfactory, and I want to talk it over with you. I know that you were once the head of a large organization, the Order of the Star, which you dissolved, and if I may ask, was this because of a personal whim, or was it motivated by a principle?"

Neither. If there is a cause for action, is it action? If you renounce because of a principle, an idea, a conclusion, is it renunciation? If you give up one thing for the sake of something greater, or for some person, is that giving up?

"Reason doesn't play a part in giving up anything; is that what you mean?"

Reason can make one behave in this manner or in that; but what reason has put together, reason can undo. If reason is the criterion of action, then the mind can never be free to act. Reason, however subtle and logical, is a process of thinking, and thinking is ever influenced, conditioned by personal fancy, by desire, or by an idea, a conclusion, whether imposed or self-induced.

"If it wasn't reason, principle or personal desire that made you do it, then was it something outside of yourself, a superior or divine agency?"

No. But perhaps it will be clear if we can approach it differently. What is your problem?

"You said that truth cannot be organized, and that no organization can lead man to truth. The organization to which I belong maintains that man can be led to truth through certain principles of action,

204

through right personal endeavour, giving oneself to good works, and so on. My problem is, am I on the right path?"

Do you think there's a path to truth?

"If I didn't think there were, I wouldn't belong to this organization. According to our leaders, this organization is based on truth; it's dedicated to the well-being of all, and it will help the villager as well as people who are highly educated and who hold responsible positions. However, when I heard you the other day, I was disturbed, and so took the first opportunity to come to see you. I hope you understand my difficulty."

Let's go into the matter slowly, step by step. First, is there a path to truth? A path implies going from one fixed point to another. As a living entity, you are changing, reshaping, pushing, questioning yourself, hoping to find a permanent, immutable truth. Isn't that so?

"Yes. I want to find truth, or God, in order to do good," he answered eagerly.

Surely, there's nothing permanent about you except what you *think* is permanent; but your thinking is also transient, is it not? And has truth a fixed place, without any movement?

"I don't know. One sees so much poverty, so much misery and confusion in the world, and in one's desire to do good, one accepts a leader or a philosophy that offers some hope. Otherwise life would be terrible."

All decent people want to do good, but most of us don't think the problem through. We say that we cannot think it through for ourselves, or that the leaders know better. But do they? Look at the various political leaders, the so-called religious leaders and the leaders of social and economic reform. They all have schemes, each saying that his scheme is the way to salvation, to the eradication of poverty, and so on; and individuals like you, who want to act in the face of all this misery and chaos, get caught in the net of propaganda and dogmatic assertions. Haven't you noticed that this very action breeds further misery and chaos?

Truth has no fixed abode; it's a living thing, more alive, more dynamic than anything the mind can think of, so there can be no path to it.

"I think I see that, sir. But are you against *all* organizations?"

It would obviously be silly to be 'against' the postal or other similar organizations. But you are not referring to such organizations, are you?

"No. I am talking about churches, spiritual groups, religious societies, and so on. The organization to which I belong embraces all religions, and anyone who is concerned with the physical and spiritual improvement of man may be a member. Of course, such organizations always have their leaders who say they know the truth, or who lead saintly lives."

Can truth be organized, with a president and secretary, or with high priests and interpreters?

"If I understand you correctly, it looks as though it can't be. Then why do these saintly leaders say that their organizations are necessary?"

It doesn't matter what the leaders say, for they are as blind as their followers, otherwise they wouldn't be leaders. What do *you* think, apart from your leaders? Are such organizations necessary?

"They may not be strictly necessary, but one does find comfort in belonging to such an organization, and in working with others of the same mind."

That's right. And there is also a sense of security in being told what to do, is there not? The leader knows, and you, the follower, do not; so under his direction you feel you can do the right thing. To have an authority over you, someone to guide you, is very comforting, especially when on all sides there is so much chaos and misery. That is why you become, not exactly a slave, but a follower, carrying out the plan laid down by the leader. It is you, the human being, who have made all this mess in the world, but you are not important; only the plan is important. But the plan is mechanical, it needs human beings to make it operate; therefore you become useful to the plan.

Then there are the priests, with their divine authority to save your soul, and from childhood you are conditioned by them to think in a certain way. Again, you as a human being are not important; it is not your freedom, not your love, that matters, but your soul, which has to be saved in accordance with the dogmas of a particular church or sect.

"I see the truth of this, all right, as you explain it. Then what is important in the midst of all this confusion?"

The important thing is to free your mind of envy, hate and violence; and for that you don't need an organization, do you? So-called religious organizations never liberate the mind, they only make it conform to a certain creed or belief.

"I need to change; there must be love in me, I must cease to be envious, and then I shall always act rightly. I won't have to be told what right action is. I see now that this is the only thing that matters, not what organization I belong to."

One may follow what is generally considered to be right action, or be told what right action is; but that does not bring about love, does it?

"No, it quite obviously does not; one is merely pursuing a pattern created by the mind. Again, I see this very clearly, sir, and I now understand why you dissolved the organization of which you were the head. One has to be a light unto oneself; following the light of another only leads one into darkness."

WHAT IS LOVE?

THE LITTLE GIRL next door was ill, and she had been crying, off and on, all day long, and far into the night. This had been going on for some time, and the poor mother was worn out. There was a small plant in the window which she used to water every evening, but for the past few days it had been neglected. The mother was alone in the house, except for a rather helpless and inefficient servant, and she seemed somewhat lost, for the child's illness was evidently serious. The doctor had driven up several times in his big car, and the mother became sadder and sadder.

A banana-plant in the garden was irrigated by the kitchen water, and the soil around it was always damp. Its leaves were dark green, and there was one very large leaf, two or three feet across and much more in length, which had so far not been torn by the winds, like the other leaves. It would sway very gently in the breeze, and it was touched only by the western sun. It was a wonderful thing to see the yellow flowers in descending circles on a long, drooping stem. These flowers would soon be young bananas, and the stem would become quite thick, for there might be dozens of them, rich, green and heavy. Now and then a shiny black bumble-bee would go in among the yellow flowers, and several black and white butterflies would come and flutter about them. There seemed to be such an abundance of life in that banana-plant, especially with the sun upon it, and with its large leaves stirring in the breeze. The little girl often used to play around it, and she was so full of fun and smiles. Sometimes we would walk together a short distance down the lane as the mother watched, and then she would go running back. We couldn't understand each other, for our words were different, but that didn't stop her from talking; so we talked.

One afternoon the mother beckoned me in. The little girl was skin and bones; she smiled weakly, then closed her eyes in utter exhaustion. She was sleeping fitfully. Through the open window came the noise of other children, shouting and playing. The mother was speechless and bereft of all tears. She wouldn't sit down, but stood by the little cot, and there was despair and longing in the air. Just then the doctor came in, and I left, with a silent promise to return.

The sun was setting behind the trees, and the huge clouds above it were brilliantly golden. There were the usual crows, and a parrot came screeching in and clung to the edge of a hole in a large, dead tree, with its tail pressed against the trunk; it hesitated, seeing a human being so close, but an instant later disappeared into the hole. There were a few villagers on the road, and a car went by, loaded with young people. A week-old calf was tied to a fence post, with its mother grazing nearby. A woman was coming down the road with a brightly-polished brass vessel on her head, and another on her hip; she was carrying water from the well. She used to go by every evening; and that evening especially, against the setting sun, she was the earth itself in motion.

Two young men had come from the town nearby. The bus had brought them to the corner, and they had walked the rest of the way. They worked in an office, they said, and so couldn't come any earlier. They had put on fresh clothes, which the old bus hadn't soiled, and they came in smiling but rather shyly, their manner hesitantly respectful. Once seated, they soon forgot their shyness, but they still weren't quite sure how to put their thoughts into words.

What sort of work do you do?

"We are both employed in the same office; I am a stenographer, and my friend keeps accounts. Neither of us has been to college, because we couldn't afford it, and neither of us is married. We don't get much pay, but as we have no family responsibilities, it's enough for our needs. If either of us ever gets married, it will be quite another matter."

"We are not very well-educated," added the second one, "and though we read a certain amount of serious literature, our reading isn't intensive. We spend a great deal of time together, and on holidays we go back to our families. There are very few in the office who are interested in serious things. A mutual friend brought us to your talk the other day, and we asked if we could see you. May I ask a question, sir?"

Of course.

"What is love?"

Do you want a definition of it? Don't you know what that word means?

"There are so many ideas about what love *should* be, that it's all rather confusing," said the first one.

What sort of ideas?

"That love shouldn't be passionate, lustful; that one should love one's neighbour as oneself; that one should love one's father and mother; that love should be the impersonal love of God, and so on. Every man gives an opinion according to his fancy."

Apart from the opinions of others, what do *you* think? Have you opinions about love too?

"It's difficult to put into words what one feels," replied the second one. "I think love must be universal; one must love all, without prejudice. It's prejudice that destroys love; it's class consciousness that creates barriers and divides people. The sacred books say that we must love one another, and not be personal or limited in our love, but sometimes we find this very difficult."

"To love God is to love all," added the first one. "There's only divine love; the rest is carnal, personal. This physical love prevents divine love; and without divine love, all other love is mere barter and exchange. Love is not sensation. Sexual sensation must be checked, disciplined; that's why I'm against birth control. Physical passion is destructive; through chastity lies the way to God."

Before we go further, don't you think we ought to find out if all these opinions have any validity? Is not one opinion as good as another? Regardless of who holds it, is not opinion a form of prejudice, a bias created by one's temperament, one's experience, and the way one happens to have been brought up?

"Do you think it is wrong to hold an opinion?" asked the second one.

To say that it is wrong or right would merely be another opinion, wouldn't it? But if one begins to observe and understand how opinions are formed, then perhaps one may be able to perceive the actual significance of opinion, judgment, agreement.

"Would you kindly explain?"

Thought is the result of influence, isn't it? Your thinking and your opinions are dictated by the way you have been brought up. You say, "This is right, and that is wrong", according to the moral pattern of your particular conditioning. We are not for the moment concerned with what is true beyond all influence, or whether there is such truth. We are trying to see the significance of opinions, beliefs, assertions, whether they be collective or personal. Opinion, belief, agreement or disagreement, are responses according to one's background, narrow or wide. Isn't that so?

"Yes, but is that wrong?"

Again, if you say it's right or wrong, you are still in the field of opinions. Truth is not a matter of opinion; a fact does not depend on agreement or belief. You and I may agree to call this object a watch, but by any other name it would still be what it is. Your belief or opinion is something that has been given to you by the society in which you live. In revolting against it, as a reaction, you may form a different opinion, another belief; but you are still on the same level, aren't you?

"I am sorry, sir, but I don't understand what you are getting at," replied the second one.

You have certain ideas and opinions about love, haven't you?

"Yes."

How did you get them?

"I have read what the saints and the great religious teachers have said about love, and having thought it over, I have formed my own conclusions."

Which are shaped by your likes and dislikes, are they not? You like or you don't like what others have said about love, and you decide which statement is right and which is wrong according to your own predilection. Isn't this what you do?

"I choose that which I consider to be true."

On what is your choice based?

"On my own knowledge and discernment."

What do you mean by knowledge? I'm not trying to trip or corner you, but together we are trying to understand why one has opinions, ideas, conclusions, about love. If once we understand this, we can go very much more deeply into the matter. So, what do you mean by knowledge?

"By knowledge I mean what I have learnt from the teachings of the sacred books."

"Knowledge embraces also the techniques of modern science, and all the information that has been gathered by man from ancient days up to the present time," added the other.

So knowledge is a process of accumulation, is it not? It is the cultivation of memory. The knowledge that we have accumulated as scientists, musicians, type-setters, scholars, engineers, makes us technicians in various departments of life. When we have to build a bridge, we think as engineers, and this knowledge is part of the tradition, part of the background, or conditioning, that influences all our thinking. Living, which includes the capacity to build a bridge, is a total action, not a separate, partial activity; yet our thinking about life, about love, is shaped by opinions, conclusions, tradition. If you were brought up in a culture which maintained that love is only physical, and that divine love is all nonsense, you would, in the same way, repeat what you had been taught, wouldn't you?

"Not always," replied the second one. "I admit it's rare, but some of us do rebel and think for ourselves."

Thought may rebel against the established pattern, but this very revolt is generally the outcome of another pattern; the mind is still caught in the process of knowledge, tradition. It is like rebelling within the walls of a prison for more conveniences, better food, and so on.

So your mind is conditioned by opinions, tradition, knowledge, and by your ideas about love, which make you act in a certain way. That is clear, isn't it?

"Yes, sir, that is clear enough," answered the first one. "But then what is love?"

If you want a definition, you can look in any dictionary; but the words which define love are not love, are they? Merely to seek an explanation of what love is, is still to be caught in words, in opinions, which are accepted or rejected according to your conditioning.

"Aren't you making it impossible to inquire into what love is?" asked the second one.

Is it possible to inquire through a series of opinions, conclusions? To inquire rightly, thought must be freed from conclusion, from the security of knowledge, tradition. The mind may free itself from one series of conclusions, and form another, which is again only a modified continuity of the old.

Now, isn't thought itself a movement from one result to another, from one influence to another? Do you see what I mean?

"I'm not at all sure that I do," said the first one.

"I don't understand it at all," said the second.

Perhaps you will, as we go along. Let me put it this way: is thinking the instrument of inquiry? Will thinking help one to understand what love is?

"How am I to find out what love is if I'm not allowed to think?" asked the second one rather sharply.

Please be a little more patient. You have thought about love, haven't you?

"Yes. My friend and I have thought a great deal about it."

If one may ask, what do you mean when you say you have thought about love?

"I have read about it, discussed it with my friends, and drawn my own conclusions."

Has it helped you to find out what love is? You have read, exchanged opinions with each other, and come to certain conclusions about love, all of which is called thinking. You have positively or negatively described what love is, sometimes adding to, and sometimes taking away from, what you have previously learnt. Isn't that so?

"Yes, that's exactly what we have been doing, and our thinking has helped to clarify our minds."

Has it? Or have you become more and more entrenched in an opinion? Surely, what you call clarification is a process of coming to a definite verbal or intellectual conclusion.

"That's right; we are not as confused as we were."

In other words, one or two ideas stand out clearly in this jumble of teachings and contradictory opinions about love. Isn't that it?

"Yes; the more we have gone over this whole question of what love is, the clearer it has become."

Is it love that has become clear, or what you *think* about it?

Let us go a little further into this, shall we? A certain ingenious mechanism is called a watch because we have all agreed to use this word to indicate that particular thing; but the word 'watch' is obviously not the mechanism itself. Similarly, there is a feeling or a state which we have all agreed to call love; but the word is not the actual feeling, is it? And the word 'love' means so many different things. At one time you use it to describe a sexual feeling, at another time you talk about divine or impersonal love, or you assert what love should or should not be, and so on.

"If I may interrupt, sir, could it be that all these feelings are just varying forms of the same thing?" asked the first one.

How does it appear to you?

"I'm not sure. There are moments when love seems to be one thing, but at other moments it appears to be something quite different. It's all very confusing. One doesn't know where one is."

That's just it. We want to be sure of love, to peg it down, so that it won't elude us; we reach conclusions, make agreements about it; we call it by various names, with their special meanings; we talk about 'my love', just as we talk about 'my property', 'my family', 'my virtue', and we hope to lock it safely away, so that we can turn to other things and make sure of them too; but somehow it's always slipping away when we least expect it.

"I don't quite follow all this," said the second one, rather puzzled.

As we have seen, the feeling itself is different from what the books say about it; the feeling is not the description, it is not the word. That much is clear, isn't it?

"Yes."

Now, can you separate the feeling from the word, and from your preconceptions of what it should and should not be?

"What do you mean, 'separate'?" asked the first one.

There is the feeling, and the word or words which describe that feeling, either approvingly or disapprovingly. Can you separate the feeling from the verbal description of it? It's comparatively easy to separate an objective thing, like this watch, from the word which describes it; but to dissociate the feeling itself from the word 'love', with all its implications, is far more arduous and requires a great deal of attention.

"What good will that do?" asked the second one.

We always want to get a result in return for doing something. This desire for a result, which is another form of conclusion-seeking, prevents understanding. When you ask, "What good will it do me if I dissociate the feeling from the word 'love'?", you are thinking of a result; therefore you are not really inquiring to find out what that feeling is, are you?

"I do want to find out, but I also want to know what will be the outcome of dissociating the feeling from the word. Isn't this perfectly natural?"

Perhaps; but if you want to understand, you will have to give your attention, and there's no attention when one part of your mind is concerned with results, and the other with understanding. In this way you get neither, and so you become more and more confused, bitter and miserable. If we don't dissociate the word, which is memory and all its reactions, from the feeling, then that word destroys the feeling; and then the word, or memory, is the ash without the fire. Isn't this what has happened to you both? You have so entangled yourselves in a net of words, of speculations, that the feeling itself, which is the only thing that has deep and vital significance, is lost.

"I am beginning to see what you mean," said the first one slowly. "We are not simple; we don't discover anything for ourselves, but just repeat what we have been told. Even when we revolt, we form new conclusions, which again have to be broken down. We really don't know what love is, but merely have opinions about it. Is that it?"

Don't *you* think so? Surely, to know love, truth, God, there must be no opinions, no beliefs, no speculations with regard to it. If you have an opinion about a fact, the opinion becomes important, not the fact. If you want to know the truth or the falseness of the fact, then you must not live in the word, in the intellect. You may have a lot of knowledge, information, about the fact, but the actual fact is entirely different. Put away the book, the description, the tradition, the authority, and take the journey of self-discovery. Love, and don't be caught in opinions and ideas about what love is or should be. When you love, everything will come right. Love has its own action. Love, and you will know the blessings of it. Keep away from the authority who tells you what love is and what it is not. No authority knows; and he who knows cannot tell. Love, and there is understanding.

Seeking and the State of Search

THE HEAVENS OPENED, and there was rain; it covered the earth. It came down in sheets, flooding the roads and visibly filling the lily-pond. The trees bent down under the weight of it. The crows were soaked and could hardly fly, and many little birds took shelter under the verandah roof. Suddenly, from nowhere, came the frogs, large and small. Those with long legs made prodigious jumps with the greatest ease. Some were brown, some had green stripes, while others were almost entirely green, and they all had bright eyes, black, round and large. When you took one in your hand, it remained there, its beady eyes looking at you; and when you put it down again, it still didn't move, but sat as though glued to the spot. The rain was still coming down; everywhere there were running streams, and the water on the path was now ankle-deep. There was no wind, but just heavy rain. In a few seconds all your clothes were soaked, and they clung to your body uncomfortably; but it was warm, and you really didn't mind getting completely wet. You looked down to keep the water out of your eyes; but the heavy drops were painful on your scalp, and you would soon have to go in. A pale purple lily, with a bright golden heart, was being torn by the force of the rain; it couldn't stand much more of such heavy beating. A green snake as thick as your finger was clinging to a branch; you could hardly see it, for it was almost the colour of the leaves, only a brighter green, with a chemical arti-ficiality about it. It had no eyelids, and its black eyes were exposed. It didn't move as you approached, but you could feel it was uncomfortable with you so close. It was of a harmless variety, about eighteen inches long, plump and amazingly supple. Even when you moved away, it still remained motionless and watchful, and from a short distance you couldn't see it at all.

The leaves of the banana-plants were being torn to shreds, the flowers were being knocked off, and it still went on raining as furiously as ever. The delicate white jasmines were on the ground, and they were quickly becoming the colour of the earth; in death they still had their goodly perfume, but only when you came near them; a little further away there was only the smell of the rain and of penetrating dampness. A bedraggled crow had taken refuge on the verandah;

215

thoroughly soaked, its wings were touching the floor, and the bluish-white skin was showing. It couldn't fly, and it looked at you, asking you not to come near. Its sharp, black beak was the only thing hard and powerful about it; everything else was soft and weak. The roar of the sea could not be heard above the patter of the rain on the roof, on the leaves, and on the fan-shaped palm. But you could feel that this noise was slowly coming to an end. Already it was raining less heavily, and you could hear the frogs croaking. Other noises became audible: voices calling, a dog barking, a car coming down the road. Everything was becoming normal again. You were of the earth, of the leaves, of the dying lily, and you too were washed clean.

He was an old man, known for his generous nature, and for his hard work. Lean and austere, he went about the country by rail, bus or on foot, talking on religious matters, and there was about him the dignity of thought and meditation. He had a beard, clean and well-trimmed, and long hair. His hands were long and thin, and he had a pleasant, friendly smile.

"Though I do not wear the saffron robe, I am a *sannyasi*, and have been all over the land, talking to many people and questioning the religious teachers everywhere. As you see, I am an old man, my beard is white, but I have tried to keep my heart young and my head clear. I left home at the age of fifteen in search of God." He smiled gently at past remembrances. "That was many years ago; and though I have read, worshipped, meditated, I have not found God. I have listened attentively to the most famous of the saintly leaders, who incessantly talk of God—listened to them, not once, but many times; I have watched their work, their social reforms, not patronizingly, but with openness of heart to see their goodness. I am neither tolerant nor intolerant. I have prayed with the crowd, and I have prayed inwardly, quietly, in solitude. As a young man, I wanted to become a social reformer, and I willingly turned my hand to good works; but I found that good works have significance only within the great whole, which is God, and while I see that social reform is necessary, it is not my all-consuming interest.

"It was not with a dry heart that I listened to these 'leaders of the people', as they are called," he went on; "but their God is not the God I am seeking. Their God is action; they preach, exhort, fast, organize

216

political meetings; they serve as the heads of committees, write articles, edit papers, and mingle with the great of the land. They are active, but they know not silence. I have sought God with them, but have not found Him. Long before the names of these men began to appear in the papers, I was seeking God alone, in caves and in the open spaces; but I have not found Him.

"Now I am an old man, and I have only a few years left. Shall I find Him? Or is He non-existent? I don't want an opinion, or the cunning arguments of a polished mind. I must know. I have listened to you many times, in the north as well as in the south, and you do not speak of God as others do, nor are you in the religious-political arena. You explain what God is not, but you do not say what He is —which is as it should be. But you give no way to Him, and that is hard to understand. I have known of you from your very young days, and I often used to wonder how it would all turn out. If it had turned out otherwise, I wouldn't be here. This is not a compliment. I want to know the truth before I leave this world."

He sat quietly, his eyes closed. There was not about him the harshness of doubt, nor the brutality of cynicism, nor the intolerance which tries to be tolerant. He was a man who had come to the end of his seeking, and still wanted to know.

There was a strange silence in the room.

Sir, is there humility when we seek? Seeking is never born of humility, is it?

"Then is it born of arrogance?"

Isn't it? The desire to achieve, to arrive, is part of the pride which conceals itself in seeking. A way must be found to bring about the efficient and equitable distribution of man's physical necessities; and it will be found, because technology will force us to find it, now or to-morrow. But apart from seeking the physical well-being of man, why do we seek at all?

"I have sought ever since my childhood because this world has very little meaning; its significance can be seen with the naked eye. I don't say it's an illusion, as some do. This world is as real as pain and sorrow. Illusion exists only in the mind, and the power to create illusion can come to an end. The mind can be cleansed of its impurities by the breath of compassion; but the cleansing of the mind is not the finding of God. I have sought Him, but have found Him not."

This daily living is a transitory thing, and one seeks permanency; or in the midst of all this madness, one hopes for something rational, sane; or one is after some kind of personal immortality; or one is pursuing fulfilment in something infinitely greater than the enrichment of passing desire. Now, all this seeking is a form of arrogance, is it not? And how are you to know reality? Will you be able to recognize it, fathom it? Is it within the measure of the mind?

"Will God come to us without our seeking Him?"

Seeking is confined to the area of thought; all seeking and finding is within the borders of the mind, is it not? The mind can imagine, speculate, can hear the noise of its own chattering, but it cannot find that which is outside of itself. Its seeking is limited to the space of its own measuring.

"Then have I only been measuring, and not really seeking?"

Seeking is always measuring, sir. There's no seeking if the mind ceases to measure, compare.

"Are you telling me that my years of seeking have been in vain?"

It's not for another to say. But the movement of the mind that sets out on the journey of seeking is ever within the wide or narrow confines of itself.

"I have sought to silence the mind, but in that too there has been no finality."

A mind that has been *made* silent is not a silent mind. It's a dead mind. Anything that has been brought to a finality by force has to be conquered again and again; there's no end to it. Only that which has an ending is beyond the reach of time.

"Is not silence to be sought? Surely, a mind that wanders must be checked and brought under control."

Can silence be sought? Is it a thing to be cultivated and gathered? To seek silence of the mind, one must already know what it is. And do we know what that silence is? We may know it through the description of another; but can it be described? Knowing is only a verbal condition, a process of recognition; and what is recognized is not silence, which is always new.

"I have known the silence of the mountains and the caves, and I have put away all thoughts save the thought of silence; but the silence of the mind I have never known. You have wisely said that speculation is empty. But there must be a state of silence; and how is that state to come into being?"

Is there a method for the coming into being of that which is not the product of imagination, of that which is not put together by the mind?

"No, I suppose there isn't. The only silence I have experienced is that which arises when my mind is completely under control; but you say this is not silence. I have tutored my mind to obedience, and have released it only under watchful care; it has been trained and made sharp through study, through argumentation, through meditation and deep thought; but the silence of which you speak has not come within the field of my experience. How is that silence to be experienced? What am I to do?"

Sir, the experiencer must cease for silence to be. The experiencer is always seeking more experiences; he wants to have new sensations, or to repeat old ones; he craves to fulfil himself, to be or become something. The experiencer is the motive-maker; and as long as there's a motive, however subtle, there's only the buying of silence; but it's not silence.

"Then how is silence to happen? Is it an accident of life? Is it a gift?"

Let's consider together the whole issue. We are always seeking something, and we use that word 'seeking' so easily. The fact that we are seeking is all-important, and not what is being sought. What one seeks is the projection of one's own desire. Seeking is not the state of search; it is a reaction, a process of denial and assertion with regard to an idea made by the mind. To seek the proverbial needle in a haystack, there must already be knowledge of the needle. Similarly, to seek God, happiness, silence, or what you will, is already to have known, formulated or imagined it. Seeking, as it's called, is always for something known. Finding is recognizing, and recognition is based on previous knowledge. This process of seeking is not the state of search. The mind that's seeking is waiting, expecting, desiring, and what it finds is recognizable, therefore already known. Seeking is the action of the past. But the state of search is entirely different, it's in no way similar to seeking; and it's not a reaction, the opposite of seeking. The two are not related in any way.

"Then what is the state of search?"

It cannot be described, but it is possible to be in that state if there is an understanding of what seeking is. We seek, out of discontent, unhappiness, fear, do we not? Seeking is a network of activities in which there's no freedom. This network has to be understood.

"What do you mean by understanding?"

Is not understanding a state of mind in which knowledge, memory, or recognition, is not immediately functioning? To understand, the mind must be still; the activities of knowledge must be in abeyance. This stillness of the mind takes place spontaneously when the teacher or the parent really wants to understand the child. When there's the intention to understand, there is attention without the distraction of the desire to attend. Then the mind is not disciplined, controlled, pulled together and *made* to be still. Its stillness is natural when there's the intention to understand. No effort, no conflict, is involved in understanding. With the understanding of the full significance of seeking, the state of search comes into being. It cannot be sought and found.

"As I have listened to you explaining, there has been a close watching of the mind. I now see the truth of what is called seeking, and I perceive that it is possible not to seek; yet the state of search is not."

Why say it is not, or it is? Being aware of the truth and the falseness of seeking, the mind is no longer caught in the machinery of seeking. There's a feeling of being unburdened, a sense of relief. The mind is still; it's no longer making effort, striving after something; but it's not asleep, nor is it waiting, expecting. It's simply quiet, awake. Isn't that so, sir?

"Please do not call me 'sir'. I am the one being instructed. What you say appears to be true."

This awakened mind is the state of search. It's no longer seeking from a motive; there's no objective to be gained. The mind has not been *made* still; there's no pressure on it to be still, and so it's still. Its stillness is not that of a leaf which is ready to dance with the next breeze; it's not a plaything of desire.

"There's awareness of a movement in that stillness."

Is this awareness not silence? We are describing, but not as the experiencer would describe. The experiencer is brought into being through many causes; he is an effect, who in turn becomes the cause of still another effect. The experiencer is both cause and effect in a never-ending series of causes and effects. To perceive the truth of this sets the mind free. There is no freedom within the network of cause-effect. Freedom is not being free from the net, but freedom is when the net is not. Freedom *from* something is not freedom; it's only a reaction, the opposite of bondage. Freedom is when bondage is understood. Truth is not something permanent, fixed, therefore it cannot be sought; truth is a living thing, it is the state of search.

"That state of search is God. There is no end to be gained and held. The seeking without finding which has gone on all these years has not brought bitterness to the heart, nor is there regret over these spent years. We are taught, we do not learn, and therein lies our misery. Understanding abolishes time and age, it sweeps away the difference between the teacher and the taught. I understand and feel greatly. We shall meet again."

"WHY DO THE SCRIPTURES CONDEMN DESIRE?"

IT WAS one of those huge, sprawling towns that are devouring the country, and to get beyond it we had to go for seemingly endless miles along shoddy streets, past factories, slums and railway sheds, through exclusive residential suburbs, until at last we saw the beginnings of the open country, where the skies were wide and the trees were tall and free. It was a beautiful day, clear and not too warm, for it had been raining recently—one of those soft, gentle rains that go deep into the earth. Suddenly, as the road crested a hill, we came upon the river, glistening in the sun as it wandered away among the green fields towards the distant sea. There were only a few boats on the river, clumsily built, with square, black sails. Many miles higher up there was a bridge for both trains and daily traffic, but at this point there was just a pontoon bridge, on which the traffic moved only one way at a time, and we saw a line of lorries, bullock-carts and motor cars, and two camels, waiting their turn to cross over. We didn't want to enter that lengthening queue, for it might be a long wait, so we took another road back, leaving the river to make its way through hills and meadows, past many a village, to the open sea.

The sky overhead was intensely blue, and the horizon was filled with enormous white clouds, with the morning sun upon them. They were fantastic in shape, and they remained motionless and distant. You couldn't get near them, even if you drove towards them for miles. By the side of the road the grass was young and green. The coming summer would burn it brown, and the country would lose its green freshness; but now everything was made new, and there was joy in the land. The road was quite rough, with potholes all over it, and though the driver avoided as many as he could, we bounced up and down, our heads almost touching the roof; but the motor was running beautifully, and there was no rattle in the car.

One's mind was aware of the stately trees, the rocky hills, the villagers, the wide blue skies, but it was also in meditation. Not a thought was disturbing it. There was no flutter of memory, no effort to hold or to resist, nor was there anything in the future to be gained. The mind was taking everything in, it was quicker than the eye, and it didn't keep what it perceived; the happening passed through it, as the breeze passes among the branches of a tree. One heard the conversation behind one, and saw the bullock-cart and the approaching lorry, yet the mind was completely still; and the movement within that stillness was the impulse of a new beginning, a new birth. But the new beginning would never be old; it would never know yesterday and to-morrow. The mind was not experiencing the new: it was itself the new. It had no continuity, and so no death; it was new, not *made* new. The fire was not from the embers of yesterday.

He had brought his friend, he said, so that with his help he could the better formulate his points. They were both rather reserved, and not given to many words, but they said they knew Sanskrit and some of its literature. Probably in their forties, they were slim and healthy-looking, with good heads and thoughtful eyes.

"Why do the Scriptures condemn desire?" began the taller one. "Practically every teacher of old seems to have condemned it, especially sexual desire, saying that it must be controlled, subjugated. They evidently regarded desire as a hindrance to the higher life. The Buddha talked of desire as the cause of all sorrow and preached the ending of it. Shankara, in his complex philosophy, said that desire and the sexual urge were to be suppressed, and all the other religious teachers have more or less maintained the same attitude. Some of the Christian saints castigated their bodies and tortured themselves in various ways, while others held that one's body, like the ass or the horse, must be well-treated but controlled. We have not read very much, but as far as we are familiar with it, all religious literature seems to insist that desire must be disciplined, subjugated, sublimated, and so on. We are just beginners in the religious life, but somehow we feel there's something missing in all this, a flower with perfume. We may be entirely wrong, and we are not pitting ourselves against the great teachers, but we would like, if we may, to talk things over with you. As far as we can make out from our reading, you have never said that desire must be suppressed or sublimated, but that it must be understood with an awareness in which there's no condemnation or justification. Though you have explained this in different ways, we find it difficult to grasp the whole meaning of it, and our talking it over with you will be of considerable help to us."

What exactly is the problem you want to discuss?

"Desire is natural, is it not, sir?" asked the other. "Desire for food, desire for sleep, desire for some degree of comfort, sexual desire, the desire for truth—in all these forms, desire is perfectly natural, and why are we told that it must be eliminated?"

Putting aside what you have been told, can we inquire into the truth and the falseness of desire? What do you mean by desire? Not the dictionary definition, but what is the significance, the content of desire? And what importance do you give to it?

"I have many desires," replied the taller one, "and these desires change in their value and importance from time to time. There are permanent as well as passing desires. A desire which I have one day may, by the very next day, be gone, or have become intensified. Even if I no longer have sexual desire, I may still want power; I may have passed beyond the sexual phase, but my desire for power remains constant."

That is so. Childish wants become mature desires with age, with habit, with repetition. The object of desire may change as we grow older, but desire remains. Fulfilment and the pain of frustration are always within the area of desire, are they not?

Now, is there desire if there's no object of desire? Are desire and its object inseparable? Do I know desire only because of the object? Let us find out.

I see a new fountain-pen, and because mine is not as good, I want the new one; so a process of desire is set going, a chain of reactions, till I get, or fail to get, what I want. An object catches the eye, and then there comes a feeling of wanting or not wanting. At what point in this process does the 'I' come in?

"That's a good question."

Does the 'I' exist before the feeling of wanting, or does it arise with that feeling? You see some object, such as a new type of fountain-pen, and a number of reactions are set going which are perfectly normal; but with them comes the desire to possess the object, and then begins another set of reactions which bring into being the 'I' who says, "I must have it". So the 'I' is put together by the feeling or desire which arises through the natural response of seeing. Without seeing, sensing, desiring, is there an 'I' as a separate, isolated entity? Or does this whole process of seeing, having a sensation, desiring, constitute the 'I'?

"Do you mean to say, sir, that the 'I' is not there first? Isn't it the 'I' who perceives and then desires?" asked the shorter one.

What do *you* say? Doesn't the 'I' separate himself only in the process of perceiving and desiring? Before this process begins, is there an 'I' as a separate entity?

"It is difficult to think· of the 'I' as merely the result of a certain physio-psychological process, for this sounds very materialistic, and it goes against our tradition and all our habits of thought, which say that the 'I', the watcher, is there first, and not that he has been 'put together'. But in spite of tradition and the sacred books, and my own wavering inclination to believe them, I see what you say to be a fact."

It's not what another may say that makes for perception of a fact, but your own direct observation and clarity of thinking; isn't that so?

"Of course," replied the taller one. "I may at first mistake a piece of rope for a snake, but the moment I see the thing clearly, there's no mistaking, no wishful thinking about it."

If that point is clear, shall we get on with the question of suppressing or sublimating desire? Now, what's the problem?

"Desire is always there, sometimes burning furiously, and sometimes dormant but ready to spring to life; and the problem is, what's one to do with it? When desire is dormant, my whole being is fairly quiet, but when it's awake, I am very disturbed; I become restless, feverishly active, till that particular desire is satisfied. I then become relatively calm—only to have desire begin all over again, perhaps with a different object. It's like water under pressure, and however high you build the dam, it's forever seeping through the cracks, going round the end, or spilling over the top. I have all but tortured myself, trying to go beyond desire, but at the end of my best efforts, desire is still there, smiling or frowning. How am I to be free of it?"

Are you trying to suppress, sublimate desire? Do you want to tame it, drug it, make it respectable? Apart from the books, ideals and *gurus,* what do you feel about desire? What is your impulse? What do you think?

"Desire is natural, isn't it, sir?" asked the shorter one.

What do you mean by natural?

"Hunger, sex, wanting comfort and security—all this is desire, and it seems so healthily sane and normal. After all, we are built like that."

If it is so normal, why are you bothered by it?

"The trouble is, there's not just one desire, but many contradictory desires, all pulling in different directions; I am torn apart inside. Two or three desires are dominant, and they override the conflicting lesser ones; but even among the major desires, there's a contradiction. It's this contradiction, with its strains and tensions, that causes suffering."

And to overcome this suffering, you are told you must control, suppress, or sublimate desire. Isn't that so? If the fulfilment of desire brought only pleasure and no suffering, you would go merrily along with it, wouldn't you?

"Obviously," put in the taller one. "But there's always some pain and fear as well, and this is what we want to eliminate."

Yes, everyone does, and that is why the whole design and background of our thinking is to continue with the pleasures while avoiding the pain of desire. Isn't this what you also are striving after?

"I'm afraid it is."

This struggle between the pleasures of desire and the suffering which also comes with it is the conflict of duality. There's nothing very puzzling about it. Desire seeks fulfilment, and the shadow of fulfilment is frustration. We don't admit that, so we all pursue fulfilment, hoping never to be frustrated; but the two are inseparable.

"Is it *never* possible to have fulfilment without the pain of frustration?"

Don't you know? Haven't you experienced the brief pleasure of fulfilment, and isn't it invariably followed by anxiety, pain?

"I have noticed that, but one tries in one way or another to keep ahead of the pain."

And have you succeeded?

"Not yet, but one always hopes to."

How to guard against such suffering is your chief concern throughout life; so you begin to discipline desire; you say, "This is the right desire, and the other is wrong, immoral." You cultivate the ideal desire, the what *should* be, while caught in the what should *not* be. The what should *not* be is the actual fact, and the what *should* be has no reality except as an imaginary symbol. This is so, isn't it?

"But however imaginary, aren't ideals necessary?" asked the shorter one. "They help us to get rid of the suffering."

Do they? Have your ideals helped you to be free from suffering, or have they merely helped you to carry on with the pleasure while ideally saying to yourself that you shouldn't? So the pain and the pleasure of desire continue. Actually, you don't want to be free of either; you want to drift with the pain and the pleasure of desire, meanwhile talking about ideals and all that stuff.

"You are perfectly right, sir," he admitted.

Let's proceed from there. Desire is not to be divided as pleasurable and painful, or as right and wrong desire. There's only desire, which appears under different forms, with different objectives. Unless you understand this, you will merely be struggling to overcome the contradictions which are the very nature of desire.

"Is there then a central desire which must be overcome, a desire from which all other desires spring?" asked the taller one.

Do you mean the desire for security?

"I was thinking of that; but there is also the desire for sex, and for so many other things."

Is there one central desire from which other desires spring like so many children, or does desire merely change its object of fulfilment from time to time, from immaturity to maturity? There's the desire to possess, to be passionate, to succeed, to be secure both inwardly and outwardly, and so on. Desire weaves through thought and action, through the so-called spiritual as well as the mundane life, does it not?

They were silent for some time.

"We can't think any further," said the shorter one. "We are stumped."

If you suppress desire, it comes up again in another form, doesn't it? To control desire is to narrow it down and be self-centred; to discipline it is to build a wall of resistance, which is always being broken down—unless, of course, you become neurotic, fixed in one pattern of desire. To sublimate desire is an act of will; but will is essentially the concentration of desire, and when one form of desire dominates another, you are back again in your old pattern of struggle.

Control, discipline, sublimation, suppression—it all involves effort of some kind, and such effort is still within the field of duality, of 'right' and 'wrong' desire. Laziness may be overcome by an act of will, but the pettiness of the mind remains. A petty mind can be very active, and it generally is, thereby causing mischief and misery for itself and others. So, however much a petty mind may struggle to overcome desire, it will continue to be a petty mind. All this is clear, isn't it?

They looked at each other.

"I think so," replied the taller one. "But please go a little slower, sir, and don't cram every sentence with ideas."

Like steam, desire is energy, is it not? And as steam can be directed to run every kind of machinery, either beneficial or destructive, so desire can be dissipated, or it can be used for understanding without there being any user of that astonishing energy. If there's a user of it, whether it be the one or the many, the individual or the collective, which is tradition, then the trouble begins; then there's the closed circle of pain and pleasure.

"If neither the individual nor the collective is to use that energy, then who *is* to use it?"

Isn't that a wrong question you're asking? A wrong question will have a wrong answer, but a right one may open the door to understanding. There's only energy; there's no question of who will use it. It's not that energy, but the user of it, who sustains confusion and the contradiction of pain and pleasure. The user, as the one and as the many, says, "This is right and that is wrong, this is good and that is bad", thereby perpetuating the conflict of duality. He is the real mischief-maker, the author of sorrow. Can the user of that energy called desire cease to be? Can the watcher not be an operator, a separate entity embodying this or that tradition, and be that energy itself?

"Isn't that very difficult?"

It's the only problem, and not how to control, discipline, or sublimate desire. When you begin to understand this, desire has quite a different significance; it is then the purity of creation, the movement of truth. But merely to repeat that desire is the supreme, and so on, is not only useless, it is definitely harmful, because it acts as a soporific, a drug to quiet the petty mind.

"But how is the user of desire to come to an end?"

If the question "How?" reflects the search for a method, then the user of desire will merely be put together in another form. What's important is the ending of the user, not how to put an end to the user. There is no 'how'. There is only understanding, the impulse that will shatter the old.

Can Politics Ever Be Spiritualized?

BEYOND THE BRIDGE is the sea, blue and distant. There are yellow sands along the curving shore, and spreading palm groves. The city people come here in their cars with their well-dressed children, who shout with the joy of being released from their tight homes and barren streets.

Early in the morning, just before the sun comes out of the sea, when the dew is heavy on the ground and the stars are still visible, this place is very beautiful. You can sit here alone, with the world of intense silence all about you. The sea is restless and dark, made angry by the moon, its waves rolling in with a fury and a roar. But in spite of the deep thunder of the sea, everything is strangely quiet; there is no breeze, and the birds are still asleep. Your mind has lost its impulse to wander the face of the earth, to move among the old, familiar landmarks, to carry on a silent soliloquy. Suddenly and unexpectedly, all that tremendous energy is drawing together, gathering itself, but not to expend itself in movement. There is movement only with the experiencer, who is seeking, gaining, losing. The gathering together of this energy, free of the pressures and influences of desire, however weakened or heightened, has brought complete inward silence. Your mind is fully lighted, without any shadow, and without casting any shadow. The morning star is very clear, steady and unblinking, and there is a glow in the eastern sky. Your mind has not moved one hair's-breadth; it is not paralysed, but the light of that inward silence has itself become action, without the words and the images of the mind. Its light is without a centre, the maker of shadow; there is only light.

The morning star is fading away, and soon a golden rim is showing beyond the stirring waters. Across the land, shadows are slowly being cast. Everything is waking up, and a soft breeze is coming from the north. You follow the path that runs by the river and joins the main road. At that hour there are very few people on it, one or two taking their morning stroll; there are almost no cars, and things are fairly quiet. The road goes through a sleepy village, where two small children are using the roadside as their toilet, laughing and talking away, unaware of the passer-by. A goat is lying down in the middle of the road, and a car goes around it. Some distance beyond the village, you pass through a gate into a well-kept garden, where there are brilliant flowers and a square pond with many lilies in it. The shadows are now deep, but there is still dew on the grass.

He was a middle-aged man from the village, and a lawyer of sorts. He didn't work very hard, he said, for he had a little property and could give some of his time to other things. At the moment he was writing a book about social conditions in this country. He had met some of the prominent people in the government, and had taken part in the latest movement of land-reform, walking with the others from village to village. His enthusiasm was very marked when he talked about political and social reform, and the whole tone of his voice changed. It became sharp, urgent, excited; his head went up, an aggressive look crept into his eyes, and his manner became assertive. Of all this he was entirely unconscious. Words and statistics came to him easily, and he seemed to gather strength as he went along. As one listened without interrupting his flow of explanations and evaluations, he suddenly realized where he was, and awkwardly stopped himself.

"I always get excited when I talk about politics and social reform; I can't help it. It's in my blood. It seems to be the same with all of us, at least in this generation: politics are in our blood. Once we have left college, our education continues chiefly through the newspapers, which for the most part are dedicated to politics. I feel that an enormous amount of good can be done through politics, and that's why I devote a great deal of my time to it. I like it, too; there's excitement in it."

As there is in drinking, in sex, in eating, in brutality, and so on. Excitement, in whatever form, gives us a sense of living, and we demand it even in religion.

"Do you think it's wrong?"

What do you think? Hate and war offer great excitement, don't they?

"Personally, I don't take politics lightly," he went on, ignoring the question; "to me it is a very serious matter, because I feel it is a marvellous instrument for bringing about essential reforms. Political action does produce results, and not in too distant a future, so there is in it a definite hope for the average man. Most religious people don't seem to realize the importance of political action, which I think is a great pity; for, as one of our leaders has said, politics must be spiritualized. You agree with this, don't you?"

A truly religious man is not concerned with politics; to him there is only action, a total religious action, and not the fragmentary activities which are called political and social.

"Are you opposed to bringing religion into politics?"

Opposition only breeds antagonism, does it not? Let us consider what we mean by religion. But first of all, what do you mean by politics?

"The whole legislative procedure: justice, planning for the welfare of the State, guaranteeing equal opportunity for all its citizens, and so on. It is the function of government to rule wisely and to prevent chaos."

Surely, reform of every kind is also a function of government; it should not be left to the whims and fancies, called ideals, of strong individuals and their groups, for this leads to the fragmentation of the State. In a two-party or multiple-party system, reformers should work either through the government, or as part of the opposition. Why do we need social reformers at all?

"Without them, many reforms already achieved would never have come into being. Reformers are necessary because they prod the government. They have greater vision than the average politician, and by their example they force the government to bring about needed reforms, or to modify its policy. Fasting is one of the means adopted by the saintly reformers to compel the government to follow their recommendations."

Which is a sort of blackmail, isn't it?

"Perhaps; but it does force the government to consider and even to carry out necessary reforms."

The saintly reformer may be mistaken, and often he is when he gets involved in politics. Because he has a certain influence with the public, the government may have to yield to his demands—sometimes with disastrous results, as has recently been shown. Since reform of every kind, through various forms of legislation, is essentially the function of a humane, intelligent government, why don't these politically-minded saints join the government, or create another political party? Is it that they want to play politics, and yet keep aloof from it?

"I think they want to spiritualize politics."

Can politics ever be spiritualized? Politics are concerned with society, which is always in conflict with itself, always deteriorating. The interrelationship of human beings constitutes society, and that relationship is actually based on ambition, frustration, envy. Society knows no compassion. Compassion is the act of a total and integrated individual.

Now, each of these political-religious reformers asserts that his is *the* way to salvation, doesn't he?

"Most of them do, but there are a few who are not so assertive."

May they not all be greatly mistaken, caught in their own conditioning, with strong prejudices and traditional bias? Is there not a tendency for each saintly political leader, with his group of followers, to bring about a further fragmentation and disintegration of the State?

"But isn't that a risk we must take? Can unity be brought about through mere legislation?"

Of course not. There may be a semblance of unity, the outward following of a universal pattern, social or political, but the unity of man can never be brought about through legislation, however enlightened. Where there's friendship, compassion, the organization of justice is unnecessary; and through the organization of justice, compassion does not necessarily come into being. On the contrary, it may banish compassion. But that's another matter.

As I was saying, why don't these saintly politicians join the government, or build up a party to carry out their policies? What's the need of these reformers, outside of the political field?

"They have more power outside of the parliament than they would have within it; they act as moral whips to the government. They do divide the people to some extent, it's true, but that's a necessary evil out of which good may come."

The problem is much deeper than that, isn't it? Political, economic and social reforms are obviously necessary; but unless we begin to understand the greater issue, which is the totality of man and his total action, such reforms only breed further mischief, necessitating still more reforms, in an endless chain by which man is held.

Now, are there not deeper urges which are compelling these 'saintly' political leaders to act as they do? Leadership implies power, the power to influence, to guide, to dominate, and subtly or assertively, these leaders are seekers after power. Power in any form is evil, and it will inevitably lead to disaster. Most people want to be led, to be told what to do, and in their confusion they bring into being leaders who are as confused as themselves.

"But why do you say that our leaders are seeking power?" he asked rather sceptically. "They are highly respectable men of good intention and good conduct."

The respectable are the conventional; they follow tradition, wide or narrow, acknowledged or unacknowledged. The respectable always have the authority of the book, of the past. They may not consciously seek power, but power comes to them through their position, their activities, and so on; and by this power they are driven. Humility is far from them. They are leaders, they have followers. He who follows another, whether it be the greatest saint or the teacher round the corner, is essentially irreligious.

"I see what you mean, sir; but why do these people seek power?" he asked, more earnestly.

Why do *you* seek power? Having power over one, or over thousands, gives an intense possessive pleasure, does it not? There's a pleasurable feeling of self-importance, of being in a position of authority.

"Yes, I know it quite well. I feel that pleasurable sense of authority when I am consulted about legal or political matters."

Why do we seek and try to maintain this exciting sense of power?

"It comes so naturally that it seems to be inbred in us."

Such an explanation blocks further and deeper inquiry, doesn't it? If you would find out the truth of the matter, you must not be satisfied by explanations, however plausible and gratifying.

Why do we want to be leaders? There must be recognition in order to feel important; if we are not recognized as such, importance has no meaning. Recognition is part of the whole process of leadership. Not only does the leader acquire importance, but also the follower. By asserting that he belongs to such-and-such a movement, led by so-and-so, the follower becomes somebody. Don't you find this to be true?

"I'm afraid I do."

As with the follower, so with the leader. Being insufficient in ourselves, empty, we proceed to fill that emptiness with a sense of possession, power, position, or with knowledge, gratifying ideologies, and so on; we crowd it with the things of the mind. This process of filling, of escaping, of becoming, whether it be conscious or otherwise, is the net of the self; it is the ego, the 'me', the entity that has identified itself with an ideology, with reform, with a certain pattern of action. In this process of becoming, which is self-fulfilment, there is always the shadow of frustration. Unless this fact is deeply understood, so that the mind is free from the act of self-fulfilment, there will ever be this evil of power, with various labels of respectability attached to it.

"If I may ask, when you yourself refused, many years ago, to continue as the head of a religious organization, had you thought all this out? You were quite young then, and how did it happen that you were able to do this?"

One has an insight, a vague feeling, of what is right, and one does it, without thinking of the consequences. Later comes the reasoned explanation; and because the act is true, the reasons will be adequate and true. But that again is a different matter. We were talking about the inner workings of leaders and followers.

The man who seeks power, or accepts power in any form, is fundamentally irreligious. He may seek power through austerity, through discipline and self-denial, which is called virtue, or through the interpretation of the sacred books; but such a man does not know the immense significance of what may be called religion.

"Then what *is* religion? I now see clearly that politics cannot be spiritualized, but that it has definite significance in its proper place, which includes the world of reform; and about that world I am still enthusiastic. But I am religious by nature, and I want to know from you what religion means."

You cannot know it from another; but what does it mean to you?

"I was brought up in Hinduism, and what it teaches I accept as religion."

That's what the Christian, the Buddhist, the Moslem also does; each accepts as religion the particular pattern of belief, dogma and ritual in which he happens to have been brought up. Acceptance implies choice, doesn't it? And is there a choice in the matter of religion?

"When I say that I accept what the religion I belong to teaches, I mean that it appeals to my reason. Is there anything wrong in that?"

It's not a matter of right or wrong, but let's understand what we're talking about. From childhood you have been influenced by your parents, and by society, to think in terms of a certain pattern of beliefs and dogmas. Later you may revolt against all that, and take on another pattern of what is called religion; but whether you revolt or not, your reason is based on your desire to be secure, to be 'spiritually' safe, and on that urge depends your choice. After all, reason or thought is also the outcome of conditioning, of bias, prejudice, of conscious or unconscious fear, and so on. However logical and efficient one's reasoning may be, it does not lead to that which is beyond the mind. For that which is beyond the mind to come into being, the mind must be totally still.

"But are you against reason?" he demanded.

Again, it is a matter of understanding, and not of being for or against something. Although one may have the capacity to think efficiently to the very end of a problem, thought is always limited; reason is incapable of going beyond a certain point. Thought can never be free, because all thinking is the response of memory; without memory, there is no thinking. Memory, or knowledge, is mechanical; being rooted in yesterday, it's always of the past. All inquiry, reasoning or unreasoning, starts from knowledge, *the what has been.* As thought is not free, it cannot go far; it moves within the limits of its own conditioning, within the boundaries of its knowledge and experience. Each new experience is interpreted according to the past, and thereby strengthens the past, which is tradition, the conditioned state. So thought is not the way to the understanding of reality.

"If one is not to use one's mind, how is it possible to find out what religion is?"

In the very process of using the mind, of thinking clearly, reasoning critically and sanely, one discovers for oneself the limitations of thought. Thought, the response of the mind in human relationship, is tethered to self-interest, positive or negative; it is bound by ambition, envy, by possessiveness, fear, and so on. Only when the mind has shaken off this bondage, which is the self, is the mind free. The understanding of this bondage is self-knowledge.

"You have not yet said what religion is. To me, religion has always been belief in God, with the whole complex of dogmas, rituals, traditions and ideals that go with it."

Belief is not the way to reality. Belief and non-belief are a matter of influence, pressure, and a mind that is under pressure, open or hidden, can never fly straight. The mind must be free from influence, from inward compulsions and urges, so that it is alone, untrammelled by the past; only then can that which is timeless come into being. There is no path to it. Religion is not a matter of dogma, orthodoxy and ritual; it is not organized belief. Organized belief kills love and friendliness. Religion is the feeling of sacredness, of compassion, of love.

"Must one abandon the beliefs, the ideals, the temple—everything with which one has been brought up? To do so would be very difficult; one is afraid to stand alone. Is such a thing really possible?"

It is possible the moment you see the urgent necessity of it. But you cannot be compelled; you must see it for yourself. Beliefs and dogmas have very little value—in fact, they are actively harmful, separating man from man and breeding animosity. What matters is for the mind to free itself from envy, from ambition, from the desire for power, because these destroy compassion. To love, to be compassionate, is of the real.

"Deep down, what you say has the ring of truth. Most of us live so much on the surface, we are so immature and subject to influence, that the real thing escapes us. And one wants to reform the world! I must begin with myself; I must cleanse my own heart, and not be carried away with the thought of reforming another. Sir, I hope I may come again."

AWARENESS AND THE CESSATION OF DREAMS

THE EASTERN SKY was more splendid than where the sun had set; there were massive clouds, fantastically shaped and seemingly lighted from within by a golden fire. Another mass of clouds was a deep, purplish blue; heavy with threat and darkness, it was shot through with flashes of lightning, twisting, sharp and brilliant. Above and beyond there were other weird shapes, incredibly beautiful and aglow with every colour imaginable. But the sun had set in a limpid sky, and towards the west there was a pure orange light. Against this sky, over the tops of the other trees, a single palm was etched, clear, motionless, darkly slender. A few children were playing about, with excitement and pleasure, in a green field. They would soon be going, for it was getting dark; already, from one of the scattered houses, someone was calling, and a child replied in a high-pitched voice. Lights were beginning to appear in the windows, and a strange stillness was creeping over the land. You could feel it coming from afar, passing over and beyond you to the ends of the earth. You sat there completely motionless, your mind going with that stillness, expanding immeasurably without a centre, without a point of recognition or reference. Seated at the edge of that meadow, your body was unmoving, but very much alive. The mind was much more so; in a state of complete silence, it was nevertheless aware of the lightning and the shouting children, of the little noises among the grass and the sounding of a distant horn. It was silent in the depths where thought could not reach it, and that silence was a penetrating bliss—a word that has little meaning except for communication—which went on and on; it was not a movement in terms of time and distance, but it was without an ending. It was strangely massive, yet it could be blown away by a breath.

The path went by a large cemetery, full of naked white slabs, the aftermath of war. It was a green, well-kept garden, enclosed by a hedge and a barbed-wire fence with a gate in it. Such gardens exist all over the earth for those who were loved, educated, killed and buried. The path continued on down a slope, where there were some tall old trees, with a small stream wandering among them. Crossing a rickety wooden bridge, you climbed another slope and followed the path out into the open country. It was quite dark now, but you knew your way, for you had been on that path before. The stars were brilliant, but the lightning-bearing clouds were coming nearer. It would still take some time for the storm to break, and by then you would have reached shelter.

"I wonder why I dream so much? I have some kind of dream practically every night. Sometimes my dreams are pleasant, but more often they are unpleasant, even frightening, and when I wake up in the morning I feel exhausted."

He was a youngish man, obviously worried and anxious. He had a fairly satisfactory job with the government, he explained, with good hopes for the future, and the need to earn a livelihood caused him no concern. He had capacity, and could always get a job. His wife was dead, and he had a small son whom he had left with a sister, for the boy was too full of mischief, he said, to bring him along. He was rather heavily built and slow of speech, with a matter-of-fact air about him.

"I am not much of a reader," he continued, "though I was good at my studies in college, and graduated with honours. But all that means nothing, except that it got me a promising job—in which I am not greatly interested. A few hours of hard work each day is enough to keep it going, and I have time to spare. I think I am normal, and I could get married again, but I am not strongly attracted to the opposite sex. I like games, and I lead a healthy, vigorous life. My work brings me into contact with some of the prominent politicians, but I am not interested in politics and all the beastly intrigues that go with it, and I deliberately keep out of it. One might climb high through favouritism and corruption, but I keep my job because I am proficient at it, and that's enough for me. I am telling you all this, not as gossip, but to give you an idea of the milieu I live in. I have a normal amount of ambition, but I am not driven crazy by it. I shall succeed if I don't fall ill, and if there isn't too much political wire-pulling. Apart from my work, I have a few good friends, and we often discuss serious things. So now you know more or less the whole picture."

If one may ask, what is it that you want to talk over?

"A friend took me to hear one of your evening talks, and with him I also attended a morning discussion. I was greatly moved by what I heard, and I want to pursue it. But what I am concerned with now is this nightly dreaming. My dreams are very disturbing, even the pleasant ones, and I want to get rid of them; I want to have peaceful nights. What am I to do? Or is this a silly question?"

What do you mean by dreams?

"When I am asleep, I have visions of various kinds; a series of pictures or apparitions arise in my mind. One night I may be about to fall over the edge of a precipice, and I wake up with a start; another night I may find myself in a pleasant valley, surrounded by high mountains and with a stream running through it; another night I may be having a terrific argument with my friends, or just missing a train, or playing a first-class game of tennis; or I may suddenly see the dead body of my wife, and so on. My dreams are rarely erotic, but they are often nightmares, full of fear, and sometimes they are fantastically complicated."

When you are dreaming, does it ever happen that there is an interpretation of it going on almost at the same time?

"No, I have never had such an experience; I just dream, and afterwards groan about it. I haven't read any books on psychology or the interpretation of dreams. I have talked the problem over with some

237

of my friends, but they are not of much help, and I feel rather wary of going to an analyst. Can you tell me why I dream, and what my dreams mean?"

Do you want an interpretation of your dreams? Or do you want to understand the complex problem of dreaming?

"Isn't it necessary to interpret one's dreams?"

There may be no need to dream at all. Surely, you must discover for yourself the truth or the falseness of the whole process which we call dreaming. This discovery is far more important than to have your dreams interpreted, is it not?

"Of course. If I could perceive for myself the full significance of dreaming, it should relieve me of this nightly anxiety and unrest. But I have never really thought about these matters, and you will have to be patient with me."

We are trying to understand the problem together, so there's no impatience on either side. We are both taking the journey of exploration, which means that we must both be alert, and not held back by any prejudice or fear which we may uncover as we go along.

Your consciousness is the totality of what you think and feel, and much more. Your purposes and motives, whether hidden or open; your secret desires; the subtlety and cunning of your thought; the obscure urges and compulsions in the depth of your heart—all this is your consciousness. It is your character, your tendencies, your temperament, your fulfilments and frustrations, your hopes and fears. Regardless of whether you believe or disbelieve in God, or in the soul, the *Atman*, in some super-spiritual entity, the whole process of your thinking is consciousness, is it not?

"I haven't thought about this before, sir, but I can see that my consciousness is made up of all these elements."

It is also tradition, knowledge and experience; it is the past in relation to the present, which makes for character; it is the collective, the racial, the totality of man. Consciousness is the whole field of thought, desire, affection and the cultivated virtues, which are not virtue at all; it is envy, acquisitiveness, and so on. Is not all this what we call consciousness?

"I may not follow in every detail, but I get the feeling of this totality," he replied hesitantly.

Consciousness is something still more: it's the battleground of contradictory desires, the field of strife, struggle, pain, sorrow. It is also the revolt against this field, which is the search for peace, for goodness, for abiding affection. Self-consciousness arises when there is awareness of conflict and sorrow, and the desire to be rid of them; also when there is awareness of joy, and the desire for more of it. All this is the totality of consciousness; it is a vast process of memory, or the past, using the present as a passage to the future. Consciousness is time— time as both the waking and the sleeping period, the day and the night.

"But can one ever be fully aware of this totality of consciousness?"

Most of us are aware of only a small corner of it, and our lives are spent in that small corner, making a lot of noise in pushing and destroying each other, with a little friendliness and affection thrown in. Of the major part we are unaware, and so there's the conscious and the unconscious. Actually, of course, there's no division between the two; it's only that we give more attention to the one than to the other.

"That much is quite clear—too clear, in fact. The conscious mind is occupied with a thousand and one things, almost all of them rooted in self-interest."

But there's the rest of it, hidden, active, aggressive and much more dynamic than the conscious, workaday mind. This hidden part of the mind is constantly urging, influencing, controlling, but it often fails to communicate its purpose during the waking hours, because the upper layer of the mind is occupied; so it gives hints and intimations during so-called sleep. The superficial mind may revolt against this unseen influence, but it is quietly brought into line again, for the totality of consciousness is concerned with being secure, permanent; and any change is always in the direction of seeking further security, the greater permanency of itself.

"I'm afraid I don't quite understand."

After all, the mind wants to be certain in all its relationships, doesn't it? It wants to be secure in its relationship with ideas and beliefs, as well as in its relationship with people and with property. Haven't you noticed this?

"But isn't that natural?"

We are educated to think that it's natural; but is it? Surely, only the mind that's not clinging to security is free to discover that which is wholly untouched by the past. But the conscious mind starts with this urge to be secure, to be safe, to make itself permanent; and the hidden or neglected part of the mind, the unconscious, is also watchful of its own interests. The conscious mind may be forced by circumstances to reform, to change itself, at least outwardly. But the unconscious, being deeply entrenched in the past, is conservative, cautious, aware of the deeper issues and of their more profound outcome; so there's a conflict between the two parts of the mind. This conflict does produce some kind of change, a modified continuity, with which most of us are concerned; but the real revolution is outside this dualistic field of consciousness.

"Where do dreams come into all this?"

We have to understand the totality of consciousness before coming to a particular part of it. The conscious mind, being occupied during its waking hours with daily events and pressures, has no time or opportunity to listen to the deeper part of itself; therefore, when the conscious mind 'goes to sleep', that is, when it's fairly quiet, not too worried, the unconscious can communicate, and this communication takes the form of symbols, visions, scenes. On waking you say, "I have had a dream", and you try to search out its meaning; but any interpretation of it will be biased, conditioned.

"Aren't there people who are trained to interpret dreams?"

There may be; but if you look to another for the interpretation of your dreams, you have the further problem of dependence on authority, which breeds many conflicts and sorrows.

"In that case, how am I to interpret them for myself?"

Is that the right question? Irrelevant questions can only produce unimportant answers. It's not a question of how to interpret dreams, but are dreams necessary at all?

"Then how can I put a stop to these dreams of mine?" he insisted.

Dreams are a device by which one part of the mind communicates with the other. Isn't that so?

"Yes, that seems fairly obvious, now that I have understood a little better the nature of consciousness."

Cannot this communication go on all the time, during the waking period as well? Isn't it possible to be aware of your own responses when you are getting into the bus, when you are with your family, when you are talking to your boss in the office, or to your servant at home? Just to be aware of all this—to be aware of the trees and the birds, of the clouds and the children, of your own habits, responses and traditions—is to observe it without judging or comparing; and if you can be so aware, constantly watching, listening, you will find that you do not dream at all. Then your whole mind is intensely active; everything has a meaning, a significance. To such a mind, dreams are unnecessary. You will then discover that in sleep there's not only complete rest and renewal, but a state which the mind can never touch. It's not something to be remembered and returned to; it's entirely inconceivable, a total renewal which cannot be formulated.

"Can I be so aware during the whole day?" he asked earnestly. "But I must, and I will be, for I honestly see the necessity of it. Sir, I have learnt a great deal, and I hope I may come again."

What Does It Mean To Be Serious?

SITTING ON the oxcart with a long slender stick in his hand was an old man, so thin that his bones were showing through. He had a kindly, wrinkled face, and his skin was very dark, burnt by many suns. The cart was heavy with firewood, and he was beating the oxen; you could hear the slap of his stick on their backs. They were coming from the country into the town, and it had been a long day. Driver and beasts were tired out, and they still had some distance to go. There was froth around the mouths of the oxen, and the old man seemed ready to drop; but there was stamina in that wiry old body, and the oxen would go on. As you walked beside the cart, the old man caught your eye, smiled, and stopped beating the oxen. They were his oxen, and he had been driving them for years; they knew he was fond of them, and the beating was a passing thing. He was stroking them now, and they continued to move at their ease. The old man's eyes told of infinite patience, and his mouth expressed weariness and endless toil. He wouldn't receive much money for his firewood, but it was enough to get by. They would rest along the roadside for the night, and make a start for home in the early morning. The cart would be empty, and the return journey would be easier. We went down the road together, and the oxen didn't seem to mind being touched by the stranger who was walking beside them. It was beginning to get dark, and presently the driver stopped, lit a lamp, hung it under his cart, and went on towards the noisy town.

Next morning the sun rose behind thick, dark clouds. It rained very often on this big island, and the earth was rich with green vegetation. There were immense trees everywhere, and well-kept gardens full of flowers. The people were well-fed, and the cattle plump and soft-eyed. On one tree there were dozens of orioles, with black wings and yellow bodies; they were surprisingly large birds, but their call was soft. They were hopping about from branch to branch, like flashes of golden light, and they seemed even more brilliant on a cloudy day. A magpie was calling in deep-throated tones, and the crows were making their usual raucous noise. It was comparatively cool, and walking would be pleasant. The temple was full of kneeling, praying people, and the grounds around it were clean. Beyond the temple was a sports club, where they were playing tennis. Children were everywhere, and among them walked the priests with their shaven heads and the inevitable fan. The streets were decorated, for there was going to be a religious procession the following day, when the moon would be full. Over the palm trees could be seen a great stretch of pale blue sky, which the clouds were rushing to cover. Among the people, along the noisy streets, and in the gardens of the well-to-do, there was great beauty; it was there everlastingly, but few cared to look.

The two of them, a man and a woman, had come from some distance to attend the talks. They could have been husband and wife, sister and brother, or just friends. They were gay and friendly, and their eyes declared the ancient culture that lay behind them. Pleasant-voiced and rather shy out of respect, they seemed surprisingly well-read, and he knew Sanskrit. He had also travelled a bit and knew the ways of the world.

"We have both been through many things," he began. "We have followed some of the political leaders, been fellow-travellers with the Communists and known at first hand their appalling brutality, gone the rounds of the spiritual teachers, and practised certain forms of meditation. We think we are serious people, but we may be deceiving ourselves. All these things were done with serious intent, but none of them seem to have great depth, though at the time we always thought they had. Both of us are active by nature, we are not the dreamy kind, but we have now come to the point when we no longer want to 'get somewhere', or participate in practices and organizational activities that have very little significance. Having found in such activities nothing more than lip-service and self-deception, we now want to understand what it is you are teaching. My father was somewhat familiar with your approach to life, and he used to talk to me about it, but I never got around to investigating the matter for myself, probably because I was 'told'—which is perhaps a normal reaction when one is young. As it happened, a friend of ours attended your talks last year, and when he recounted to us something of what he had heard, we decided to come. I don't know where to start, and perhaps you can help us out."

Though his companion hadn't said a word, her eyes and her manner indicated that she was giving full attention to what was being said.

Since you have said that you are both serious, let us begin from there. I wonder what we mean when we talk about being serious? Most people are serious about something or other. The politician with his schemes, and in his attaining of power; the schoolboy in his desire to pass an examination; the man who is out to make money; the professional man, and the man who is dedicated to some ideology, or is caught in the net of a belief—they are all serious in their own way. The neurotic is serious, and so also is the *sannyasi*. What then does it mean to be serious? Please don't think I am quibbling, but if we could understand this thing, we might learn a great deal about ourselves; and after all, that is the right beginning.

"I am serious," said his companion, "in wanting to clarify my own confusion, and it is for this reason that I have gone around seeking the help of those who say they can guide me towards that clarification. I have tried to forget myself in good works, in bringing some happiness to others, and in that effort I have been serious. I am also serious in my desire to find God."

Most people are serious about something. Negatively or positively, their seriousness always has an object, religious or otherwise, and upon the hope of attaining that object their seriousness depends. If for any reason the hope of attaining the object of their gratification is removed, are they still serious? One is serious in achieving, in gaining, in succeeding, in becoming; it is the end that makes one serious, the thing that one hopes to get or to avoid. So the end is important, and not the understanding of what it is to be serious. We are concerned, not with love, but with what love will do. The doing, the result, the achievement, is all-important, and not love itself, which has its own action.

"I don't quite understand how there can be seriousness unless one is serious *about* something," he replied.

"I think I see what you mean," said his companion. "I want to find God, and it is important for me to find Him, otherwise life has no meaning; it's only a bewildering chaos, full of misery. I can understand life only through God, who is the end and the beginning of all things; He alone can guide me in this welter of contradictions, and that's why I am serious about finding Him. But you are asking, is this seriousness at all?"

Yes. The understanding of living, with all its complications, is one thing, and the search for God is another. In saying that God, the ultimate end, will give meaning to life, you have brought into being —haven't you?—two opposing states: living, and God. You are struggling to find something away from life. You are serious about achieving a goal, an end, which you call God; and is that seriousness? Perhaps there is no such thing as finding God first, and then living; it may be that God is to be found in the very understanding of this complex process called life.

We are trying to understand what we mean by seriousness. You are serious about a formulation, a self-projection, a belief, which has nothing to do with reality. You are serious about the things of the mind, and not about the mind itself, who is the maker of these things. In giving your seriousness to achieving a particular result, are you not pursuing your own gratification? That's what everyone is serious about: getting what he wants. And is that all we mean by seriousness?

"I have never before looked at it in this way," she exclaimed. "Evidently I am not really serious at all."

Don't let's jump to conclusions. We are trying to understand what it means to be serious. One can see that to pursue fulfilment in any form, however noble or stupid, is not to be really serious. The man who drinks to escape from his sorrow, the man who is after power, and the man who is seeking God, are all on the same path, though the social significance of their pursuits may differ. Are such people serious?

"If not, then I'm afraid none of us are," he replied. "I always took it for granted that I was serious in my various undertakings, but now I am beginning to see that there is an altogether different kind of seriousness. I don't think I am able to put it into words yet, but I am beginning to get the feeling of it. Will you please go on?"

"I am a bit lost in all this," put in his companion. "I thought I was understanding it, but it eludes me."

When we are serious, we are serious *about* something; that is so, isn't it?

244

"Yes."

Now, is there a seriousness which is not directed towards an end and does not build up resistance?

"I don't quite follow."

"The question in itself is quite simple," he explained. "Wanting something, we set about getting it, and in this effort we consider ourselves to be serious. Now, he's asking, is that really seriousness? Or is seriousness a state of mind in which end-gaining and resistance do not exist?"

"Let me see if I understand this," she replied. "As long as I am trying to get or to avoid something, I am concerned about myself. End-gaining is really self-interest; it is a form of indulgence, blatant or refined, and you are saying, sir, that indulgence is not seriousness. Yes, that is now quite clear to me. But then what is seriousness?"

Let's inquire and learn about it together. You are not being taught by me. Being taught, and being free to learn, are two entirely different things, are they not?

"Please go a little slowly. I am not very bright, but I will get it by perseverance. I am also a bit stubborn—a sober virtue, but one that can be a nuisance. I hope you will be patient with me. In what way is being taught different from being free to learn?"

In being taught, there's always the teacher, the *guru* who knows, and the disciple who does not know; thus a division is forever maintained between them. This is essentially an authoritarian, hierarchical outlook, in which love does not exist. Though the teacher may talk about love, and the disciple assert his devotion, their relationship is unspiritual, deeply immoral, leading to a great deal of confusion and suffering. This is clear, isn't it?

"Frighteningly clear," he put in. "You have abolished at one stroke the whole structure of religious authority; but I see you are right."

"But one needs guidance, and who will act as a guide?" asked his companion.

Is there any need for guidance when we are constantly learning, not from anyone in particular, but from everything as we go along? Surely, we seek guidance only when we want to be safe, secure, comfortable. If we are free to learn, we shall learn from the falling leaf, from every kind of relationship, from being aware of the activities of our own minds. But most of us are not free to learn, because we are so used to being taught; we are told what to think by books, by our parents, by society, and like a gramophone we repeat what's on the record.

"And the record is generally very badly scratched," he added. "We have played it so often. Our thinking is entirely second-hand."

Being taught has made one repetitive, mediocre. The urge to be guided, with its implications of authority, obedience, fear, lack of love, and so on, can only lead to darkness. Being free to learn is quite another matter. And there can be no freedom to learn when there's already a conclusion, an assumption; or when one's outlook is based on experience as knowledge; or when the mind is held in tradition, tethered to a belief; or when there is the desire to be secure, to achieve a particular end.

"But it's impossible to be free of all that!" she ejaculated.

You don't know if it's possible or impossible until you have tried.

"Whether one likes it or not," she insisted, "one's mind is taught; and if, as you say, a mind that's taught cannot learn, what is one to do?"

The mind can be aware of its own bondage, and in that very awareness it is learning. But first of all, is it clear to us that a mind that's blindly held in what it has been taught, is incapable of learning?

"In other words, you are saying that as long as I merely follow tradition, I cannot learn anything new. Yes, that much is clear enough. But how am I to be free of tradition?"

Not so fast, please. The gatherings of the mind prevent the freedom to learn. To learn, there must be no accumulation of knowledge, no piling up of experiences as the past. Do you yourself see the truth of this? Is it a fact to you, or just something I have said, with which you may agree or disagree?

"I think I see it to be a fact," he put in. "Of course, you don't mean that we must throw away all the knowledge that science has gathered, that would be absurd. The point is, if we want to learn, we cannot assume anything."

Learning is a movement, but not from one fixed point to another, and this movement is impossible if the mind is burdened with an accumulation of the past, with conclusions, traditions, beliefs. This accumulation, though it may be called the *Atman,* the soul, the higher self, and so on, is the 'me', the ego, the self. The self and its maintenance prevent the movement of learning.

"I am beginning to understand what is meant by the movement of

246

learning," she said slowly. "As long as I'm enclosed within my own desire for security, for comfort, for peace, there can be no movement of learning. Then how am I to be free of this desire?"

Isn't that a wrong question? There's no method by which to be free. The very urgency and importance of being able to learn will free the mind from conclusions, from the self which is put together by words, by memory. The practising of a method, the 'how' and its discipline, is another form of accumulation; it never frees the mind, but only sets it going in a different pattern.

"I seem to understand something of all this," he said, "but so much is involved, I wonder if I shall ever really get to the bottom of it."

It's not as bad as all that. With the understanding of one or two central facts, the whole picture becomes clear. A mind that's taught, or desires to be guided, cannot learn. We now see this quite plainly, so let's go back to the question of seriousness, with which we started.

We saw that the mind is not serious if it has some end to be gained or avoided. Then what is seriousness? To find out, one must be aware that one's mind is turned outward or inward in order to fulfil itself, to gain or to become something. It's this awareness that sets the mind free to learn what it means to be serious; and to learning there is no end. To a mind that's learning, the heavens are open.

"I have learnt a great deal in this brief conversation," said his companion, "but shall I be able to learn further without your help?"

Do you see how you are blocking yourself? If one may say so, you are greedy for more, and this greed is preventing the movement of learning. Had you been aware of the significance of what you were feeling and saying, it would have opened the door to that movement. There is no 'further' learning, but just learning as you go along. Comparison arises only when there is accumulation. To die to everything that you have learnt is to learn. This dying is not a final act: it is to die from moment to moment.

"I have seen and understood, and goodness will flower from it."

Is There Anything Permanent?

THE HOUSE stood on a hill overlooking the main road, and beyond the road was the dull grey sea, which never seemed to have life. It was not like the sea in other parts of the world—blue, restless, immense—but was always either brown or grey, and the horizon seemed so close. One was glad it was there, for a cool breeze generally came from it when the sun was going down. On rare occasions there would be not a breath of air, and then it was suffocatingly hot; the smell of tar would come up from the road, along with the exhaust fumes of the ceaseless traffic.

There was a small garden below the house, with many flowers, and it was a delight to the passers-by. From the overhanging bushes, yellow flowers fell on the roadside, and occasionally a pedestrian would stoop to pick up a fallen blossom. Children went by with their nurses, but most of them were not allowed to pick up the flowers; the road was dirty, and they mustn't touch dirty things!

Not far away there was a temple by a pond, and around the pond there were benches. People were always sitting on those benches, and on the brick steps leading down to the water. From an open space at the edge of the pond, four or five steps led up into the temple. The temple, the steps and the open space were kept very clean, and people removed their footwear before coming there. Each worshipper rang the bell that was hanging from the roof, placed flowers near the idol, folded his hands in prayer, and went away. It was fairly quiet there, and although you could see the traffic, the noise didn't come that far.

Every evening, after the sun had set, a young man would come and sit near the entrance of the shrine. Freshly bathed and wearing clean clothes, he looked well-educated, and was probably an office-worker of some kind. He would sit there cross-legged for an hour or more, with his back straight and his eyes closed; in his right hand, under a newly-washed cloth which was still damp, he would be holding a string of beads. His covered fingers would move from one bead to the next as his lips pronounced the words of each prayer. Apart from this, he never moved a muscle, and he would sit there, lost to the world, till it was quite dark.

There was always a vendor or two near the entrance of the temple, selling nuts, flowers and coconuts. One evening three young men came and sat there. They all appeared to be under twenty. Suddenly one of them got up and began to dance, while another beat out the rhythm on a tin. He had on only a singlet and a loin-cloth, and he was showing off. He danced with extraordinary agility, moving his hips and arms with easy grace. He must have watched not only the Indian dances, but also the dancing that went on at the fashionable club near by. Quite a crowd had gathered by now, and they were encouraging him; but he needed no encouragement, and the dance was getting rather crude. All this time the man of prayers was sitting there, his body erect, with only his lips and his fingers moving. The little temple pool was reflecting the light of the stars.

We were in a small, bare room overlooking a noisy street. There was a mat on the floor, and we all sat around it. Through the open window could be seen a single palm tree on which a kite was perched, with its fierce eyes and its sharp, overhanging beak. There were three men and two women in the group that had come. The women sat on one side, opposite the men, and never spoke; but they listened attentively, and often their eyes would glisten with understanding, and a slight smile would appear on their lips. They were all quite young, and all had been to college, and now each of them had a job or a profession. They were all good friends and called each other by familiar names, and they had evidently talked over together a great many things. One of the men had the feel of the artist about him, and it was he who began.

"I always think," he said, "that very few artists are really creative. Some of them know how to handle colour and brush; they have learnt design and are masters of detail; they know anatomy to perfection, and are astonishingly capable on canvas. Equipped with capacity and technique, and moved by a deep creative impulse, they paint. But presently they become known and established, and then something happens to them—money and flattery, probably. Creative vision is gone, but they still have their superb technique, and for the rest of their lives they juggle with it. Now it's pure abstraction, now it's double-faced women, now it's a war scene with a few lines, space and dots. That period passes, and a new period is begun: they become sculptors, ceramists, church builders, and so on. But the inward glory is lost, and they know only outward glamour. I'm not an artist, I don't even know how to hold a brush; but I have a feeling there's something enormously significant that we all miss."

"I'm a lawyer," said one of the others, "but the practice of law is to me only a means of livelihood. I know it's rotten, one has to do so many dirty things to get on, and I would give it up tomorrow were it not for family responsibilities, and one's own fear—which is a greater burden than the responsibilities. From childhood I have been attracted to religion; I almost became a *sannyasi*, and even now I try to meditate every morning. Most definitely I feel that the world is too much with us. I am neither happy nor unhappy; I just exist. But in spite of everything, there's a deep yearning for something greater than this shoddy existence. Whatever it is, I feel it is there, but my will seems to be too weak and ineffectual to break through the mediocrity in which I live. I have tried going away, but I had to come back— because of the family, and all the rest of it. I am inwardly torn in two directions. I could escape from this conflict by losing myself in the dogmas and rituals of some church or temple, but all that seems so silly and infantile. Mere social respectability, with its immoral morality, means nothing to me; but I am respected in my law practice, and I could go ahead in that profession—but that's even a greater escape than the temple or the church. I have studied the books and the double-talk of Communism, and its chauvinistic nonsense is a terrible thing. Everywhere I go—at home, in court, on solitary walks —this inward agony is with me, like a disease for which there's no remedy. I have come here with my friends, not to find a remedy, for I have read what you say about such things, but if possible to understand this inward fever."

"When I was a boy, I always wanted to be a doctor," said the third one, "and I'm a doctor now. I can and do make quite a bit of money; I could probably make more, but what for? I try to be very conscientious with my patients, but you know how it is. I treat the well-to-do, but I also have patients without a penny, and there are so many of them that even if I could treat a thousand a day, there would still be more. I can't give all my time to them, so I see the rich in the mornings, and the poor in the afternoons, and sometimes far into the night; and with so much work, one does tend to become somewhat callous. I try to take as much trouble with the poor as with the well-to-do, but I find I am becoming less sympathetic and am losing that sensitivity which is so essential to the medical practitioner. I use all the right words, and have developed a good 'bedside manner', but inwardly I am drying up. The patients may not know this, but I know it all too well. I loved my patients at one time, especially the wretchedly poor; I really felt for them, with all their filth and disease. But over the years I have slowly been losing all that; my heart is becoming dry, my sympathy withering. I went away for a time in the hope that a complete change and rest would kindle the flame again;

but it's no good. The fire simply isn't there, and I have only the dead ashes of memory. I attend to my patients, but my heart is empty of love. It has done me good to tell you all this—but that's only a relief, it's not the real thing. And can the real thing ever be found?"

All of us were silent. The kite had flown away and a large crow had taken its place on the palm tree. Its powerful black beak was shining in the sun.

Aren't all these problems interrelated? One has to distrust similarity; but these three problems are not essentially dissimilar, are they?

"Come to think of it," replied the lawyer, "it looks like my two friends and I are in the same boat. We are all after the same thing. We may call it by different names—love, creativity, something greater than this tawdry existence—but it's really the same thing."

"Is it?" asked the artist. "At moments I have felt the astonishing beauty and vastness of life; but those moments soon pass, and a void is left. This void has its own vitality, but it's not the same as the other. The other is beyond the measure of time, beyond all word and thought. When that otherness comes into being, it's as though one had never existed; all the pettiness of life, the tortures of daily existence, are gone, and only that state remains. I have known that state, and I must somehow revive it. I am not concerned with anything else."

"You artists," said the doctor, "think that you are set apart from the rest of us. You are above other men; you have a special gift with special privileges; you are supposed to see more, feel more, live more intensely. But I don't think you are so very different from the engineer, or the lawyer, or the doctor, who may also live intensely. I used to suffer with my patients; I loved them, I knew what they were going through, their fears, their hopes and despairs. I felt as intensely for them as you might feel for a cloud, for a flower, for a leaf blown by the wind, or for the human face. Your intensity of feeling is not different from mine, or from that of our friend here. It is this intensity of feeling that matters, not what one feels intensely *about*. The artist likes to think that his particular expression of it is something far superior, nearer heaven, and I know the world holds its breath when it utters that word 'artist'; but you are as human as the rest of us, and our intensity is as keen, alive, vibrant, as yours. I am not belittling the artist, nor am I jealous of him; I am only saying that intensity of feeling is the important thing. Of course, it may be wrongly directed, and then the result is chaos and suffering both for oneself and for others, particularly if one happens to be in a position of power. The point is, you and I are after the same thing—you in wanting to recapture what you call the beauty and vastness of life, and I in wanting to love again."

"And I also am seeking it, in wanting to break through the mediocrity of my life," added the lawyer. "This ache which I feel is similar to yours; I may not be able to put it into words, or on canvas, but it's as intense as the colour you see in that flower. I, too, long for something infinitely more than all this, something that will bring peace and fullness."

"All right, I yield; both of you are right," admitted the artist. "Vanity is sometimes stronger than reason. We are all vain in our own peculiar ways, and how it hurts to admit it! Of course we are in the same boat, as you say. We all want something beyond our petty selves, but this pettiness creeps up on us and overwhelms us."

Then what's the problem we want to talk over? Is it clear to all of us?

"I think so," replied the doctor. "I should like to put it this way. Is there a permanent state of love, of creativity, a permanent ending of sorrow? We would all agree to this statement of the question, wouldn't we?"

The others nodded in assent.

"Is there a state of love, or creative peace," went on the doctor, "which, once having been attained, will never degenerate, never be lost?"

"Yes, that's the question," agreed the artist. "There is this extraordinary height of exhilaration which comes unexpectedly, and fades away like a fragrance. Can this intensity remain, without the reaction of dull emptiness? Is there a state of inspiration which does not yield to time and mood?"

You are asking a great deal, aren't you? If necessary, we shall consider later what that state is. But first of all, is there anything permanent?

"There must be," said the lawyer. "It would be very depressing and rather frightening to discover that there's nothing permanent."

We may find that there's something much more significant than permanency. But before we go into this, do we see that there must be no conclusion, no apprehension, no wish which will project a pattern of thought? To think clearly, one must not start from a supposition, a belief, or an inner demand, must one?

"I'm afraid this is going to be exceedingly difficult," replied the artist. "I have such a clear and definite memory of the state I have experienced, that it's almost impossible to put it aside."

"Sir, what you say is perfectly true," said the doctor. "If I am to discover a new fact, or perceive the truth of something, my mind cannot be cluttered with what has been. I see how necessary it is for the mind to set aside all that it has known or experienced; but considering the nature of the mind, is such a thing possible?"

"If there must be no inner demand," said the lawyer, thinking aloud, "then I must not wish to break through my present petty condition, or think of some other state, which can only be the outcome of what has been, a projection of what I already know. But isn't this almost impossible?"

I don't think so. If I want to understand you, surely I can have no prejudices or conclusions about you.

"That is so."

If for me the all-important thing is to understand you, then this very sense of urgency overrides all my prejudices and opinions about you, doesn't it?

"There can of course be no diagnosis until after an examination of the patient," said the doctor. "But is such an approach possible in an area of human experience where there's so much self-interest?"

If there's the intensity to understand the fact, the truth, then everything is possible; and everything becomes a hindrance if this intensity is not there. That much is clear, isn't it?

"Yes, at least verbally," replied the artist. "Perhaps I shall slip into it more as we go along."

We are trying to find out if there is, or is not, a permanent state —not what we would like, but the actual fact, the truth of the matter. Everything about us, within as well as without—our relationships, our thoughts, our feelings—is impermanent, in a constant state of flux. Being aware of this, the mind craves permanency, a perpetual state of peace, of love, of goodness, a security that neither time nor events can destroy; therefore it creates the soul, the *Atman,* and the visions of a permanent paradise. But this permanency is born of impermanency, and so it has within it the seeds of the impermanent. There is only one fact: impermanence.

"We know that the cells of the body are undergoing a constant change," said the doctor. "The body itself is impermanent; the organism wears out. Nevertheless, one feels there's a state untouched by time, and it's that state one is after."

Let us not speculate, but stick to facts. Thought is aware of its own impermanent nature; the things of the mind are transient, however much one may assert that they are not. The mind itself is the result of time; it has been put together through time, and through time it can be taken apart. It can be conditioned to think that there's a permanency, and it can also be conditioned to think that there's nothing enduring. Conditioning itself is impermanent, as is observable every day. The fact is that there's impermanency. But the mind craves for permanency in all its relationships, it wants to perpetuate the family name through the son, and so on. It cannot abide the uncertainty of its own state, and so it proceeds to create certainty.

"I am aware of this fact," said the doctor. "I once knew what it meant to love my patients, and while love was there I didn't care two pins whether it was permanent or impermanent; but now that it's gone, I want it to be made enduring. The desire for permanency arises only when one has experienced impermanence."

"But is there no lasting state of what may be called creative inspiration?" asked the artist.

Perhaps we shall understand that presently. Let us first see very clearly that the mind itself is of time, and that whatever the mind puts together is impermanent. It may, in its impermanence, have had a momentary experience of something which it now calls the permanent; and having once experienced that state, it remembers and desires more of it. So, from what it has known, memory puts together and projects that which it calls the permanent; but that projection is still within the scope of the mind, which is the field of the transient.

"I realize that whatever is born of the mind must be in a constant state of flux," said the doctor. "But when love was there, it was not born of the mind."

But now it has become a thing of the mind through memory, has it not? The mind now demands that it be revived; and what is revived will be impermanent.

"That's perfectly right, sir," put in the lawyer, "I see it quite clearly. My ache is the ache of remembering the things that should not be,

254

and longing for the things that should be. I never live in the present, but either in the past or in the future. My mind is always time-bound."

"I think I am getting this," said the artist. "The mind, with all its cunning, with its intrigues, its vanities and envies, is a whirlpool of self-contradictions. Occasionally it may catch a hint of something beyond its own noise, and what it has caught becomes a remembrance. It is with these ashes of remembrance that we live, treasuring things that are dead. I have been doing this, and what folly it is!"

Now, can the mind die to its remembrances, its experiences, to all the things it has known? Without seeking the permanent, can it die to the impermanent?

"I must understand this," said the doctor. "I have known love—you will all forgive me for using that word—and I cannot 'know' it again because my mind is held by the remembrance of what has been. It is this remembrance that it wants to make permanent, the remembrance of what it has known; and remembrance, with its associations, is nothing but ashes. Out of dead ashes, no new flame can be born. Then what? Please let me go on. My mind is living on memories, and the mind itself is memory, the memory of what has been; and this memory of what has been wants to be made permanent. So there is no love, but only the memory of love. But I want the real thing, not just the memory of it."

Wanting the real thing is still the urge of memory, isn't it?

"You mean I mustn't want it?"

"That's right," replied the artist. "Wanting it is a craving born of memory. You didn't want or cling to the real thing when it was there; it was simply there, like a flower. But as it faded, the craving for it began. To want it is to have the ashes of remembrance. The supreme moment which I have been longing for is not the real. My longing arises from the remembrance of something that once happened, and so I am back in the fog of memory, which I now see is darkness."

Craving is remembrance; there is no craving without the known, which is the memory of what has been, and it is this craving that sustains the 'me', the self, the ego. Now, can the mind die to the known—the known which is demanding to be made permanent? This is the real problem, isn't it?

"What do you mean by dying to the known?" asked the doctor.

To die to the known is to have no continuity of yesterday. That

255

which has continuance is only memory. What has no continuity is neither permanent nor impermanent. Permanency or continuity comes into being only when there's fear of transiency. Can there be an ending of consciousness as continuity, a dying to the total feeling of becoming without gathering again in the very act of dying? There is this feeling of becoming only when there is the memory of what has been and what should be, and then the present is used as a passage between the two. Dying to the known is the complete stillness of the mind. Thought under the pressure of craving can never be still.

"I followed with understanding up to the point when you mentioned dying," said the lawyer. "Now I am confused."

Only that which has an ending can be aware of the new, of love, or the supreme. What has continuance, 'permanence', is memory of the things that have been. The mind must die to the past, though the mind is put together by the past. The totality of the mind must be completely still, without any pressure, influence or movement from the past. Only then is the other possible.

"I shall have to ponder over this a great deal," said the doctor. "It will be real meditation."

Why This Urge To Possess?

It had been raining for days, and it still didn't look as though it were going to clear up. The hills and the mountains were under dark clouds, and the green shore across the lake was hidden by a thick fog. There were puddles everywhere, and the rain came through the half-open windows of the car. Leaving the lake behind and winding its way into the hills, the road passed a number of little towns and hamlets, and then climbed the side of a mountain. By now the rain had stopped, and as we went higher, the snow-clad peaks began to show themselves, sparkling in the morning sun.

Presently the car stopped, and you walked along a footpath that led away from the road, among the trees and into the open meadows. The air was still and cold, and it was surprisingly silent; there were not the usual cows with their bells. You met no other human beings on that path, but in the damp earth there were the footprints of heavy shoes with rows of nails. The path was not too soggy, but the pines were heavy with rain. Coming to the edge of a cliff, you could see far below a stream flowing from the distant glaciers. It was fed by several waterfalls, but their noise didn't reach that far, and there was complete silence.

You couldn't help being quiet too. It wasn't an enforced quietness; you became quiet naturally and easily. Your mind no longer went on its endless wanderings. Its outward movement had stopped, and it was on an inward journey, a journey that led to great heights and astonishing depths. But soon even this journey stopped, and there was neither an outward nor an inward movement of the mind. It was completely still, yet there was movement—a movement wholly unrelated to the going out and the coming back of the mind, a movement that had no cause, no end, no centre. It was a movement within the mind, through the mind, and beyond the mind. The mind could follow all its own activities, however intricate and subtle, but it was unable to follow this other movement, which did not originate from itself.

So the mind was still. It was not *made* still; its stillness had not been arranged, nor was it brought about by any desire to be still. It was simply still, and because it was still, there was this timeless movement. The mind could never capture it and put it among its remembrances; it would if it could, but there was no recognition of this movement. The mind did not know it, for it had never known it; therefore the mind was still, and this timeless movement went on beyond recall.

The sun was now behind the distant peaks, which were again covered by the clouds.

"I have been looking forward to this talk for many days, and now that I'm here, I don't know where to begin."

He was a young man, rather tall and lean, and he carried himself well. He had been to college, he said, but didn't do very well there, only just scraping through, and it was thanks to his father's wire-pulling that he had managed to get a good job. His job had a future, as every job had if you worked hard, but he wasn't too keen on it; he would stay on, and that was about all. What with all this mess the world was in, it didn't seem to matter much anyway. He was married, and had a small son—rather a nice child, and surprisingly intelligent, he added, considering the mediocrity of his parents. But when the boy grew up, he would probably become like the rest of the world, chasing success and power, if by that time there was still a world left.

257

"As you see, I can easily enough talk about some things, but what I really want to talk about seems so complex and difficult. I have never before talked about it to anyone, not even to my wife, and I suppose that makes it all the harder to talk about it now; but if you have patience, I will come to it."

He paused for a moment or two, and then went on.

"I am an only son, and was rather pampered. Though I am fond of literature, and would like to write, I have neither the gift nor the drive to carry it through. I am not entirely stupid, and could make something of my life, but I have one consuming problem: I want to possess people, body and soul. It's not just possession that I seek, but complete domination. I can't bear that there should be any freedom for the person possessed. I have watched others, and though they also are possessive, it's all so lukewarm, without any real intensity behind it. Society and its notion of good manners hold them within bounds. But I have no bounds; I just possess, without any qualifying adjectives. I don't think anyone can know what agonies I go through, to what tortures I subject myself. It isn't mere jealousy, it's literally hell-fire. Something will have to snap, though so far nothing has. Outwardly I manage to control myself, and I probably seem normal enough; but I am raging inside. Please don't think I'm exaggerating; I only wish I were."

What makes us want to possess, not only people, but things and ideas? Why this urge to own, with all its struggle and pain? And when once we do possess, it doesn't put an end to the problem, but only awakens other issues. If one may ask, do you know why you want to possess, and what possession means?

"To possess property is different from possessing people. As long as our present government lasts, the personal ownership of property will be permitted—not too much, of course, but at least a few acres, a house or two, and so on. You can take measures to safeguard your property, to keep it in your own name. But with people it's different. You can't pin them down, or lock them up. Sooner or later they slip out of your grasp, and then the torture begins."

But why this urge to possess? And what do we mean by possessing? In possessing, in feeling that you own, there is pride, a certain sense of power and prestige, is there not? There is pleasure in knowing that something is yours, be it a house, a piece of cloth, or a rare picture. The possession of capacity, talent, the ability to achieve, and the recognition that it brings—these also give you a sense of importance, a secure outlook on life. As far as people are concerned, to possess and to be possessed is often a mutually satisfactory relationship. There is also possession in terms of beliefs, ideas, ideologies, is there not?

"Aren't we entering too wide a field?"

But possession implies all this. You may want to possess people, another may possess a whole series of ideas, while someone else may be satisfied with owning a few acres of land; but however much the objects may vary, all possession is essentially the same, and each will defend what he owns—or in the very yielding of it, will possess something else at another level. Economic revolution may limit or abolish the private ownership of property, but to be free from the psychological ownership of people or ideas is quite another matter. You may get rid of one particular ideology, but you will soon find another. At all costs, you must possess.

Now, is there ever a moment when the mind is not possessing or being possessed? And why does one want to possess?

"I suppose it is because in owning one feels strong, safe; and of course there's always a gratifying pleasure in ownership, as you say. I want to possess persons for several reasons. For one thing, having power over another gives me a feeling of importance. In possession there's also a sense of well-being; one feels comfortably secure."

Yet with it all there is conflict and sorrow. You want to keep on with the pleasure of possessing, and avoid the pain of it. Can this be done?

"Probably not, but I go on trying. I ride on the stimulating wave of possession, knowing perfectly well what is going to happen; and when the fall comes, as it always does, I pick myself up and get on the next wave."

Then you have no problem, have you?

"I want this torture to end. Is it really impossible to possess completely and forever?"

It seems impossible with regard to property and ideas; and isn't it much more so in regard to people? Property, ideologies and deep-rooted traditions are static, fixed, and they can be defended for long periods of time through legislation and various forms of resistance; but people are not like that. People are alive; like you, they also want to dominate, to possess or be possessed. In spite of codes of morality and the sanctions of society, people do slip out of one pattern of possession

259

into another. There's no such thing as complete possession of anything, at any time. Love is never possession or attachment.

"Then what am I to do? Can I be free from this misery?"

Of course you can, but that's entirely another matter. You are aware that you possess; but are you ever aware of a moment when the mind is neither possessing nor being possessed? We possess because in ourselves we are nothing, and in possessing we feel we have become somebody. When we call ourselves Americans, Germans, Russians, Hindus, or what you will, the label gives us a sense of importance, so we defend it with the sword and with the cunning mind. We are nothing but what we possess—the label, the bank account, the ideology, the person —and this identification breeds enmity and endless strife.

"I know all this well enough; but you said something which struck a chord in me. Am I ever aware of a moment when the mind is neither possessing nor being possessed? I don't think I am."

Can the mind cease possessing, or being possessed by, the past and the future? Can it be free from both the influence of experience, and the urge to experience?

"Is that ever possible?"

You will have to find out; you will have to be fully aware of the ways of your own mind. You know the truth of possession, its sorrow and pleasure, but you stop there and try to overcome the one by the other. You do not know a moment when the mind is neither possessing nor being possessed, when it is totally free from the influence of what has been, and from the desire to become. To inquire into and discover for yourself the truth of this freedom is the liberating factor, and not the will to be free.

"Am I capable of such difficult inquiry and discovery? In a curious way, I am. I have been cunning and purposeful in possessing, and with that same energy I can now begin to inquire into the freedom of the mind. I should like to come back, if I may, after I have experimented with this."

DESIRE AND THE PAIN OF CONTRADICTION

TWO MEN were engaged in digging a long, narrow grave. It was fine, sandy soil, without too much clay, and the digging was easy. Now they were trimming the corners and making it neat all round. Some palm trees overhung the grave, and they had big bunches of golden coconuts. The men wore only loin-cloths, and their bare bodies were shining in the early morning sun. The light soil was still damp from the recent rains, and the leaves of the trees, stirred by a gentle breeze, were sparkling in the clear morning air. It was a lovely day, and as the sun had only just come over the tree-tops, it still wasn't too hot. The sea was pale blue and very calm, and the white waves were coming in lazily. There wasn't a cloud in the sky, and the waning moon was in midheaven. The grass was very green, and the birds were everywhere, calling to each other in different notes. There was great peace over the land.

Across the narrow ditch the men placed two long planks, and across these in turn a solid rope. Their bright loin-cloths and dark, sunburnt bodies had given life to the empty grave; but now they were gone, and the soil was quickly drying in the sun. It was quite a big cemetery, without much order, but well-kept. The rows of white slabs with names carved upon them had been discoloured by the many rains. Two gardeners worked there all day long, watering, trimming, planting and weeding. One was tall, and the other was short and plump. Except for a cloth on their heads against the burning sun, they too wore only loin-cloths, and their skin was nearly black. On rainy days the soiled cloth around their loins was still their only garment, and the rains washed their dark bodies. The tall one was now watering a flowering bush which he had just planted. From a large, round, earthenware pot with a narrow neck, he was sprinkling the water over the leaves and flowers. The pot glistened in the sun as the muscles in his dark body moved with ease, and the way he stood had grace and dignity. It was a beautiful thing to watch. The shadows were long in the morning sun.

Attention is a strange thing. We never look but through a screen of words, explanations and prejudices; we never listen save through judgments, comparisons and remembrances. The very naming of the flower, or the bird, is a distraction. The mind is never still to look, to listen. The moment it looks, it is off on its restless wanderings; in the very act of listening there is an interpretation, a recollection, an enjoyment, and attention is denied. The mind may be absorbed by the thing it sees or listens to, as a child is by a toy, but this is not attention. Nor is concentration attention, for concentration is the way of exclusion and resistance. There is attention only when the mind is not absorbed by an inward or outward idea or object. Attention is the complete good.

He was a middle-aged man, nearly bald, with clear, observant eyes, and his face was lined with worry and anxiety. The father of several children, he explained that his wife had died with the birth of the last child, and now they were all living with some relative. Although he was still employed, his salary was small, and it was difficult to make ends meet, but somehow they got through each month without too much strain. The eldest son was earning his own way, and the second was in college. He himself came of a family that had the austere traditions of many centuries, and this background now stood him in good stead. But for the coming generation, things were going to be very different; the world was changing rapidly, and the old traditions were crumbling. In any case, life would have its own way, and it was futile to grumble. He hadn't come to talk about his family, or the future, but about himself.

"Ever since I can remember, I seem to have been in a state of contradiction. I have always had ideals, and have always fallen far short of them. From my earliest years I have felt a pull towards the monastic life, the life of solitude and meditation, and I have ended up with a family. I once thought that I would like to be a scholar, but instead I have become an office drudge. My whole life has been a series of disturbing contrasts, and even now I am in the midst of self-contradictions which bother me greatly; for I want to be at peace with myself, and I don't seem able to harmonize these conflicting desires. What am I to do?"

Surely, there can never be a harmony or integration of opposing desires. Can you harmonize hate and love? Can ambition and the desire for peace ever be brought together? Mustn't they always be contradictory?

"But cannot conflicting desires be brought under control? Cannot these wild horses be tamed?"

You have tried, haven't you?

"Yes, for many years."

And have you succeeded?

"No, but that is because I haven't properly disciplined desire, I haven't tried hard enough. The fault is not with discipline, but with him who fails in discipline."

Is not this very disciplining of desire the breeder of contradiction? To discipline is to resist, to suppress; and is not resistance or suppression the way of conflict? When you discipline desire, who is the 'you' that is doing the disciplining?

"It's the higher self."

Is it? Or is it merely one part of the mind trying to dominate the other, one desire suppressing another desire? This suppression of one part of the mind, by another which you call the 'higher self', can only lead to conflict. All resistance is productive of strife. However much one desire may suppress or discipline another, that so-called higher desire breeds other desires which soon are in revolt. Desire multiplies itself; there isn't just one desire. Haven't you noticed this?

"Yes, I have noticed that in disciplining a particular desire, other desires spring up around it. You have to go after them one by one."

And so spend a lifetime pursuing and holding down one desire after another—only to find at the end that desire still remains. Will is desire, and it can tyrannically dominate all other desires; but what is thus conquered has to be conquered again and again. Will can become a habit; and a mind that functions in the groove of habit is mechanical, dead.

"I'm not sure I understand all the finer points of what you are explaining, but I am aware of the entanglements and contradictions of desire. If there were only one contradiction in me, I could put up with its strife, but there are several of them. How am I to be at peace?"

To understand is one thing, and to desire to be at peace is another. With understanding there does come peace, but the mere desire to be at peace only strengthens desire, which is the source of all conflict. A strong, dominant desire never brings peace, but only builds an imprisoning wall around itself.

"Then how is one to get out of this net of self-contradictory desires?"

Is the 'how' an inquiry, or the demand for a method by which to put an end to contradiction?

"I suppose I am asking for a method. But isn't it only through the patient and rigorous practice of a proper method that one can end this strife?"

Again, any method implies an effort to control, suppress or sublimate desire, and in this effort, resistance in different forms, subtle or brutal, is built up. It's like living in a narrow passage that shuts you away from the vastness of life.

"You seem to be very much against discipline."

I am only pointing out that a disciplined, moulded mind is not a free mind. With the understanding of desire, discipline loses its significance. The understanding of desire is of far greater significance than discipline, which is mere conformity to a pattern.

"If there's to be no discipline, then how is the mind to be free from desire, which brings all these contradictions?"

Desire does not bring contradictions. Desire *is* contradiction. That is why it's important to understand desire.

"What do you mean by understanding desire?"

It is to be aware of desire, without naming it, without rejecting or accepting it. It is to be simply aware of desire, as you would be of a child. If you would understand a child, you must observe it, and such observation is not possible if there's any sense of condemnation, justification or comparison. Similarly, to understand desire, there must be this simple awareness of it.

"Will there then be the cessation of self-contradiction?"

Is it possible to guarantee anything in these matters? And this very urge to be sure, safe—is it not another form of desire?

Sir, have you ever known a moment when there has been no self-contradiction?

"Perhaps in sleep, but not otherwise."

Sleep is not necessarily a state of peace, or of freedom from self-contradiction—but that's another matter.

Why have you never known such a moment? Haven't you experienced total action—an action involving your mind and your heart as well as your body, the totality of your whole being?

"Unfortunately, I have never known such a pure moment. Complete self-forgetfulness must be a great bliss, but it has never happened to me, and I think very few are ever blessed in that manner."

Sir, when the self is absent, do we not know love—not the love that is called personal or impersonal, worldly or divine, but love without the interpreting mind?

"Sometimes, when I am sitting at my desk in the office, a strange feeling of 'otherness' does come over me—but it's such a rare thing. If only it would last and not fade away."

How acquisitive we are! We want to hold that which cannot be held; we want to remember that which is not the stuff of memory. All this wanting, pursuing, reaching, which is the desire to be, to become,

264

makes for contradiction, the building up of the self. The self can never know love; it can only know desire, with its contradictions and miseries. Love is not a thing to be pursued, to be gained; it is not to be bought through the practice of virtue. All such pursuits are the ways of the self, of desire; and with desire there is always the pain of contradiction.

"What Am I To Do?"

The wind was blowing fresh and cool. It was not the dry air of the surrounding semi-desert, but came from the mountains far away. Those mountains were among the highest in the world, a great chain of them running from north-west to south-east. They were massive and sublime, an incredible sight when you saw them in the early morning, before the sun was on the sleeping land. Their towering peaks, glowing a delicate rose, were startlingly clear against the pale blue sky. As the sun climbed higher, the plains were covered with long shadows. Soon those mysterious peaks would disappear in the clouds, but before they withdrew, they would leave their blessing on the valleys, the rivers and the towns. Though you could no longer see them, you could feel that they were there, silent, immense and timeless.

A beggar was coming down the road, singing; he was blind, and a child was leading him. People passed him by, and occasionally someone would drop a coin or two into the tin he was holding in one hand; but he went on with his song, heedless of the rattle of the coins. A servant came out of a big house, dropped a coin in the tin, muttered something, and went back again, shutting the gate behind him. The parrots were off for the day in their crazy and noisy flight. They would go to the fields and the woods, but towards evening they would return for the night to the trees along the road; it was safer there, though the street-lights were almost among the leaves. Many other birds seemed to remain all day in the town, and on a big lawn some of them were trying to catch the sleepy worms. A boy went by, playing his flute. He was lean and barefooted; there was a swagger in his walk, and his feet didn't seem to mind where they trod. He *was* the flute, and the song was in his eyes. Walking behind him, you felt that he was the first boy with a flute in all the world. And, in a way, he was;

for he paid no attention to the car that rushed past, nor to the police-man standing at the corner, heavy with sleep, nor to the woman with a bundle on her head. He was lost to the world, but his song went on.

And now the day had begun.

The room was not very large, and the few who had come rather crowded it. They were of all ages. There was an old man with his very young daughter, a married couple, and a college student. They evidently didn't know each other, and each was eager to talk about his own problem, but without wanting to interfere with the others. The little girl sat beside her father, shy and very quiet; she must have been about ten. She had on fresh clothes, and there was a flower in her hair. We all sat for awhile without saying a word. The college student waited for age to speak, but the old man preferred to let others speak first. At last, rather nervously, the young man began.

"I am now in my last year at college, where I have been studying engineering, but somehow I don't seem to be interested in any particular career. I simply don't know what I want to do. My father, who is a lawyer, doesn't care what I do as long as I do *something*. Of course, since I am studying engineering, he would like me to be an engineer; but I have no real interest in it. I have told him this, but he says the interest will come when once I get working at it for a livelihood. I have several friends who studied for different careers, and who are now earning their own way; but most of them are already becoming dull and weary, and what they will be like a few years hence, God only knows. I don't want to be like that—and I'm sure I will be, if I become an engineer. It isn't that I'm afraid of the exams. I can pass them easily enough, and I'm not boasting. I just don't want to be an engineer, and nothing else seems to interest me either. I have done a spot of writing, and have dabbled in painting, but that kind of thing doesn't carry very far. My father is only concerned with pushing me into a job, and he could get me a good one; but I know what will happen to me, if I accept it. I feel like throwing up everything and leaving college without waiting to take the final exams."

That would be rather silly, wouldn't it? After all, you are nearly through college; why not finish it? There's no harm in that, is there?

"I suppose not. But what am I to do then?"

Apart from the usual careers, what would you really like to do? You must have some interest, however vague it may be. Somewhere, deep down, you know what it is, don't you?

"You see, I don't want to become rich; I have no interest in raising a family, and I don't want to be a slave to a routine. Most of my friends who have jobs, or who have embarked upon a career, are tied to the office from morning till night; and what do they get out of it? A house, a wife, some children—and boredom. To me, this is really a frightening prospect, and I don't want to be caught in it; but I still don't know what to do."

Since you have thought so much about all this, haven't you tried to find out where your real interest lies? What does your mother say?

"She doesn't care what I do as long as I am safe, which means being securely married and tied down; so she backs father up. On my walks I have thought a great deal about what I would really like to do, and I have talked it over with friends. But most of my friends are bent on some career or other, and it's no good talking to them. Once they are caught in a career, whatever it may be, they think it's the right thing to do—duty, responsibility, and all the rest of it. I just don't want to get caught in a similar treadmill, that's all. But what is it I would really like to do? I wish I knew."

Do you like people?

"In a vague sort of way. Why do you ask?"

Perhaps you might like to do something along the line of social work.

"Curious you should say that. I have thought of doing social work, and for a time I went around with some of those who have given their lives to it. Generally speaking, they are a dry, frustrated lot, frightfully concerned about the poor, and ceaselessly active in trying to improve social conditions, but unhappy inside. I know one young woman who would give her right eye to get married and lead a family life, but her idealism is destroying her. She's caught in the routine of doing good works, and has become dreadfully cheerful about her boredom. It's all idealism without flare, without inward joy."

I suppose religion, in the accepted sense, means nothing to you?

"As a boy I often used to go with my mother to the temple, with its priests, prayers and ceremonies, but I haven't been there for years."

That too becomes a routine, a repetitious sensation, a living on words and explanations. Religion is something much more than all that. Are you adventurous?

"Not in the usual meaning of that word—mountain climbing, polar exploration, deep-sea diving, and so on. I'm not being superior, but to me there's something rather immature about all that. I could no more climb mountains than hunt whales."

What about politics?

"The ordinary political game doesn't interest me. I have some Communist friends, and have read some of their stuff, and at one time I thought of joining the party; but I can't stomach their double-talk, their violence and tyranny. These are the things they actually stand for, whatever may be their official ideology and their talk of peace. I went through that phase quickly."

We have eliminated a great deal, haven't we? If you don't want to do any of these things, then what's left?

"I don't know. Am I still too young to know?"

It's not a matter of age, is it? Discontent is part of existence, but we generally find a way to tame it, whether through a career, through marriage, through belief, or through idealism and good works. One way or another, most of us manage to smother this flame of discontent, don't we? After successfully smothering it, we think at last we are happy—and we may be, at least for the time being. Now, instead of smothering this flame of discontent through some form of satisfaction, is it possible to keep it always burning? And is it then discontent?

"Do you mean I should remain as I am, dissatisfied with everything about me and within myself, and not seek some satisfying occupation that will let this fire burn out? Is that what you mean?"

We are discontented because we think we should be contented; the idea that we should be at peace with ourselves makes discontentment painful. You think you ought to *be* something, don't you?—a responsible person, a useful citizen, and all the rest of it. With the understanding of discontent, you may be these things and much more. But you want to do something satisfying, something which will occupy your mind and so put an end to this inner disturbance; isn't that so?

"It is in a way, but I now see what such occupation leads to."

The occupied mind is a dull, routine mind; in essence, it's mediocre. Because it's established in habit, in belief, in a respectable and profitable routine, the mind feels secure, both inwardly and outwardly; therefore it ceases to be disturbed. This is so, isn't it?

"In general, yes. But what am I to do?"

You may discover the solution if you go further into this feeling of discontent. Don't think about it in terms of being contented. Find out why it exists, and whether it shouldn't be kept burning. After all, you are not particularly concerned about earning a livelihood, are you?

"Quite bluntly, I am not. One can always live somehow or other."

So that's not your problem at all. But you don't want to be caught in a routine, in the wheel of mediocrity; isn't that what you are concerned about?

"It looks like it, sir."

Not to be thus caught demands hard work, incessant watching, it means coming to no conclusions from which to continue further thinking; for to think from a conclusion is not to think at all. It's because the mind starts from a conclusion, from a belief, from experience, from knowledge, that it gets caught in routine, in the net of habit, and then the fire of discontent is smothered.

"I see that you are perfectly right, and I now understand what it is that has really been on my mind. I don't want to be like those whose life is routine and boredom, and I say this without any sense of superiority. Losing oneself in various forms of adventure is equally meaningless; and I don't want to be merely contented either. I have begun to see, however vaguely, in a direction which I never knew even existed. Is this new direction what you were referring to the other day in your talk when you spoke of a state, or a movement, which is timeless and ever creative?"

Perhaps. Religion is not a matter of churches, temples, rituals and beliefs; it's the moment-by-moment discovery of that movement, which may have any name, or no name.

"I'm afraid I have taken more than my share of the available time," he said, turning to the others. "I hope you don't mind."

"On the contrary," replied the old man. "I for one have listened very attentively, and have profited a great deal; I, too, have seen something beyond my problem. In listening quietly to the troubles of another, our own burdens are sometimes lightened."

He was silent for a minute or two, as if considering how to express what he wanted to say.

"Personally, I have reached an age," he went on, "when I no longer ask what I am going to do; instead, I look back and consider what I have done with my life. I too went to college, but I was not as thoughtful as our young friend here. Upon graduating from college, I went in search of work, and once having found a job, I spent the next forty years and more in earning a livelihood and maintaining a rather large family. During all that time I was caught in the office routine to which you have referred, and in the habits of family life, and I know its pleasures and tribulations, its tears and passing joys. I have grown old with struggle and weariness, and in recent years there has been a fast decline. Looking back on all that, I now ask myself, 'What have you done with your life? Apart from your family and your job, what have you actually accomplished?' "

The old man paused before answering his own question.

"Over the years, I joined various associations for the improvement of this and that; I belonged to several different religious groups, and left one for another; and I hopefully read the literature of the extreme left, only to find that their organization is as tyrannically authoritarian as the church. Now that I have retired, I can see that I have been living on the surface of life; I have merely drifted. Though I struggled a little against the strong current of society, in the end I was pulled along by it. But don't misunderstand me. I'm not shedding tears over the past; I don't bemoan the things that have been. I am concerned with the few years that I still have left. Between now and the fast-approaching day of my death, how am I to meet this thing called life? That is my problem."

What we are is made up of what we have been; and what we have been also shapes the future, without definitely giving line and sub-stance to every thought and action. The present is a movement of the past to the future.

"What has been my past? Practically nothing at all. There have been no great sins, no towering ambition, no overwhelming sorrow, no degrading violence. My life has been that of the average man, neither hot nor cold; it has been an even flow, a thoroughly mediocre life. I have built up a past in which there's nothing to be either proud or ashamed of. My whole existence has been dull and empty, without much meaning. It would have been the same, had I lived in a palace, or in a village hut. How easy it is to slip into the current of mediocrity! Now, my question is, can I stem in myself this current of mediocrity? Is it possible to break away from my pettily enlarging past?"

What is the past? When you use the word 'past', what does it signify?

"It seems to me that the past is chiefly a matter of association and memory."

Do you mean the totality of memory, or just the memory of everyday incidents? Incidents that have no psychological significance, while they may be remembered, do not take root in the soil of the mind. They come and go; they do not occupy or burden the mind. Only those remain which have psychological significance. So what do you mean by the past? Is there a past that remains solid, immovable, from which you can cleanly and sharply break away?

"My past is made up of a multitude of little things put together, and its roots are shallow. A good shock, like a strong wind, could blow it away."

And you are waiting for the wind. Is that your problem?

"I'm not waiting for anything. But must I go on like this for the rest of my days? Can I not break away from the past?"

Again, what is the past from which you want to break away? Is the past static, or is it a living thing? If it's a living thing, how does it get its life? Through what means does it revive itself? If it's a living thing, can you break away from it? And who is the 'you' that wants to break away?

"Now I'm getting confused," he complained. "I have asked a simple question, and you counter it by asking several more complicated ones. Would you kindly explain what you mean?"

You say, sir, that you want to be free from the past. What is this past?

"It consists of experiences and the memories one has of them."

Now, these memories, you say, are on the surface, they are not deep-rooted. But may not some of them have roots deep in the unconscious?

"I don't think I have any deep-rooted memories. Tradition and belief have deep roots in many people, but I follow them only as a matter of social convenience. They don't play a very significant part in my life."

If the past is to be dismissed so easily, there's no problem; if only the outer husk of the past remains, which can be brushed off at any time, then you have already broken away. But there's more to the problem than that, isn't there? How are you to break through your mediocre life? How are you to shatter the pettiness of the mind? Isn't this also your problem, sir? And surely, the 'how' in this case is a furtherance of inquiry, not the demand for a method. It's the practising of a method, based on the desire to succeed, with its fear and authority, that has brought about pettiness in the first place.

"I came with the intention of dispelling my past, which is without much significance, but I am being confronted with another problem."

Why do you say that your past is without much significance?

"I have drifted on the surface of life, and when you drift, you can't have deep roots, even in your family. I see that to me life hasn't meant very much; I have done nothing with it. Only a few years are now left to me, and I want to stop drifting, I want to make something of what remains of my life. Is this at all possible?"

What do you want to make of your life? Doesn't the pattern of what you want to be, evolve from what you *have* been? Surely, your pattern is a reaction from what has been; it is an outcome of the past.

"Then how am I to make anything of life?"

What do you mean by life? Can you act upon it? Or is life incalculable, and not to he held within the boundaries of the mind? Life is everything, isn't it? Jealousy, vanity, inspiration and despair; social morality, and the virtue which is outside the realm of cultivated righteousness; knowledge gathered through the centuries; character, which is the meeting of the past with the present; organized beliefs, called religions, and the truth that lies beyond them; hate and affection; the love and compassion which are not within the field of the mind—all this and more is life, is it not? And you want to do something with it, you want to give it shape, direction, significance. Now, who is the 'you' that wants to do all this? Are you different from that which you seek to change?

"Are you suggesting that one should just go on drifting?"

When you want to direct, to shape life, your pattern can only be according to the past; or, being unable to shape it, your reaction is to drift. But the understanding of the totality of life brings about its own action, in which there is neither drifting nor the imposition of a pattern. This totality is to be understood from moment to moment. There must be the death of the past moment.

"But am I capable of understanding the totality of life?" he asked anxiously.

If you do not understand it, no one else can understand it for you. You cannot learn it from another.

"How shall I proceed?"

Through self-knowledge; for the totality, the whole treasure of life, lies within yourself.

"What do you mean by self-knowledge?"

It is to perceive the ways of your own mind; it is to learn about your cravings, your desires, your urges and pursuits, the hidden as well as the open. There is no learning where there is the accumulation of knowledge. With self-knowledge, the mind is free to be still. Only then is there the coming into being of that which is beyond the measure of the mind.

The married couple had been listening the whole time; they had been awaiting their turn, but never interrupted, and only now the husband spoke up.

"Our problem was that of jealousy, but after listening to what has already been said here, I think we may be capable of resolving it. Perhaps we have understood more deeply by quietly listening than we would have by asking questions."

Fragmentary Activities and Total Action

Two crows were fighting, and they meant business. They were flopping about on the ground with their wings locked, and their sharp, black beaks were tearing at each other. One or two of their companions were cawing at them from a nearby tree, and suddenly the whole neighbourhood of crows was there, making an awful noise and trying to stop the fight. There must have been dozens of them, but in spite of their anxious and angry calls, the fight went on. A shout didn't stop it; then a loud clap of the hands scared them all away, even the fighters, who continued to fly at each other in and out among the branches of the surrounding trees. But it was all over. A black cow tied to a stake had placidly looked in the direction of the fight, and then gone on with her feeding. She was a small animal, as cows go, and very friendly, with big, limpid eyes.

A procession came along the road. It was a funeral. Half a dozen cars were led by a hearse, in which could be seen the coffin, a highly polished affair with many silver fittings. Arriving at the cemetery, all the people got out of their cars, and the coffin was carried slowly to the grave, which had been dug earlier that morning. Twice around the grave they went, and then carefully laid the coffin on two solid planks which spanned the open trench. All knelt as the priest pronounced his blessing, and the coffin was gently lowered into its final resting place. There was a long pause; then each one threw in a handful of the freshly dug soil, and the diggers, in their bright loin-cloths, began shoveling it into the grave, which was soon filled. A wreath of white flowers, already withering in the hot sun, was placed upon the grave, and the people then solemnly departed.

It had been raining recently, and the grass in the cemetery was dazzlingly green. All around it were palm and banana trees, and flowering bushes. It was a pleasant place, and children would come to play on the grass under the trees, where there were no graves. Early in the morning, long before the sun was up, there was heavy dew on the grass, and the tall palms stood out against the starlit sky. The breeze from the north was fresh, and it brought with it the long moan of a distant train. Otherwise it was very quiet; there were no lights in the surrounding houses, and the rattle of lorries on the road had not yet begun.

Meditation is the flowering of goodness; it is not the cultivation of goodness. What is cultivated never endures; it passes away, and has to be started again. Meditation is not for the meditator. The meditator knows how to meditate; he practises, controls, shapes, struggles, but this activity of the mind is not the light of meditation. Meditation is not put together by the mind; it's the total silence of the mind in which the centre of experience, of knowledge, of thought, is not. Meditation is complete attention without an object in which thought is absorbed. The meditator can never know the goodness of meditation.

No longer young, he was a man well-known for his political idealism and his good works. Deep in his heart there was the hope of finding something far greater than these, but he was one of those to whom righteous action had always been the indication of goodness. He was constantly embroiled in reform, which he regarded as the means to an ultimate end: the goodness of society. An odd mixture of piety and activity, he lived in the shell of his own well-reasoned thought; yet he had heard a whisper of something beyond it. He had come with a friend, who was active with him in social reform. The friend was a short, wiry man, and there was about him an air of aggression held in check. He must have seen that aggression is not the right way to proceed, but he couldn't quite cover it up; it was behind his eyes, and it showed unknowingly when he smiled. As we sat down together in that room, neither of them seemed to notice the delicate blossom that a passing breeze had brought in through the window. It was lying on the floor, and the sun was upon it.

"My friend and I have not come here to discuss political action," the first one began. "We are well aware of what you think about it. To you, action is not political, reformatory or religious; there is only action, a total action. But most of us do not think like that. We think in compartments, which are sometimes watertight, and sometimes pliable, yielding; but our action is always fragmentary. We just don't know what total action is. We know only the activities of the part, and we hope by putting these various parts together to make the whole."

Is it ever possible to make the whole by assembling the parts, except in mechanical things? There you have a blue-print, a design to help you to put the parts together. Have you a similar design by which to bring about the perfection of society?

"We have," the friend replied.

Then you already know what the future will be for man?

"We are not so conceited as all that, but we do want certain obvious reforms brought about, to which no one can object."

Surely, reform will always be fragmentary. To be active in doing 'good' without understanding total action is in the long run to do harm, isn't it?

"What is total action?"

It is certainly not a putting together of various separate activities. To understand total action, fragmentary activity must cease. It's impossible to see at one sweep the whole expanse of the heavens by going from one small window to another. One must abandon all windows, mustn't one?

"That sounds fine intellectually, but when you see the hungry, the miserably poor, you boil inside and want to do something."

Which is most natural. But mere reform is always in need of further reform, and to carry on these various fragmentary activities, without understanding total action, seems so mischievous and destructive.

"How are we to understand this total action of which you speak?" asked the other.

Obviously, one has first to abandon the part, the fragmentary, which is the group, the nation, the ideology. Holding on to these, one hopes to understand the whole, which is impossible. It is like an ambitious man

275

trying to love. To love, the desire for success, for power and position, must cease. One can't have both. Similarly, the mind, whose very thinking is fragmentary, is incapable of discovering this total action.

"Then how can one ever discover it at all?" demanded the friend.

There is no formula for its discovery. The feeling of being whole, complete, is very different from the intellectual description of it. We don't feel this total being, and we try to bring together the fragments, hoping thereby to have the whole. Sir, if one may ask, why do you do anything?

"I feel and think, and action flows from it."

Doesn't this lead to contradiction in your various activities?

"Often it does, but one can avoid that contradiction by sticking to a definite course of action."

In other words, you shut out all activities which have no relation to the one you have chosen. Sooner or later, won't this create confusion?

"Perhaps. But what is one to do?" he asked rather irritably.

Is that merely a verbal question, or do you begin to feel that sticking to a chosen pattern of action is exclusive and harmful? It is because you don't *feel* the necessity for total action that you play around with activities which are contradictory. But to feel the necessity for total action, you must inquire deeply within yourself. There's no inquiry if there's no humility. To learn, there must be humility; but you already know, and how can a man who knows be humble? When there's humility, you can't be a reformer, or a politician.

"Then we can't do anything, and we shall be driven into slavery by those of the extreme left whose ideology promises a paradise on earth! They will take power and liquidate us. But such an eventuality can definitely be avoided through intelligent legislation, through reform, and through the gradual socialization of industry. This is what we are after."

"But what about humility?" asked the first one. "I see its importance, but how is one to come by it?"

Surely, not through a method. To practise humility is to cultivate pride. A method implies success, and success is arrogance. The difficulty is that most of us want to be somebody, and this partial, reformatory activity gives us an opportunity to satisfy that urge. Economic or political revolution is still partial, fragmentary, leading to further tyranny and misery, as has recently been shown. There's only one total revolution, the religious, and it has nothing to do with organized religion, which is another form of tyranny. But why is there no humility?

"For the simple reason that if one were humble, one would not be able to do anything," asserted the friend. "Humility is for the recluse, not for the man of action."

You haven't moved away from your conclusions, have you? You came with them, and you will leave with them; and to think from conclusions is obviously not to think at all.

"What prevents humility?" asked the first one.

Fear. Fear of saying "I don't know"; fear of not being a leader, of not being important; fear of not being in the show, whether it be the traditional show, or the latest ideology.

"Am I afraid?" he asked musingly.

Can another answer that question? Mustn't one discover the truth of the matter for oneself?

"I suppose I have been in the limelight for so long that I have taken it for granted that the activities in which I am engaged are the good and the true. You are perfectly right. There's a certain amount of modification and adjustment on our part, but we dare not think too deeply, because we want to be among the leaders, or at least with the leaders; we don't want to be the forgotten men."

Surely, all this indicates that you are really not interested in the people, but in ideologies, schemes and Utopias. You do not love the people, or feel sympathy for them; you love yourself, through your personal identification with certain theories, ideals and reformatory activities. *You* remain, clothed in a different respectability. You help the people in the name of something, for the good of something. You are actually concerned, not with helping the people, but with advancing the plan or the organization which you assert will help the people. Isn't this where your real interest lies?

They remained silent and departed.

FREEDOM FROM THE KNOWN

IT WAS a very clear, starry night. There was not a cloud in the sky. The dull roar of the neighbouring city had subsided, and there was a great stillness, unbroken even by the hoot of an owl. The waning moon was just above the tall palms, which were very still, bewitched by the silence. Orion was well up in the western sky, and the Southern Cross was over the hills. Not a house had a light in it, and the narrow road was deserted and dark.

Suddenly, from somewhere among the trees, there came the sound of wailing. At first it was muffled, and produced a strange impression of mystery and fear. As it drew nearer, the wailing became sharp and noisy, and it sounded artificial; the sadness didn't ring quite true. Into the open at last came a procession of people with lamps, and the wailing went on louder than ever. They were carrying on their shoulders what appeared, in the pale moonlight, to be a dead body. Going slowly along a path that crossed the open ground and turned to the right, the procession disappeared again among the trees. The wailing grew fainter, and finally stopped. Again there was complete silence—that strange silence which comes when the world is asleep, and which has a quality of its own. It wasn't the silence of the forest, of the desert, of far, isolated places; nor was it the silence of a fully awakened mind. It was the silence of toil and weariness, of sorrow and the surface-flutter of joy. This silence would pass with the coming dawn, and would return with the coming again of the night.

The next morning our host inquired, "Did that procession last night disturb you?"

What was it?

"When someone is seriously ill, they call an M.D., but to be on the safe side, they also bring in a man who is supposed to be able to drive away the evil of death. After chanting over the sick man and doing all kinds of fantastic things, the exorcist himself lies down and gives every appearance of going through the pangs of death. Then he is tied on a litter, carried in a procession with much wailing to the burial or burning place, and left there. Presently his assistant unties the cords, and he comes back to life; the chanting over the sick man is resumed, and then they all quietly go back to their homes. If the patient recovers, the magic has worked; if he does not, then the evil has been too strong."

The elderly man who had come was a *sannyasi,* a religious ascetic who had given up the world. His head was shaven, his only garment a newly-washed loin-cloth of saffron, and he carried a long staff, which he laid beside him as he sat on the floor with the ease of long practice. His body was slim and well-disciplined, and he leaned slightly forward as though he were listening, but his back was perfectly straight. He was very clean, his face was clear and fresh, and he had about him the dignity of other-worldliness. When he spoke he looked up, but otherwise he kept his eyes down. There was something very pleasant and friendly about him. He had travelled on foot all over the land, going from village to village and from town to town. He walked only in the mornings, and towards evening, not when the sun was hot. Being a *sannyasi* and a member of the highest caste, he had no trouble in getting food, for he was received with respect and fed with care. When, on rare occasions, he travelled by train, it was always without a ticket, for he was a holy man, and he had the air of one whose thoughts were not of this world.

"From one's youth the world has had little attraction, and when one left the family, the house, the property, it was for always. One has never returned. It has been an arduous life, and the mind is now well-disciplined. One has listened to spiritual teachers in the north and in the south; one has gone on pilgrimages to different shrines and temples, where there was holiness and right teaching. One has searched in the silence of secluded places, far from the haunts of men, and one knows the beneficial effects of solitude and meditation. One has witnessed the upheavals this country has passed through in recent years—the turning of man against man, of sect against sect, the killing, and the coming and going of the political leaders, with their schemes and promised benefits. The cunning and the innocent, the powerful and the weak, the wealthy and the poor—they have always coexisted, and always will; for that is the way of the world."

He was silent for a minute or two, and then continued.

"In the talk of the other evening, it was said that the mind must be free from ideas, formulations, conclusions. Why?"

Can search begin from a conclusion, from that which is already known? Must not search begin in freedom?

"When there's freedom, is there any need to search? Freedom is the end of search."

Surely, freedom from the known is only the beginning of search. Unless the mind is free from knowledge as experience and conclusion, there is no discovery, but only a continuance, however modified, of what has been. The past dictates and interprets further experience, thereby strengthening itself. To think from a conclusion, from a belief, is not to think at all.

"The past is what one is now, and it is made up of the things that one has put together through desire and its activities. Is there a possibility of being free of the past?"

Isn't there? Neither the past nor the present is ever static, fixed, finally determined. The past is the result of many pressures, influences and conflicting experiences, and it becomes the moving present, which is also changing, being transformed under the ceaseless pressure of many different influences. The mind is the result of the past, it is put together by time, by circumstances, by incidents and experiences based on the past. But everything that happens to it, outwardly and inwardly, affects it. It does not continue as it was, nor will it be as it is.

"Is this always so?"

Only a specialized thing is set forever in a mould. The seed of rice will never, under any circumstances, become wheat, and the rose can never become the palm. But fortunately the human mind is not specialized, and it can always break away from what has been; it needn't be a slave to tradition.

"But karma is not so easily disposed of; that which has been built up through many lives cannot quickly be broken."

Why not? What has been put together through centuries, or only yesterday, can be undone immediately.

"In what manner?"

Through the understanding of this chain of cause-effect. Neither cause nor effect is ever final, unchangeable—that would be everlasting enslavement and decay. Each effect of a cause is undergoing many influences from within and from without, it is constantly changing, and it becomes in its turn the cause of still another effect. Through the understanding of what is actually taking place, this process can be stopped instantaneously, and there is freedom from that which has been. Karma is not an ever-enduring chain; it's a chain that can be broken at any time. What was done yesterday can be undone today; there's no permanent continuance of anything. Continuance can and must be dissipated through the understanding of its process.

"All this is clearly seen, but there's another problem which must be clarified. It is this. Attachment to family and to property ceased long ago; but the mind is still attached to ideas, to beliefs, to visions."

Why?

"It was easy to shake off attachment to worldly things, but with the things of the mind, it's a different matter. The mind is made up of thought, and thought exists in the form of ideas and beliefs. The mind

280

dare not be empty, for if it were empty, it would cease to be; therefore it is attached to ideas, to hopes, and to its belief in the things that lie beyond itself."

You say it was easy to shake off attachment to family and property. Why then is it not easy to be free of attachment to ideas and beliefs? Are not the same factors involved in each case? A man clings to family and property because without them he feels lost, empty, alone; and it is for the same reason that the mind is attached to ideas, visions, beliefs.

"That is so. Being physically alone, in solitary places, causes one no concern, for one is alone even among the multitude; but the mind shrinks from being without the things of the mind."

This shrinking is fear, is it not? Fear is caused, not by the fact of being outwardly or inwardly alone, but by anticipation of the *feeling* of being alone. We are afraid, not of the fact, but of the anticipated effect of the fact. The mind foresees and is afraid of what *might* be.

"Then is fear always of the anticipated future, and never of the fact?"

Isn't it? When there is fear of what has been, that fear is not of the fact itself, but of its being discovered, shown up, which again is in the future. The mind is afraid, not of the unknown, but of losing the known. There is no fear of the past; but fear is caused by the thought of what the effects of that past might be. One is afraid of the inner aloneness, the sense of emptiness, that might arise if the mind no longer had something to cling to; so there is attachment to an ideology, a belief, which prevents the understanding of what *is*.

"This also is clearly seen."

And must not the mind be alone, empty? Must it not be untouched by the past, by the collective, and by the influence of one's own desire?

"That is yet to be discovered."

TIME, HABIT AND IDEALS

THERE HAD been heavy rains, several inches a day for over a week, and the river was running very high. It was already over its banks, and some of the villages were flooded. The fields were under water, and the cattle had to be moved to higher ground. A few more inches and it would be over the bridge, and then there would really be trouble;

but just as it was reaching the danger point, the rains stopped and the river began to go down. Some monkeys who had taken refuge in the trees were isolated, and they would have to remain there for a day or so.

Early one morning, when the waters had subsided, we set out across the open country, which was flat almost up to the foot of the mountains. The road went past village after village, and past farms equipped with modern machines. It was spring, and along the road the fruit trees were in bloom. The car was running smoothly. There was the purr of the motor, and the hum of rubber tyres on the road; and yet there was an extraordinary silence everywhere, among the trees, on the river, and over the planted earth.

The mind is silent only with the abundance of energy, when there is that attention in which all contradiction, the pulling of desire in different directions, has ceased. The struggle of desire to be silent does not make for silence. Silence is not to be bought through any form of compulsion; it is not the reward of suppression or even sublimation. But the mind that is not silent is never free; and it is only to the silent mind that the heavens are opened. The bliss which the mind seeks is not found through its seeking, nor does it lie in faith. Only the silent mind can receive that blessing which is not of church or belief. For the mind to be silent, all its contradictory corners must come together and be fused in the flame of understanding. The silent mind is not a reflective mind. To reflect, there must be the watcher and the watched, the experiencer heavy with the past. In the silent mind there is no centre from which to become, to be, or to think. All desire is contradiction, for every centre of desire is opposed to another centre. The silence of the total mind is meditation.

He was a youngish man, with a large head, clear eyes and capable-looking hands. He spoke with ease and self-assurance, and he had brought along his wife, a dignified lady who evidently wasn't going to say anything. She had probably come under his persuasion, and preferred to listen.

"I have always been interested in religious matters," he said, "and early in the morning, before the children are up and the household bustle begins, I spend a considerable period of time in the practice of meditation. I find meditation very helpful in gaining control of the mind and in cultivating certain necessary virtues. I heard your dis-

282

course on meditation a few days ago, but as I am new to your teachings, I was not quite able to follow it. But that's not what I came to talk about. I came to talk about time—time as a means to the realization of the Supreme. As far as I can see, time is necessary for the cultivation of hose qualities and sensibilities of mind which are essential, if enlightenment is to be attained. This is so, isn't it?"

If one begins by assuming certain things, is it then possible to seek out the truth of the matter? Do not conclusions prevent clarity of thought?

"I have always taken it for granted that time is necessary to attain liberation. This is what most of the religious books maintain, and I have never questioned it. One gathers that individuals here and there have realized that exalted state instantaneously; but they are only the few, the very few. The rest of us must have time, short or long, in which to prepare the mind to receive that bliss. But I quite see what you mean when you say that to think clearly, the mind must be free of conclusions."

And it is extremely arduous to be free of them, is it not?

Now, what do we mean by time? There is time by the clock, time as the past, the present and the future. There is time as memory, time as distance, journeying from here to there, and time as achievement, the process of becoming something. All this is what we mean by time. And is it ever possible for the mind to be free of time, to go beyond its limitations? Let's begin with chronological time. Can one ever be free of time in the factual, chronological sense?

"Not if one wants to catch a train! To be sanely active in this world, and to maintain some kind of order, chronological time is essential."

Then there is time as memory, habit, tradition; and time as effort to achieve, to fulfil, to become. It obviously takes time to learn a profession, or acquire a technique. But is time also necessary for the realization of the Supreme?

"It seems to me that it is."

What is it that is achieving, realizing?

"I suppose it's what you call the 'me'."

Which is a bundle of memories and associations, both conscious and unconscious. It's the entity who enjoys and suffers, who has practised virtues, acquired knowledge, gathered experience, the entity who has known fulfilment and frustration, and who thinks there is the soul, the *Atman,* the Higher Self. This entity, this 'me', this ego, is the product of time. Its very substance is time. It thinks in time, functions in time, and builds itself up in time. This 'me', which is memory, thinks that through time it will reach the Supreme. But its 'Supreme' is something it has formulated, and is therefore also within the field of time, is it not?

"The way you unfold it, it does seem that the maker of effort and the end for which he is striving are equally within the sphere of time."

Through time you can achieve only that which time has created. Thought is the response of memory, and thought can realize only that which thought has put together.

"Are you saying, sir, that the mind must be free from memory, and from the desire to achieve, to realize?"

We shall come to that presently. If we may, let us approach the problem differently. Take violence, for example, and the ideal of non-violence. It's said that the ideal of non-violence is a deterrent to violence. But is it? Let's say I am violent, and my ideal is *not* to be violent. There is an interval, a gap between what I actually am, and what I *should* be, the ideal. To cover this intervening distance takes time; the ideal is to be achieved gradually, and during this interval of the gradual approach I have the opportunity to indulge in the pleasure of violence. The ideal is the opposite of what I am, and all opposites contain the seeds of their own opposites. The ideal is a projection of thought, which is memory, and the practising of the ideal is a self-centred activity, just as violence is. It has been said for centuries, and we go on repeating, that time is necessary to be free from violence; but it's a mere habit, and there's no wisdom behind it. We are still violent. So time is not the factor of freedom; the ideal of non-violence does not free the mind from violence. And cannot violence just cease —not to-morrow, or ten years hence?

"Do you mean instantaneously?"

When you use that word, aren't you still thinking or feeling in terms of time? Can violence cease, that's all, not in any given moment?

"Is such a thing possible?"

Only with the understanding of time. We are used to ideals, we are in the habit of resisting, suppressing, sublimating, substituting, all of which involves effort and struggle through time. The mind thinks in habits; it is conditioned to gradualism, and has come to regard time as a means of achieving freedom from violence. With the understanding of the falseness of that whole process, the truth of violence is seen, and *this* is the liberating factor, not the ideal, or time.

"I think I understand what you are saying, or rather, I feel the truth of it. But isn't it very difficult to free the mind from habit?"

It is difficult only when you *fight* habit. Take the habit of smoking. To fight that habit is to give it life. Habit is mechanical, and to resist it is only to feed the machine, give more power to it. But if you consider the mind and observe the formation of its habits, then with the understanding of the larger issue, the lesser becomes insignificant and drops away.

"Why does the mind form habits?"

Be aware of the ways of your own mind, and you will discover why. The mind forms habits in order to be secure, safe, certain, undisturbed, in order to have continuity. Memory is habit. To speak a particular language is a process of memory, habit; but what is expressed in the language, a series of thoughts and feelings, is also habitual, based on what you have been told, on tradition, and so on. The mind moves from the known to the known, from one certainty to another; so there's never freedom from the known.

This brings us back to what we started with. It's assumed that time is necessary for the realization of the Supreme. But what thought can think about is still within the field of time. The mind cannot possibly formulate the unknown. It can speculate about the unknown, but its speculation is not the unknown.

"Then the problem arises, how is one to realize the Supreme?"

Not by any method. To practise a method is to cultivate another set of time-binding memories; but realization is possible only when the mind is no longer in bondage to time.

"Can the mind free itself from its self-created bondage? Is not an outside agency necessary?"

When you look to an outside agency, you are back again in your conditioning, in your conclusions. Our only concern is with the question, "Can the mind free itself from its self-created bondage?" All other questions are irrelevant and prevent the mind from attending to that one question. There is no attention when there's a motive, the pressure to achieve, to realize; that is, when the mind is seeking a result, an end. The mind will discover the solution of this problem, not through arguments, opinions, convictions or beliefs, but through the very intensity of the question itself.

Can God Be Sought Through Organized Religion?

THE EVENING sun was on the green rice-fields and on the tall palms. The fields curved around the palm groves, and a stream, running through the fields and the groves, caught the golden glow and became alive. The earth was very rich. It had rained a great deal, and the vegetation was thick; even the fence-posts were putting out green leaves. The sea was full of fish, and there was no starvation in the land; the people were well-fed, the cattle fat and indolent. There were children everywhere, with little on, and the sun had made them dark.

It was a lovely evening, cool after the hot, sunny day. A breeze was coming across the hills, and the waving palms gave shape and beauty to the sky. The little car was chugging up a hill, and the small child sharing the front seat had made herself comfortable. She was too shy to say a word, but she was all eyes, taking everything in. There were many people on the road, some well-covered and others almost naked. A man wearing only a string and a piece of cloth was standing in the stream near the bank. He ducked under the water several times, rubbed himself, ducked some more, and came out. Soon it was quite dark, and the headlights of the car lighted up the people and the trees.

It's strange how the mind is always occupied with its own thoughts, with watching and listening. It is never really empty; and if by chance it seems so, it's only blank, or day-dreaming. It may be occupied with wanting to be empty, but it's never empty; and being so completely full, no other movement is possible. Becoming aware of its state of constant occupation, it tries to be unoccupied, empty. The method, the practice, which promises peace, becomes the new occupation of the mind. Some thought—of the office, of the family, of the future—perpetually fills the mind. It's always crowded, cluttered up with the things of its own or another's making; there is a ceaseless movement which has little significance.

An occupied mind is a petty mind, whether its occupation is with God, with envy, or with sex. Loneliness, the self-centred movement of the mind, is a deeper occupation, and this is covered over with activity. The mind is never rich in complete emptiness; there is always a corner which is active, planning, chattering, busy.

The total emptiness of the mind, when even its darkest recesses are exposed, has an intensity which is not the fury of being occupied, and it is not diminished by the resistance which occupation brings. There being nothing to resist or overcome, this intensity is effortless silence. The occupied mind does not know this silence. Even those moments when it is not occupied are only breaks in the activity of its occupation, which are soon mended. This silence of emptiness is not the opposite of occupation. All opposites are within the pattern of struggle. It is not a result, an effect, for it has no motive, no cause. All cause-effect is within the sphere of self-centred activity. The self, with its occupation, can never know this intensity of silence, nor what is in it and beyond it.

Three men had come from the distant town by train and bus. One, considerably older than the other two, with a well-kept beard, was the spokesman, though the others were in no way subservient to him. Slow and deliberate in speech, he was able to quote freely from the well-established authorities. He was never impatient, and there was an air of tolerance about him. Of the two younger men, one was nearly bald, and the other had heavy hair. The balding one seemed not yet to have made up his mind about serious matters, and was willing to examine what was said; but here and there definite patterns of thought could be noticed. He smiled widely as he talked, but did not gesticulate. The other was rather shy, and spoke very little.

"Is it not possible to find God through the established religious organizations?" inquired the older man.

If one may ask, why are you putting this question? Is it a serious problem in itself, or merely an opening to a serious problem? If there's a more serious problem behind it, wouldn't it be simpler to proceed directly to that?

"For the present this question is quite a serious one, at least for us. We all heard you two years ago, when last you were here, and it then seemed to us that you were far too drastic in your reasoning about organized religions. My two friends and I belong to one; but it has slowly dawned upon us that you may be right, and we want to talk it over with you seriously."

First of all, what does it mean to be serious? We are serious, in a passing way, about so many things. Since you have all taken the trouble to come here, wouldn't it be well to begin by understanding what we mean by seriousness?

"Perhaps we are not as serious as you would want us to be, but we do give as much time as possible to the search for God."

Is time spent in doing something an indication of seriousness? The business man, the office worker, the scientist, the carpenter—they all give a great deal of time to their respective occupations. You would consider them serious, would you not?

"In a way, yes. But the seriousness with which we carry on the search for God is entirely different. It's difficult to put into words."

Seriousness in the one case is outer, superficial, whereas in the other, it is inner, deeper, requiring far greater insight, and so on; is that it?

"That's more or less what he means," put in the balding one. "We devote as much time as possible to meditation, to reading the sacred books and attending religious gatherings. In short, we are very serious in our search for God."

Again, is time the factor of seriousness? Or does seriousness depend on the state of the mind?

"I don't quite understand what you mean by 'the state of the mind'."

However serious a petty or immature mind may be, it is ever limited, shallow, dependent, subject to influence. To be concerned with only a part of life is to be only partially serious; but the mind that is concerned with the totality of life will approach all things with serious intent. Such a mind is totally serious, earnest.

"I think you mean that we never approach life as a whole," said the older one, "and I'm afraid you're right."

The partial approach finds a partial answer, and however serious one may be, one's seriousness will always be fragmentary. Such a mind cannot find the truth of anything.

"Then how is one to have this total seriousness?"

The 'how' is not at all important. There is no method or practice that can awaken this feeling—the feeling of the mind intent upon understanding the totality of its own being. We will come upon this feeling, I hope, as we proceed with our talk. But you began by asking if God can be found through organized religion.

"Yes, that was our question," the balding one replied. "All we know of religion is what has been drilled into us from childhood. Throughout the centuries, organized religions have taught us to believe in this or that. Practically every saint we know of has followed the religion of

288

his fathers and depended on the authority of its sacred books. The three of us here belong to one of the traditional religious organizations, but since listening to you, we have come to doubt—or at least, I have come to doubt—the point of belonging to any religious organization at all. This is what we would like to talk about."

What does organization imply? We organize in order to co-operate in doing something. Organization is necessary for effective action if you and I wish to do something together. We have to organize, put ourselves in right relationship, if we are to carry out effectively some political, social, or economic plan. Are religious organizations on the same or a similar footing? And what do you mean by religion?

"To me, religion is the way of life," replied the third one. "The way of life is laid down for us by our spiritual teachers and the sacred books, and the following of it in our daily life constitutes religion."

Is religion a matter of following a pattern laid down by another, however great? To follow is merely to conform, to imitate, in the hope of receiving a comforting reward; and surely that is not religion. The releasing of the individual from envy, greed and violence, from the desire for success and power, so that his mind is freed from self-contradictions, conflicts, frustrations—is not this the way of religion? And only such a mind can discover the true, the real. Such a mind is in no way influenced, it is not under any pressure, and so it is able to be still; and it is only when the mind is totally still that there is a possibility of the coming into being of that which is beyond the measure of the mind. But organized religions merely condition the mind to a particular pattern of thought.

"But we were brought up to think within the pattern, with its code of morality," said the balding one. "The temple or the church, with its worship, its ceremonies, its beliefs and dogmas—to us, this has always been religion, and you are destroying it without putting anything in its place."

What is false must be put away if what is true is to be. The aloneness of the mind is essential; and the way of religion is the disentanglement of the mind from the pattern which is put together by the collective, by the past. At present the mind is caught in the collective morality, with its acquisitiveness, its ambition, its respectability and pursuit of power. The understanding of all this has its own action, which frees the mind-feeling from the collective, and then it is capable of love, compassion. Only then is there the sublime.

"But we are not yet capable of such immense understanding," said the older one. "We still need the co-operation and guidance of others to help us along in the right direction. This co-operation and guidance is provided by what we call organized religion."

Do you actually need the help of another to be free from envy, ambition? And when you do have the help of another, is there freedom? Or does freedom come only with self-knowledge? Is self-knowledge a matter of guidance, of organized help? Or are the ways of the self to be discovered from moment to moment in our daily relationships? Dependence on another, or on an organization, breeds fear, does it not?

"There may be a few who are strong enough to stand alone and combat the world, but the vast majority of us need the comforting supports of organized religion. Our lives, on the whole, are empty, dull, without much significance, and it seems better to fill this emptiness with religious beliefs, rather than to fill it with stupid amusements, or with the sophistication of worldly thoughts and desires."

In filling that emptiness with religious beliefs, you have filled it with words, haven't you?

"We are supposed to be educated people," said the balding one. "We have been to college, we have fairly good jobs, and all the rest of it. Moreover, religion has always been of the deepest interest to us. But I see now that what we considered to be religion is not religion at all. On the other hand, to break out of this prison of the collective requires more energy and understanding than most of us possess; so what are we to do? If we left the religious organization to which we belong, we would feel lost, and sooner or later we would pick up another belief with which to deceive ourselves and fill our own emptiness. The attraction of the old way is strong, and we lazily follow it. But in talking all this over, certain things have become clear to me as never before; and perhaps that very clarity will produce its own action."

ASCETICISM AND TOTAL BEING

WE WERE flying very high, over fifteen thousand feet. The plane was crowded, without an empty seat. People from all over the world were in it. Far below, the sea was the colour of new spring grass, delicate and enchanting. The island from which we had taken off was dark green; the black roads and the red paths, winding through the palm groves and the thick, green vegetation, were clear and sharp, and the red-roofed houses were pleasant to look upon. The sea gradually became grey-green, and then blue. Now we were above the clouds, and they hid the earth, stretching mile upon mile as far as the eye could see. Overhead the sky was pale blue, vast and all-enclosing. A slight wind was behind us, and we were flying fast, better than three hundred and fifty miles an hour. Suddenly the clouds parted, and there, far below, was the barren, red earth, with but little vegetation. Its red was like the glow of a forest on fire. There was no forest, but the earth itself was aflame, not with fire, but with colour; it was intense and startling. Soon we were flying over fertile land, with villages and hamlets scattered among the green fields. The earth was now divided after man's heart, and each cultivated section was held, possessed. It was like an endless, multicoloured carpet, but each colour belonged to somebody. A river wound its way through it all, and along its banks there were trees, casting the long shadows of the morning. Far away were the mountains, stretching right across the land. It was beautiful country; there was space and age.

Beyond the noise of the propellers and the chattering of the people, and beyond its own chattering, the mind was in movement. It was a completely silent journey, not in time and space, but into itself. This inward movement was not the outward journeying of the mind within the narrow or extensive field of its own making, of its own clamorous past. It was not a journey undertaken by the mind; it was an altogether different movement. The totality of the mind, not just a part of it, the hidden as well as the open, was completely still. The recording of this fact, here, is not the fact; the fact is wholly different from the words which record it. That stillness was not in the measure of time. Becoming and being have no relationship with each other; they move in entirely different directions; the one does not lead to the other. In the stillness of being, the past as the watcher, as the experiencer, is not. There is no activity of time. It's not a remembrance that is communicating, but the actual movement itself—the movement of silence into the measureless. It's a movement that does not start from a centre, that does not go from one point to another; it has no centre, no observer. It's a journey of the total being, and the total being has no contradiction of desire. In this journey of the whole, there is no point of departure and no point of arrival. The whole mind is still, and this stillness is a movement which is not the journeying of the mind.

The drenching rain had come and gone, but there was still the sound of falling water everywhere. In the room it was very damp, and it would take several days for things to dry out. The man who had come had deep-set eyes, and a good body. He had renounced the world and its ways; and while he did not wear the robes of that renunciation, there was stamped on his face the thought of other things. He had not shaved recently, for he had been travelling, but he was freshly washed, and so were his clothes. Pleasant and friendly of manner, with expressive hands, he sat gravely silent for a considerable time, testing out the atmosphere, feeling his way. Presently he explained.

"I heard you many years ago, quite by chance, and something of what you said has always remained with me: that reality is not come by through discipline, or through any form of self-torture. Since that time I have been all over the land, seeing and hearing many things. I have rigidly disciplined myself. To overcome physical passion has not been too difficult, but other forms of desire have not been so easy to put away. I have practised meditation every day for many years, without being able to get beyond a certain point. But what I want to discuss with you is self-discipline. Control of the body and the mind is essential—and to a great extent they *have* been controlled. But in talking over with a fellow-pilgrim the process of self-discipline, I have perceived the dangers of it. He has hurt himself physically in overcoming his sexual passion. One can go too far in that direction. But moderation in self-discipline is not easy. Achievement of any kind brings a sense of power. There is an exhilarating excitement in conquering others, but much more so in dominating oneself."

Asceticism has its delights, just as worldliness has.

"That is perfectly true. I know the pleasures of asceticism, and the sense of power it gives. As all ascetics and saints have always done, I have suppressed the bodily urges in order to make the mind sharp and quiescent. I have subjected the senses, and the desires that arise from them, to rigorous discipline, so that the spirit might be liberated. I have denied every form of comfort to the body, and slept in every kind of place; I have eaten any kind of food, except meat, and have fasted for days at a time. I have meditated long hours with one-pointed en-

292

deavour; yet in spite of all this struggle and pain, with its sense of power and inward joy, the mind does not seem to have gone beyond a certain point. It's as though one came up against a wall, and do what one may, it will not be broken down."

On this side of the wall are the visions, the good acts, the cultivated virtues, the worship, the prayers, the self-denial, the gods; and all these things have only the significance that the mind gives to them. The mind is still the dominant factor, is it not? And is the mind capable of going beyond its own barriers, beyond itself? Isn't that the question?

"Yes. After thirty strenuously purposeful and disciplined years devoted to meditation and complete self-denial, why has this enclosing wall not been broken down? I have talked to many other ascetics who have had the same experience. There are, of course, those who assert that one must be still more arduous in self-denial, more purposeful in meditation, and so on; but I know I can do no more. All my efforts have only led to this present state of frustration."

No amount of toil and effort can break down this seemingly impenetrable wall; but perhaps we shall be able to understand the problem if we can look at it differently. Is it possible to approach the problems of life totally, with the whole of one's being?

"I don't think I know what you mean."

Are you at any moment aware of your whole being, the totality of it? The totality is not realized by bringing together the many conflicting parts, is it? Can there be the feeling of the whole of your being —not the speculative whole, not what you think of or formulate as the whole, but the actual feeling of the whole?

"Such a feeling may be possible, but I have never experienced it."

At present, a part of the mind is trying to capture the whole, is it not? One part is struggling against another part, one desire against another desire. The hidden mind is in conflict with the open; violence is attempting to become non-violent. Frustration is followed by hope, fulfilment and another frustration. That is all we know. There is the ceaseless pursuit of fulfilment, in whose very shadow is frustration; so we never know or experience wholeness of being. The body is against feeling; feeling is against thought; thought is pursuing the what *should* be, the ideal. We are broken up into fragments, and by bringing the various fragments together, we hope to make the whole. Is it ever possible to do this?

"But what else is there to do?"

For the moment, let's not be concerned with action; perhaps we shall come to that later. This feeling of the totality of your being, of your body, mind and heart, is not the bringing together of all these fragments. You cannot make contradictory desires into a harmonious whole. To attempt to do so is an act of the mind, and the mind itself is only a part. A part cannot create the whole.

"I see this; but then what?"

Our inquiry is not to find out what to do, but to discover this feeling of the whole of one's being—actually to experience it. This feeling has its own action. When there is action without this feeling, then the problem arises of how to bridge the gulf between the fact and what *should* be, the ideal. Then we never feel completely, there is always a withholding; we never think totally, there is always fear; we never act freely, there is always a motive, something to be gained or avoided. Our living is always partial, never whole, and thereby we make ourselves insensitive. Through suppression of desire, through mere control of the mind, through denial of his bodily needs, the ascetic makes himself insensitive.

"Must not our desires be tamed?"

When they are tamed by suppressing them, they lose their vigour, and in this process the perceptions are dulled, the mind is made insensitive; though freedom is sought, one has not the energy to find it. One needs abundant energy to find truth, and this energy is dissipated through the conflict which results from suppression, conformity, compulsion. But yielding to desire also breeds self-contradiction, which again dissipates energy.

"Then how is one to conserve energy?"

The desire to conserve energy is greed. This essential energy cannot be conserved or accumulated; it comes into being with the cessation of contradiction within oneself. By its very nature, desire brings about contradiction and conflict. Desire is energy, and it has to be understood; it cannot merely be suppressed, or made to conform. Any effort to coerce or discipline desire makes for conflict, which brings with it insensitivity. All the intricate ways of desire must be known and understood. You cannot be taught and you cannot learn the ways of desire. To understand desire is to be choicelessly aware of its movements. If you destroy desire, you destroy sensitivity, as well as the intensity that is essential for the understanding of truth.

"Is there not intensity when the mind is one-pointed?"

Such intensity is a hindrance to reality, because it is the result of limiting, narrowing down the mind through the action of will; and will is desire. There is an intensity which is wholly different: the strange intensity which comes with total being, that is, when one's whole being is integrated, not put together through the desire for a result.

"Will you say something more about this total being?"

It is the feeling of being whole, undivided, not fragmented—an intensity in which there is no tension, no pull of desire with its contradictions. It is this intensity, this deep, unpremeditated impulse, that will break down the wall which the mind has built around itself. That wall is the ego, the 'me', the self. All activity of the self is separative, enclosing, and the more it struggles to break through its own barriers, the stronger those barriers become. The efforts of the self to be free only build up its own energy, its own sorrow. When the truth of this is perceived, only then is there the movement of the whole. This movement has no centre, as it has no beginning and no end; it's a movement beyond the measure of the mind—the mind that is put together through time. The understanding of the activities of the conflicting parts of the mind, which make up the self, the ego, is meditation.

"I see what I have been doing all these years. It has always been a movement from the centre—and it's this very centre that must be broken up. But how?"

There is no method, for any method or system becomes the centre. The realization of the truth that this centre must be broken up is the breaking up of it.

"My life has been an incessant struggle, but now I see the possibility of ending this conflict."

THE CHALLENGE OF THE PRESENT

THIS LANE went down to the sea from the wide, well-lit road, passing between the garden walls of many rich houses. It was quiet there, for the walls seemed to shut out the noise of the town. The lane curved in and out a great deal, and on the white walls the shadows danced when the breeze stirred in the trees. The breeze was laden with many odours: the tang of the sea, the smell of the evening meal, the perfume of jasmine, and the fumes of exhaust. Now it was coming from the sea, and there was a strange intensity. A large white flower was growing in the dark soil beside the path, and the evening was full of its fragrance. The path continued downward, and it wasn't long before it met another road which ran along the sea. A young man was sitting beside the road, and he had a dog on a leash. They were both resting. It was a large, powerful dog, sleek and well-fed. Its owner must have considered the dog more important than the man, for the man was wearing soiled clothes and had a frightened, dejected look. It was the dog who was important, not the man, and the dog seemed to know it. Dogs of good breed are snobbish, anyway. Two people came along, talking and laughing, and the dog growled threateningly as they passed; but they paid no attention, for the dog was on a leash and firmly held. A small boy was carrying something very heavy, and he could only just manage it; but he was surprisingly cheerful, and he smiled as he went by.

It was now fairly quiet; no cars were passing, and there was no one on the road. Gradually the intensity grew. It was not induced by the quietness of the evening, or the starlit sky, or the dancing shadows, or the dog on a leash, or the fragrance of the passing breeze; but all these things were within that intensity. There was only intensity, simple and clear, without a cause, without a god, without the whisper of a promise. It was so strong that the body was momentarily incapable of any movement. All the senses had a heightened sensitivity. The mind, that strange and complex thing, was drained of all thought and so was completely awake; it was a light in which there was no shadow. One's whole being was aflame with an intensity that consumed the movement of time. The symbol of time is thought, and in that flame the noise of a passing bus and the perfume of the white flower were consumed. Sound and fragrance wove into each other, but were two distinct, separate flames. Without a tremor, and without the watcher, the mind was aware of this timeless intensity; it was itself the flame, clear, intense, innocent.

He and his wife were there in the small room, whose only window gave upon a blank wall in front of which stood the brown trunk of a large tree. You saw only the massive trunk and not the spreading branches. He was a big, well-built man, and rather heavy. His smile

296

was quick and friendly, but his keen eyes could show anger, and his tongue could be very sharp. He had evidently read a great deal, and was now trying to go beyond knowledge. His wife was clear-eyed, with a pleasant face; she too was large, but not flabby. She took little part in the conversation, but listened with apparent interest. They had no children.

"Is it ever possible to free the mind from memory?" he began. "Is not memory the very substance of the mind—memory being the knowledge and experience of centuries? Does not every experience strengthen memory? In any case, I have never been able to understand why one should be free from the past, as you seem to maintain. The past is rich with pleasant associations and remembrances. Fortunately one can often forget the unpleasant or sorrowful incidents, but the pleasant memories remain. There would be great poverty of being if all the experience and knowledge one has gained were to be put aside. It would be a poor mind indeed that had no depth of knowledge and experience. It would be a primitive mind."

If you do not feel the necessity of being free from the past, then it is not a problem, is it? Then the richness of the past, with all its sufferings and joys, will be maintained. But is the past a living thing? Or does the movement of the present give life to the past? The present, with its demanding intensity and changeful swiftness, is a constant challenge to the mind. The present and the past are always in conflict unless the mind is capable of meeting wholly the swift present. Conflict arises only when the mind, burdened with the past, the known, the experienced, responds incompletely to the challenge of the present, which is always new, changing.

"Can the mind ever respond completely to the present? It seems to me that one's mind is always coloured by the past; and is it ever possible to be wholly free of this coloration?"

Let us go into it and find out. The past is time, is it not?—time as experience, knowledge; and all further experience strengthens the past.

"How?"

When an event takes place in one's life and one has what we call an experience, this experience is immediately translated in terms of the past. If one has a particular religious belief, that belief may bring about certain experiences which in turn strengthen the belief. The superficial mind may adjust itself to the pressures and demands of its immediate environment; but the hidden part of the mind is heavily conditioned by the past, and it is this conditioning, this background that dictates the experience. The whole movement of consciousness is the response of the past, is it not? The past is essentially static, dormant, it has no action of its own; but it comes to life when any challenge is offered to it; it responds. All thinking is the response of the past, of accumulated experience, knowledge. So all thinking is conditioned; freedom is beyond the power of thought.

"Then how is the mind ever to be free of its own limitations?"

If one may ask, why should the mind—which is itself the past, the result of time—be free? What is the motive behind your question? Why does it arise at all? Is it a theoretical or an actual problem?

"I think it is both. There is the speculative curiosity to know, as one might want to know about the structure of matter, and it's also a personal problem. It's a problem to me in the sense that there seems to be no way out of my conditioning. I may break out of one pattern of thought, but in that very process another pattern is formed. Does the breaking up of the old ever bring the new into being?"

If it is recognizable as the new, is it the new? Surely, that which is recognized as the new is still the outcome of the past. Recognition is born of memory. It is only when the past ceases that the new can be.

"But is it possible for the mind to break through the curtain of the past?"

Again, why are you asking this question?

"As I said, one is curious to know; and there is also the desire to be free of certain unpleasant and painful memories."

Mere curiosity does not lead very far. And to hold on to the pleasant, while trying to get rid of the unpleasant, only makes the mind dull, superficial; it does not bring freedom. The mind must be free from both, not just from the unpleasant. Enslavement to pleasant memories is obviously not freedom. The desire to hold on to what is pleasant breeds conflict in life; this conflict further conditions the mind, and such a mind can never be free. As long as the mind is caught in the stream of memory, pleasant or unpleasant; as long as it is held in the chain of cause-effect; as long as it is using the present as a passage from the past to the future, it can never be free. Freedom is then merely an idea, not an actuality. The truth of this must be seen, and then your question will have quite a different significance.

"If I see the truth of it, will there be freedom?"

Speculation is vain. The truth must be seen, the actual fact that there's no freedom as long as the mind is a prisoner of the past must be *experienced*.

"Has a man who is free in this ultimate sense any relationship to the stream of causation and time? If not, then what is the good of this freedom? What value or significance has such a man in this world of joy and pain?"

It's strange how we nearly always think in terms of utility. Are you not asking this question from the boat adrift on the stream of time? And from there you want to know what significance a free man has for the people in the boat. Probably none at all. Most people are not interested in freedom; and when they meet a man who is free, they either make of him a deity and place him in a shrine, or they put him away in stone or in words—which is to destroy him. But surely your concern is not with such a man. Your concern is with freeing the mind of the past—the mind that is you.

"When once the mind is free, then what is its responsibility?"

The word 'responsibility' is not applicable to such a mind. Its very existence has an explosive action on time, on the past. It is this explosive action that is of the highest importance. The man who remains in the boat and asks for help wants it in the pattern of the past, in the field of recognition, and to this the free mind has no reply; but that explosive freedom acts on the bondage of time.

"I don't know what I can say to all this. I really came with my wife out of curiosity, and I find myself becoming deeply serious. At some depth of myself I am serious, and I am discovering it for the first time. Many of my generation have turned away from the recognized religions, but deep down there is the religious feeling, with very little opportunity for it to come out. One must avail oneself of the present opportunity."

SORROW FROM SELF-PITY

AT THIS time of the year, in this warm climate, it was spring. The sun was exceptionally mild, for a light wind was coming from the north where the mountains were fresh in the snow. A tree beside the road, bare a week ago, was now covered with new green leaves which sparkled in the sun. The new leaves were so tender, so delicate, so small in the vast space of the mind, of the earth and the blue sky; yet within a short time they seemed to fill the space of all thought. Further along the road there was a flowering tree which had no leaves, but only blossoms. The breeze had scattered the petals on the ground, and several children were sitting among them. They were the children of the chauffeurs and other servants. They would never go to school, they would always be the poor people of the earth; but among the fallen petals beside the tarred road, those children were part of the earth. They were startled to see a stranger sitting there with them, and they became suddenly silent; they stopped playing with the petals, and for a few seconds they were as still as statues. But their eyes were alive with curiosity, friendliness and apprehension.

In a small, sunken garden by the roadside there were quantities of bright flowers. Among the leaves of a tree in that garden a crow was shading itself from the midday sun. Its whole body was resting on the branch, the feathers covering its claws. It was calling or answering other crows, and within a period of ten minutes there were five or six different notes in its cawing. It probably had many more notes, but now it was satisfied with a few. It was very black, with a grey neck; it had extraordinary eyes which were never still, and its beak was hard and sharp. It was completely at rest and yet completely alive. It was strange how the mind was totally with that bird. It was not observing the bird, though it had taken in every detail; it was not the bird itself, for there was no identification with it. It was *with* the bird, with its eyes and its sharp beak, as the sea is with the fish; it was with the bird, and yet it went through and beyond it. The sharp, aggressive and frightened mind of the crow was part of the mind that spanned the seas and time. This mind was vast, limitless, beyond all measure, and yet it was aware of the slightest movement of the eyes of that black crow among the new, sparkling leaves. It was aware of the falling petals, but it had no focus of attention, no point from which to attend. Unlike space which has always something in it—a particle of dust, the earth, or the heavens—it was wholly empty, and being empty it could attend without a cause. Its attention had neither root nor branch. All energy was in that empty stillness. It was not the energy that is built up with intent, and which is soon dissipated when pressure is taken

300

away. It was the energy of all beginning; it was life that had no time as ending.

Several people had come together, and as each one tried to state some problem, the others began to explain it and to compare it with their own trials. But sorrow is not to be compared. Comparison breeds self-pity, and then misfortune ensues. Adversity is to be met directly, not with the idea that yours is greater than another's.

They were all silent now, and presently one of them began.

"My mother has been dead for some years. Quite recently I have lost my father also, and I am full of remorse. He was a good father, and I ought to have been many things which I was not. Our ideas clashed; our respective ways of life kept us apart. He was a religious man, but my religious feeling is not so obvious. The relationship between us was often strained, but at least it was a relationship, and now that he is gone I am stricken with sorrow. My sorrow is not only remorse, but also the feeling of suddenly being left alone. I have never had this kind of sorrow before, and it is quite acute. What am I to do? How am I to get over it?"

If one may ask, do you suffer for your father, or does sorrow arise from having no longer the relationship to which you had grown accustomed?

"I don't quite understand what you mean," he replied.

Do you suffer because your father is gone, or because you feel lonely?

"All I know is that I suffer, and I want to get away from it. I really don't understand what you mean. Will you please explain?"

It is fairly simple, is it not? Either you are suffering on behalf of your father, that is, because he enjoyed living and wanted to live, and now he is gone; or you are suffering because there has been a break in a relationship that had significance for so long, and you are suddenly aware of loneliness. Now, which is it? You are suffering, surely, not for your father, but because you are lonely, and your sorrow is that which comes from self-pity.

"What exactly is loneliness?"

Have you never felt lonely?

"Yes, I have often taken solitary walks. I go for long walks alone, especially on my holidays."

Isn't there a difference between the feeling of loneliness, and being alone as on a solitary walk?

"If there is, then I don't think I know what loneliness means."

"I don't think we know what anything means, except verbally," someone added.

Have you never experienced for yourself the feeling of loneliness, as you might a toothache? When we talk of loneliness, are we experiencing the psychological pain of it, or merely employing a word to indicate something which we have never directly experienced? Do we really suffer, or only think we suffer?

"I want to know what loneliness is," he replied.

You mean you want a description of it. It's an experience of being completely isolated; a feeling of not being able to depend on anything, of being cut off from all relationship. The 'me', the ego, the self, by its very nature, is constantly building a wall around itself; all its activity leads to isolation. Becoming aware of its isolation, it begins to identify itself with virtue, with God, with property, with a person, country, or ideology; but this identification is part of the process of isolation. In other words, we escape by every possible means from the pain of loneliness, from this feeling of isolation, and so we never directly experience it. It's like being afraid of something round the corner and never facing it, never finding out what it is, but always running away and taking refuge in somebody or something, which only breeds more fear. Have you never felt lonely in this sense of being cut off from everything, completely isolated?

"I have no idea at all what you are talking about."

Then, if one may ask, do you really know what sorrow is? Are you experiencing sorrow as strongly and urgently as you would a toothache? When you have a toothache, you act; you go to the dentist. But when there is sorrow you run away from it through explanation, belief, drink, and so on. You act, but your action is not the action that frees the mind from sorrow, is it?

"I don't know what to do, and that's why I'm here."

Before you can know what to do, must you not find out what sorrow actually is? Haven't you merely formed an idea, a judgment, of what sorrow is? Surely, the running away, the evaluation, the fear, prevents you from experiencing it directly. When you are suffering from a toothache, you don't form ideas and opinions about it; you just have it and you act. But here there is no action, immediate or remote, because you are really not suffering. To suffer and to understand suffering, you must look at it, you must not run away.

"My father is gone beyond recall, and so I suffer. What must I do to go beyond the reaches of suffering?"

We suffer because we do not see the truth of suffering. The fact and our ideation about the fact are entirely distinct, leading in two different directions. If one may ask, are you concerned with the fact, the actuality, or merely with the idea of suffering?

"You are not answering my question, sir," he insisted. "What am I to do?"

Do you want to escape from suffering, or to be free from it? If you merely want to escape, then a pill, a belief, an explanation, an amusement may 'help', with the inevitable consequences of dependence, fear, and so on. But if you wish to be free from sorrow, you must stop running away and be aware of it without judgment, without choice; you must observe it, learn about it, know all the intimate intricacies of it. Then you will not be frightened of it, and there will no longer be the poison of self-pity. With the understanding of sorrow there is freedom from it. To understand sorrow there must be the actual experiencing of it, and not the verbal fiction of sorrow.

"May I ask just one question?" put in one of the others. "In what manner should one live one's daily life?"

As though one were living for that single day, for that single hour.

"How?"

If you had only one hour to live, what would you do?

"I really don't know," he replied anxiously.

Would you not arrange what is necessary outwardly, your affairs, your will, and so on? Would you not call your family and friends together and ask their forgiveness for the harm that you might have done to them, and forgive them for whatever harm they might have done to you? Would you not die completely to the things of the mind, to desires and to the world? And if it can be done for an hour, then it can also be done for the days and years that may remain.

"Is such a thing really possible, sir?"

Try it and you will find out.

INSENSITIVITY AND RESISTANCE TO NOISE

THE SEA was calm and the horizon clear. It would be an hour or two before the sun would come up behind the hills, and the waning moon set the waters dancing; it was so bright that the neighbourhood crows were up and cawing, which wakened the cocks. Presently the crows and the cocks became silent again; it was too early even for them. It was a strange silence. It was not the silence that comes after noise, or the brooding stillness before a storm. It was not a 'before and after' silence. Nothing was moving, nothing stirring among the bushes. There was the totality of silence, with its penetrating intensity. It was not the hem of silence, but the very being of it, and wiped out all thought, all action. The mind felt this measureless silence and itself became silent—or rather it moved into silence without the resistance of its own activity. Thought was not evaluating, measuring, accepting silence, but it was itself silence. Meditation was effortless. There was no meditator, no thought pursuing an end; therefore silence was meditation. This silence had its own movement, and it was penetrating into the depths, into every corner of the mind. Silence *was* the mind; the mind had not become silent. Silence had planted its seed in the very heart of the mind, and though the crows and the cocks were again heralding the dawn, this silence would never end. The sun was now coming up beyond the hills; long shadows lay across the earth, and the heart would follow them all day.

The woman who lived next door was quite young, and she had three children. Her husband would return from his office in the late afternoon, and after games they would all smile over the wall. One day she came with one of her children, purely out of curiosity. She hadn't much to say, nor was there much to say. She talked of many things —of clothes, of cars, of education and drinking, of parties and club life. There was a whisper among the hills, but it disappeared before you could get to it. There was something beyond the words, but she hadn't time to listen. The child became restless and fidgety.

"I wonder why you waste your time on such people?" he inquired as he came in. "I know her, a social butterfly, good at cocktail parties, with a certain amount of taste and money. I am surprised she came to see you at all. A sheer waste of your time, but perhaps she will get something out of it. You must know that type of woman: clothes and jewels, with primary interest in herself. I really came to talk about something else, of course, but seeing *her* here rather upset me. Sorry to have talked about her."

304

A youngish man with good manners and a cultured voice, he was precise, orderly and rather fussy. His father was well-known in the political field. He was married and had two children, and was earning enough to make ends meet. He could make more money easily, he said, but it wasn't worth it; he would put his children through college, and after that they would have to look after themselves. He talked about his life, the vagaries of fortune, the ups and downs of his existence.

"Living in town has become a nightmare to me," he went on. "The noise of a big city bothers me beyond all reason. The rumpus of the children in the house is bad enough, but the roar of a city, with its buses, its cars and tram-cars, the hammering that goes on in the construction of new buildings, the neighbours with their blaring radios—this whole hideous cacophony of noise is most destructive and shattering. I can't seem to adjust myself to it. It's twisting my mind, and even physically it tortures me. At night I stuff something in my ears, but even then I know the noise is there. I'm not quite a 'case' yet, but I shall become one if I don't do something about it."

Why do you think noise is having such an effect on you? Are not noise and quietness related to each other? Is there noise without quietness?

"All I know is that noise in general is driving me nearly crazy."

Suppose you hear the persistent barking of a dog at night. What happens? You set in motion the mechanism of resistance, do you not? You are fighting the noise of the dog. Does resistance indicate sensitivity?

"I have many such fights, not only with the noise of dogs, but with the noise of radios, the noise of children in the house, and so on. We live on resistance, don't we?"

Do you really hear the noise, or are you only aware of the disturbance it creates in you, and which you resist?

"I don't quite follow you. Noise disturbs me, and one naturally resists the cause of one's disturbance. Is not this resistance natural? We resist almost everything that is painful or sorrowful."

And at the same time we set about cultivating the pleasurable, the beautiful; we don't resist that, we want more of it. It's only the unpleasant, the disturbing things that we resist.

"But as I said, isn't this very natural? All of us do it instinctively."

I am not saying it is abnormal; it is so, an everyday fact. But in

305

resisting the unpleasant, the ugly, the disturbing, and accepting only what is pleasurable, do we not bring about constant conflict? And does not conflict make for dullness, insensitivity? This dual process of acceptance and opposition makes the mind self-centred in its feelings and activities, does it not?

"But what is one to do?"

Let's understand the problem, and perhaps such understanding will bring about its own action in which there is no resistance or conflict. Doesn't conflict, inner and outer, make the mind self-centred and therefore insensitive?

"I think I understand what you mean by self-centredness; but what do you mean by sensitivity?"

You are sensitive to beauty, are you not?

"That's one of the curses of my life. It's almost painful for me to see something lovely, to look at a sunset over the sea, or the smile of a child, or a beautiful work of art. It brings tears to my eyes. On the other hand, I loathe dirt, noise and untidiness. At times I can hardly bear to go out into the streets. The contrasts tear me apart inwardly, and please believe me, I am not exaggerating."

But is there sensitivity when the mind takes delight in the beautiful and stands in horror of the ugly? We are not now considering what is beauty and what is ugliness. When there is this contrasting conflict, this heightened appreciation of the one and resistance to the other, is there sensitivity at all? Surely, wherever there is conflict, friction, there is distortion. Is there not distortion when you lean towards beauty and shrink from ugliness? In resisting noise, are you not cultivating insensitivity?

"But how is one to put up with what is hideous? One cannot tolerate a bad smell, can one?"

There is the dirt and squalor of a city street, and the beauty of a garden. Both are facts, actualities. In resisting the one, do you not become insensitive to the other?

"I see what you mean; but then what?"

Be sensitive to both the facts. Have you ever tried listening to noise —listening to it as you would listen to music? But perhaps one never listens to anything at all. You cannot listen to what you hear if you resist it. To listen there must be attention, and where there is resistance there is no attention.

"How am I to listen with what you call attention?"

How do you look at a tree, at a beautiful garden, at the sun on the water, or at a leaf fluttering in the wind?

"I don't know, I just love to look at such things."

Are you self-conscious when you look at something in that manner? "No."

But you are when you resist what you see.

"You are asking me to listen to noise as though I loved it, aren't you? Well, I *don't* love it, and I don't think it's ever possible to love it. You can't love an ugly, brutal character."

That is possible and it has been done. I am not suggesting that you should love noise; but is it not possible to free the mind from all resistance, from all conflict? Every form of resistance intensifies conflict, and conflict makes for insensitivity; and when the mind is insensitive, then beauty is an escape from ugliness. If beauty is merely an opposite, it is not beauty. Love is not the opposite of hate. Hate, resistance, conflict do not engender love. Love is not a self-conscious activity. It is something outside the field of the mind. Listening is an act of attention, as observing is. If you do not condemn noise, you will find it ceases to disturb the mind.

"I am beginning to understand what you mean. I shall try it as I leave this room."

THE QUALITY OF SIMPLICITY

THE RAIN-WASHED hills were sparkling in the morning sun and the sky behind them was very blue. The valley, full of trees and streams, was high up among the hills; not too many people lived there, and it had the purity of solitude. There were a number of white buildings with thatched roofs, and many goats and cattle; but it was out of the way, and you wouldn't ordinarily come upon it unless you knew or had been told of its existence. At its entrance a dustless road went by, and as a rule no one came into this valley without some definite purpose. It was unspoiled, secluded and far away, but that morning it seemed especially pure in its solitude, and the rains had washed away the dust of many days. The rocks on the hills were still wet in the morning sun, and the hills themselves seemed to be watching, waiting. These hills extended from east to west, and the sun rose and set among them. There was one which rose against the blue sky like a temple sculptured out of the living rock, square and splendid. A path wound its way from one end of the valley to the other, and at a certain point along this path the sculptured hill could be seen. Set further back than the other hills, it was darker, heavier, endued with great strength. By the side of the path a stream gently whispered, moving eastward towards the sun, and the wide wells were full of water which held hope for the summer and beyond. Innumerable frogs were making a loud noise all along that quiet stream, and a large snake crossed the path. It was in no hurry and moved lazily, leaving a trail in the soft, damp earth. Becoming aware of the human presence, it stopped, its black, forked tongue darting in and out of its pointed mouth. Presently it resumed its journey in search of food, and disappeared among the bushes and the tall, waving grass. It was a lovely morning, and pleasant under a big mango tree which stood by an open well. The fragrance of freshly washed leaves was in the air, and the smell of the mango. The sun didn't come through the heavy leaves, and you could sit there for a long time on a slab of rock which was still damp.

The valley was in solitude and so was the tree. These hills were some of the oldest on earth, and so they too knew what it is to be alone and far away. Loneliness is sad with the creeping desire to be related, not to be cut off; but this sense of solitude, this aloneness was related to everything, part of all things. You were not aware that you were alone, for there were the trees, the rocks, the murmuring water. You are only aware of your loneliness, not of your solitude; and when you are aware of your solitude, you have become lonely. The hills, the streams, that man passing by, were all part of this solitude whose purity held all impurity within itself, and was not soiled by it. But impurity could not share this solitude. It is impurity that knows loneliness, that is burdened with the sorrow and pain of existence. Sitting there under the tree, with large ants crossing your leg, in that measureless solitude there was the movement of timeless age. It wasn't a space-covering movement, but a movement within itself, a flame within the flame, a light within the emptiness of light. It was a movement that would never stop, for it had no beginning and so no cause to end. It was a movement that had no direction, and so it covered space. There under the tree all time stood still, like the hills, and this movement covered it and went beyond it; so time could never overtake this movement. The mind could never touch the hem of it; but the mind *was* this movement. The watcher could not race with it, for he was able only to follow his own shadow and the words that clothed it. But under that tree, in that aloneness, the watcher and his shadow were not.

The wells were still full, the hills were still watching and waiting, and the birds were still flying in and out among the leaves.

A man and his wife and their friend were sitting in the sunlit room. There were no chairs, but only a straw mat on the floor, and we all sat around it. Of the two windows, one looked out on a blank, weather-beaten wall, and through the other were visible some bushes which needed watering. One was in bloom, but without scent. The husband and wife were fairly well-to-do, and they had grown-up children who were living their own lives. He was retired, and they had a little place of their own in the country. They rarely came to town, he said, but they had come especially to hear the talks and discussions. During the three weeks of the meetings their particular problem had not been touched upon, and so they were here. Their friend, an oldish, grey-headed man who was growing bald, lived in town. He was a well-known lawyer with an excellent practice.

"I know you don't approve of our profession, and sometimes I think you are right," said the lawyer. "Our profession is not what it should be; but what profession is? The three professions of lawyer, soldier and policeman are, as you say, detrimental to man and a disgrace to society—and I would include the politician. Being in it, I can't at this late date get out of it, though I have given considerable thought to the matter. But I am not here to talk about this, though I would like very much to avail myself of another opportunity to do so. I came with my friends because their problem interests me too."

"What we want to talk about is rather complex, at least as far as I can see," said the husband. "My lawyer friend and I have been interested for many years in religious matters—not in mere ritualism and conventional beliefs, but in something much more than the usual paraphernalia of religions. Speaking for myself, I may say that I have meditated for a number of years on various questions pertaining to the inner life, and I always find myself wandering about in circles. For the present I do not want to talk over the implications of meditation, but to go into the question of simplicity. I feel one must be simple, but I'm not sure I know what simplicity is. Like most people, I am a very complex being; and is it possible to become simple?"

To become simple is to continue in complexity. It is not possible to become simple, but one can approach complexity with simplicity.

"But how can the mind, which is very complex, approach any problem simply?"

Being simple and becoming simple are two entirely distinct processes, each leading in a different direction. Only when the desire to become ends is there the action of being. But before we go into all that, may one ask why you feel that you must have the quality of simplicity? What is the motive behind this urge?

"I really don't know. But life is getting more and more complicated; there is greater struggle, with growing indifference and wider superficiality. Most people are living on the surface and making a lot of noise about it, and my own life is not very deep; so I feel I must become simple."

Simple in outward things, or inwardly?

"In both ways."

Is the outward manifestation of austerity—having very few clothes, taking only one meal a day, doing without the usual comforts, and so on—an indication of simplicity?

"Outward austerity is necessary, is it not?"

We will find the truth or the falseness of that presently. Do you think it is simplicity to have a mind cluttered with beliefs, with desires and their contradictions, with envy and the pursuit of power? Is there simplicity when the mind is occupied with its own advancement in virtue? Is an occupied mind a simple mind?

"When you put it that way, it becomes obvious that it is not a simple mind. But how can one's mind be cleansed of its accumulations?"

We haven't come to that yet, have we? We see that simplicity is not a matter of outward expression, and that as long as the mind is crowded with knowledge, experiences, memories, it is not truly simple. Then what is simplicity?

"I doubt that I can give a correct definition of it. These things are very difficult to put into words."

We are not seeking a definition, are we? We will find the right words when we have the feeling of simplicity. You see, one of our difficulties is that we try to find an adequate verbal expression without feeling the quality, the inwardness of the thing. Do we ever feel anything directly? Or do we feel everything through words, through concepts and definitions? Do we ever look at a tree, at the sea, at the sky, without forming words, without a remark about them?

"But how is one to feel the nature or quality of simplicity?"

Are you not preventing yourself from feeling its nature by asking for a method which will bring it about? When you are hungry and there is food before you, you do not ask "How am I to eat?" You just eat. The 'how' is always a digression from the fact. The feeling of simplicity has nothing to do with your opinions, words and conclusions about that feeling.

"But the mind, with its complexities, is always interposing what it thinks it knows about simplicity."

Which prevents it from staying with the feeling. Have you ever tried to stay with a feeling?

"What do you mean by staying with a feeling?"

You stay with a feeling of pleasure, don't you? Having tasted it, you try to hold on to it, you scheme to continue with it, and so on. Now, can one stay with the feeling which the word 'simplicity' represents?

"I don't think I know what that feeling is, so I can't stay with it."

Is there the feeling apart from the reactions aroused by that word 'simplicity'? Is there the feeling separate from the word, the term, or are they inseparable? The feeling itself and the naming of it are almost simultaneous, aren't they? The word is always put together, made up, but the feeling is not; and it is very arduous to separate the feeling from the word.

"Is such a thing ever possible?"

Is it not possible to feel intensely, purely, without contamination? To feel intensely *about* something—about the family, about the country, about a cause—is comparatively easy. Intense feeling or enthusiasm may arise through identifying oneself with a belief or an ideology, for example. Of this one knows. One may see a flock of white birds in the blue sky and almost faint with the intense feeling of such beauty, or one may recoil with horror at the cruelty of man. All such feelings are aroused by a word, by a scene, by an act, by an object. But is there not an intensity of feeling without an object? And is not that feeling incomparably great? Is it then a feeling, or something entirely different?

"I'm afraid I don't know what you are talking about, sir. I hope you don't mind my telling you so."

Not at all. Is there a state without cause? If there is, then can one feel it out, not verbally or theoretically, but actually be aware of that state? To be thus acutely aware, verbalization in every form, and all identification with the word, with memory, must wholly cease. Is there a state without cause? Is not love such a state?

"But love is sensual, and beyond that it is divine."

We are back again in the same confusion, are we not? To divide love as *this* and *that* is worldly; from this division there is profit. To love without the verbal-moral hedge around it is the state of compassion, which is not aroused by an object. Love is action, and all else is reaction. An act born of reaction only breeds conflict and sorrow.

"If I may say so, sir, this is all beyond me. Let me be simple, and then perhaps I shall understand the profound."

QUEST BOOKS
are published by
The Theosophical Society in America,
Wheaton, Illinois 60189-0270,
a branch of a world organization
dedicated to the promotion of the unity of
humanity and the encouragement of the study of
religion, philosophy, and science, to the end that
we may better understand ourselves and our place in
the universe. The Society stands for complete
freedom of individual search and belief.
For further information about its activities,
write, call 1-800-669-1571, or consult its Web page:
http: / / www.theosophical.org

The Theosophical Publishing House
is aided by the generous support of
THE KERN FOUNDATION,
a trust established by Herbert A. Kern
and dedicated to Theosophical education.